Evidence and Inquiry

For HB

Evidence and Inquiry

*Towards Reconstruction in
Epistemology*

Susan Haack

BLACKWELL
Oxford UK & Cambridge USA

First published 1993
Reprinted 1994
First published in paperback 1995
Reprinted 1995 (twice)

Blackwell Publishers Ltd
108 Cowley Road
Oxford OX4 1JF, UK

Blackwell Publishers Inc.
238 Main Street
Cambridge, Massachusetts 02142
USA

British Library Cataloguing in Publication Data

A CIP catalogue record for this book is available from
the British Library.

Library of Congress Cataloging-in-Publication Data
Haack, Susan
    Evidence and inquiry : towards reconstruction in epistemology /
Susan Haack.
      p. cm.
    Includes bibliographical references and index.
    ISBN 0–631–11851–9 (hb.) — 0–631–19679–X (pb.)
    1. Knowledge, Theory of.   2. Evidence.   I. Title.
BD161.H133   1993
121—dc20   93–6589
                                                     CIP

Typeset in 10 on 12pt Plantin
by Graphicraft Typesetters Ltd, Hong Kong
Printed and bound in Great Britain by Hartnolls Limited, Bodmin, Cornwall

This book is printed on acid-free paper

[L]et us remember how common the folly is, of going from one faulty extreme into the opposite.

Thomas Reid *Essays on the Intellectual Powers*, VI, 4

Contents

Preface

This book has been many years in the writing. It was begun, about a decade ago, at the University of Warwick, and finished at the University of Miami.

Substantial parts of the final version of the book were completed with the help of Max Orovitz awards from the University of Miami for the summers of 1991 and 1992.

The book draws upon, develops, substantially revises, and in some cases repudiates, earlier published work. Chapter 1 draws upon, and substantially revises, 'Theories of Knowledge: an Analytic Framework', *Proceedings of the Aristotelian Society*, 1982–3. Chapter 2 draws upon, and substantially revises, some material from 'C. I. Lewis', in *American Philosophy*, ed. Marcus Singer, 1985. Chapter 4 is a development of 'Double-Aspect Foundherentism: a New Theory of Empirical Justification', delivered at the American Philosophical Association meetings in December 1991 and published in *Philosophy and Phenomenological Research*, 1993. Chapter 5 draws on two pieces, 'Epistemology *With* a Knowing Subject', *Review of Metaphysics*, 1979, and 'What is "the Problem of the Empirical Basis", and Does Johnny Wideawake Solve It?', *British Journal for the Philosophy of Science*, 1991. Chapter 6 supercedes 'The Relevance of Psychology to Epistemology', *Metaphilosophy*, 1975, and goes beyond 'The Two Faces of Quine's Naturalism', *Synthese*, 1993. Chapters 8 and 9 both draw in some measure upon 'Recent Obituaries of Epistemology', *American Philosophical Quarterly*, 1990. Chapter 10 substantially improves, I hope, on 'Rebuilding the Ship While Sailing on the Water', in *Perspectives on Quine*, eds Barrett and Gibson, 1990.

I would like to express my thanks to all the many people who have helped me, in various ways and at various stages. For first urging me to write a book on epistemology, to Nicholas Rescher. For reading and commenting with care and intelligence on large chunks of the manuscript, to Mark Migotti. For helpful correspondence, to W. P. Alston, Donald Campbell, John Clendinnen, Luciano Floridi, Peter Hare, Dirk Koppelberg, Henry Kyburg, Rita Nolan, Hilary Putnam, Sidney Ratner, Paul Roth, Ralph Sleeper, Ernest Sosa, and Andrew Swann – and to David Stove, additionally, for supplying the splendid dialogue which now opens chapter 9. For helpful conversations, to A. Phillips-Griffiths and David Miller at Warwick; and, at Miami, to Leonard Carrier, Edward Erwin, Alan Goldman, Harvey Siegel and Risto Hilpinen – and to Howard Pospesel, additionally, for his patience in teaching me to word-process. For helpful comments and criticisms, to the audiences who, over the years, heard various versions of various parts of this work – and to the generations of students who learned epistemology with me. To Adrian Larner, for a good-natured joke at my expense ('Professor Haack, exponent of the Neologistic Typographical School of Philosophy') which I have adopted as an accurate self-description. To Lucia Palmer, for the shrewd comment about my style of philosophizing which prompted me to adapt a title of Dewey's for my subtitle. To Lissette Castillo, for transforming my rough sketches into artwork. To Mark Stricker, Kurt Erhard and Joanne Waugh, for help with proofreading, footnotes and references. To Alison Truefitt for her intelligent copy-editing.

And most of all, to Howard Burdick – for everything.

Introduction

This book is intended as a contribution to the epistemology of empirical knowledge.

There are strong trends in philosophy today markedly hostile to the traditional projects of epistemology, projects which a great clamour of voices, from enthusiasts of the latest developments in cognitive science or neurophysiology, through radical self-styled neo-pragmatists, to followers of the latest Paris fashions, would have us believe are illegitimate, fundamentally misconceived. I disagree. I hope my subtitle has already made my position clear: what epistemology needs is not *de*construction, but *re*construction.

The problems of the epistemological tradition, I shall be arguing, are legitimate; formidably difficult, but not in principle insoluble. So the problems I shall be tackling are familiar enough; most centrally: what counts as good, strong, supportive evidence for a belief? (the 'project of explication' of criteria of evidence or justification, as I shall call it); and: what is the connection between a belief's being well-supported by good evidence, and the likelihood that it is true? (the 'project of ratification'). But the answers I shall be offering will be unfamiliar. By breaking out of some false dichotomies which have informed recent work, I shall argue, it is possible to avoid the all-too-familiar difficulties which face foundationalism, coherentism, reliabilism, critical rationalism, etc., etc. – difficulties which have encouraged the idea that there must be something fundamentally wrong with the whole epistemological enterprise.

I shall be offering a new explication of epistemic justification, a theory which is neither foundationalist nor coherentist in structure, but 'foundherentist', as I shall call it, allowing both for pervasive mutual support among beliefs and for the contribution of experience to empirical justification; neither purely causal nor purely logical in content, but a double-aspect theory, partly causal and partly evaluative; and essentially gradational, taking as *explicandum* not 'A is justified in believing that p iff . . .' but 'A is more/less justified in believing that p depending upon . . .'. And I shall be offering a new approach to the project of ratification, an approach which will be neither purely a priori nor purely empirical in character, but very modestly naturalistic, allowing the contributory relevance both of empirical considerations about human beings' cognitive capacities and limitations, and of considerations of a logical, deductive character.

In what follows I shall draw a good deal on the analogy of a crossword puzzle – which, I shall argue, better represents the true structure of relations of evidential support than the model of a mathematical proof so firmly entrenched in the foundationalist tradition. This analogy, if I am right, sheds light on how it is possible for there to be mutual support among beliefs without vicious circularity. But it also foreshadows a certain difficulty about the organization of the book. I am unable to proceed in a simple, linear fashion, but find myself obliged to go up and back, weaving and interweaving the interconnecting threads of my argument.

Furthermore, because I am trying to transcend the false dichotomies which have informed much recent work, the option is not open to me of organizing what I have to say along the elegantly simple lines of, say, BonJour's *The Structure of Empirical Knowledge*, which depends upon the twin dichotomies of foundationalism versus coherentism and externalism versus internalism – the first of which is not exhaustive, and the second of which is not robust enough to carry any serious weight. Nor, because of the complex interconnections among the rejected dichotomies, is the option open to me of structuring what I have to say by first explaining the reasons for, and the consequences of, rejecting one dichotomy, then the reasons for, and consequences of, rejecting the next, and so on.

The fantasy of presenting my argument in operatic style, with different but related themes being sung simultaneously in different voices, is appealing – but, of course, unrealizable. Instead, having no option but to write a book in the linear style of books, I have no option, either, but to acknowledge the inevitability of more-than-occasional anticipations of themes only later spelled out properly, and retracing of argumentative steps back to themes already introduced to reveal their interconnections with already-introduced ideas. Not to try the reader's patience more than is inevitable, I offer here a sketch-map of the somewhat zig-zag path I shall follow.

I begin (chapter 1) by focusing on the familiar rivalry of

foundationalism versus coherentism, offering as precise an account as possible of the various versions of each style of theory, and as sharp an account as possible of the arguments used by each party against the other. In fact, I argue, both parties have good critical arguments; neither kind of theory will do. But they do not exhaust the field; a third possibility, foundherentism, remains to be explored, and can withstand the strongest arguments of coherentists against foundationalism, and vice versa.

To relieve the abstractness of this opening manoeuvre somewhat, I then present detailed case-studies of specific foundationalist and coherentist programmes. First (chapter 2) is a critique of C. I. Lewis's foundationalist theory, a critique which begins by showing that Lewis's arguments really establish, not foundationalism, but the indispensable role of experience in empirical justification; and which proceeds by showing how Lewis's own half-awareness of this prompts him to make modifications which lead him away from foundationalism in the direction of foundherentism.

Next (chapter 3) is a critique of BonJour's coherence theory, a critique which begins by showing that BonJour's account falls to the familiar objection that coherence within a belief-set is insufficient to guarantee any connection with the world; and which proceeds by showing how BonJour's own half-awareness of this seduces him into an ambiguity which, resolved in the only way which promises any success in the project of ratification, also leads him away from coherentism in the direction of foundherentism. There follows a critique of Davidson's defence of coherentism – not, of course, for purposes of completeness, for a comprehensive survey is obviously impossible – but rather, to show how the assumption that justification must be either a purely logical or else a purely causal notion contributes to creating the illusion that foundationalism and coherentism exhaust the options.

It is then time to articulate my intermediate style of theory (chapter 4). Here several key themes will come together: the gradational character of justification; the distinction of the state and the content sense of 'belief' and the need for a double-aspect conception of evidence; the foundherentist structure of the theory and the crossword analogy which informs it. This begins my positive contribution to the project of explication.

Since a significant part of the argument against the traditionally rival theories is their failure adequately to account for the relevance of experience to empirical justification (coherentism can allow no role to experience, foundationalism only a forced and unnatural one), the foundherentist account of the evidence of the senses requires particularly careful articulation. This is undertaken in chapter 5, using as foil a case-study of Popperian 'epistemology without a knowing subject', and one of its chief stumbling-blocks, the 'problem of the empirical basis'. My thesis, that this problem is not only unsolved by Popper, but insoluble within a Popperian framework, is reinforced by an analysis of the failure of Watkins' recent rescue effort. Diagnosis and resolution of the Popperian impasse is possible within foundherentism because foundherentism transcends Popper's dichotomies of causal versus logical and inductivist versus deductivist approaches, and because its conception of perception is more realist, and more realistic, than the sense-datum theory to which Watkins resorts.

My (broadly Peircean) account of perception is supported, on the one hand, by an argument that the familiar dichotomies of direct versus indirect theories of perception, realist versus irrealist conceptions, are too crude, and that the truth lies between the usual rivals; and, on the other, by its consonance with some plausible psychological theorizing. Watkins' account, by contrast, is not well-motivated by the psychological work to which he refers; and his appeals to psychology violate the epistemic ordering which his Popperian approach requires, but mine does not.

As the last couple of sentences indicate, mine is, in a sense, a naturalistic epistemology: it is not wholly a priori, since it relies on empirical assumptions about human beings' cognitive capacities and limitations, and so acknowledges the contributory relevance to epistemology of natural-scientific studies of cognition. But this modest naturalism is very different from the much more radical, scientistic approaches which also go by the title, 'naturalistic epistemology'. So chapter 6 opens by distinguishing various styles of naturalism: most important, the aposteriorist reformist style of naturalism of which mine is a restricted version; the scientistic reformist style of naturalism which maintains that traditional epistemological problems can simply be handed over to the sciences to resolve; and the revolutionary scientistic style of naturalism which maintains that traditional epistemological problems are illegitimate, and should be replaced by new, natural-scientific projects. Much of this chapter is devoted to showing how an ambiguity in Quine's use of 'science', between 'our presumed empirical knowledge' and 'the natural sciences', leads him to shift from an initial reformist aposteriorist naturalism ('epistemology is part of our presumed empirical knowledge') to a reformist scientism ('epistemology is part of the natural sciences of cognition'); and then, under pressure from the implausibility of the idea that psychology, or biology, or any natural science could tell us, for instance, why predictive power is indicative of the truth of a theory, to a revolutionary scientism in which the old epistemological problems are transmuted into new projects which *are* susceptible of resolution by the sciences.

As Quine makes his first shift, from aposteriorist to scientistic reformist naturalism, he also shifts his focus away from the concept of evidence and on to the reliability of belief-forming processes. As this suggests, the idea that substantial epistemological questions can be resolved within the sciences of cognition seems to find its most hospitable environment in the context of a reliabilist conception of justification. So in chapter 7 I take the opportunity to explain why the advantages of reliabilism over my evidentialist foundherentism are more apparent than real, before arguing that even if reliabilism were correct it would be a mistake to imagine – as Alvin Goldman claims – that it falls to psychology to supply a substantive theory of justification, to adjudicate between foundationalism and coherentism, to determine whether there is such a thing as a priori knowledge, etc., etc.

The attentive reader will gather from the tone of my discussion of Goldman that I suspect that his hopes of a close co-operation of epistemology with the more prestigious field of cognitive psychology are motivated less by good arguments than by intellectual fashion. This fashion finds a much more radical, indeed bizarre, expression in the work of some recent revolutionaries who, claiming that *they* represent the culmination of the new tradition of naturalistic epistemology, argue that recent work in the sciences of cognition has shown the traditional projects of epistemology to be completely misconceived. Pausing briefly to disentangle these revolutionary scientistic naturalists' arguments from their rhetoric, I argue (chapter 8) that neither the work in cognitive psychology and AI to which Stich appeals, nor the work in connectionist neurophysiology to which the Churchlands appeal, has any tendency to suggest, as they claim, that people don't have beliefs. It is not science, but preconceptions in the philosophy of mind, upon which the no-belief thesis depends; and those preconceptions (Paul Churchland's insistence that intentional states are real only if 'smoothly reducible' to physical states, Stich's insistence that they are real only if 'autonomously describable') are, I argue, false. After taking the opportunity to articulate my sign-mediation account of belief and to show its consonance with a conception of human beings as physical organisms in a physical environment, I complete the argument against revolutionary scientism by showing that Stich's and Churchland's position is not just ill-motivated, but self-defeating.

The task of defending the legitimacy of epistemology is not yet complete, however. Since the time of *Philosophy and the Mirror of*

Nature, Rorty has maintained that the traditional epistemological projects are misconceived and should simply be abandoned; and now Stich has shifted his allegiance from revolutionary scientistic naturalism to the vulgar pragmatist party. The purpose of chapter 9 is to show that neither has any good arguments against epistemology; and that, since Rorty's 'edifying' philosophy masks a cynicism which would undermine not only epistemology, but all forms of inquiry, while Stich's liberated post-analytic epistemology turns out to consist in a search for more efficient techniques of self-deception, the poverty of these revolutionaries' post-epistemological utopias indicates just how indispensable epistemology really is. The critique of Rorty provides an opportunity for a critical analysis of contextualism, relativism, tribalism and conventionalism in epistemology, and for a classification of conceptions of truth – irrealist, pragmatist, minimally realist, strongly realist and transcendentalist. The critique of Stich provides an opportunity to investigate the internal connections between the concepts of belief, justification, inquiry and truth, and to explain why truth is valuable. Finally, the challenge implicit in my referring to these writers as 'vulgar pragmatists' – that their claim to be the philosophical descendants of classical pragmatism is unwarranted – is argued explicitly.

The vulgar pragmatists' attempts to undermine the project of ratification fail; it makes perfectly good sense (*pace* Rorty) to ask whether these or those criteria of justification are truth-indicative, and truth-indicative is (*pace* Stich) what criteria of justification need to be to be good. The remaining task, then, is to offer what reassurance I can that the foundherentist criteria *are* truth-indicative (chapter 10). By way of preliminary, I distinguish my enterprise, which focuses on criteria of evidence or justification, from the enterprise of giving guidelines for the conduct of inquiry; and argue that, while a kind of pluralism may well be plausible with respect to the latter, the fashionable thesis that different cultures or communities have widely divergent standards of evidence is at least an exaggeration, and possibly altogether false. This comports with the partial dependence of my ratification of the foundherentist criteria on empirical presuppositions about the cognitive capacities of human beings, of all normal humans, that is. This is the a posteriori component of my ratificatory argument, the part which focuses on the foundherentist account of experiential evidence. The other part, however, the part which focuses on the foundherentist characterization of evidential support, will be, rather, of a logical, deductive character.

Descartes's attempted proof that what is clearly and distinctly perceived is true is a classic ratificatory effort. I do not aspire so high, but aim only to give reasons for thinking that, if any indication of truth is possible for us, satisfaction of the foundherentist criteria is an indication of the truth of a belief. If I am right, this more modest task can be achieved without sacrificing realism with respect to truth – and without arguing in a vicious circle.

In general, I hope, there is no need for elaborate explanation for my choice of topics. There is, however, one nest of issues my neglect of which I should explain: the question of the analysis of knowledge, of the relation of knowledge to justified true belief, the resolution of the 'Gettier paradoxes'. This nexus of problems will be barely touched upon, not given the central place it enjoys in some contemporary work. In part, this is because I find myself with relatively little to say about it; in part, also, because the little I do have to say about it is, in a sense, negative: my conjecture being that Gettier-type 'paradoxes' arise because of a mismatch between the concept of knowledge, which, though vague and shifting, is surely categorical, and the concept of justification, which is essentially gradational. If so, there may be no intuitively satisfactory analysis of knowledge to be had, no sharp line to be drawn between cases where a subject does, and cases where he doesn't, know, no ideal point of equilibrium which precludes our having knowledge by luck without precluding our having knowledge altogether. And to me, at any rate, the question: what counts as better or worse evidence for believing something? seems both deeper and more important than the question: supposing that what one believes is true, how good does one's evidence have to be before one can count as knowing?[1] (I suspect, indeed, that part of the explanation of the present disillusionment with epistemology is just plain *boredom* with the Gettier problem.)

I have focused the book on (what I regard as) important and interesting epistemological questions. I have adopted a structure consonant with the pattern of evidential support suggested by the crossword puzzle analogy which is a recurrent theme. I would have liked, also, to have written in a tone appropriate to the pervasively fallibilistic tenor of the position I am presenting; but to do this would have been so much at odds with the conventions of contemporary philosophical writing as to run the risk of speaking too diffidently to be listened to at all. So sometimes I sound more confident than I feel.

One aspect of my presentation will inevitably irritate some readers, and perhaps will alienate some altogether. But I do not apologize for my allegiance to the Neologistic Typographical School of Philosophy. Because many of the familiar dichotomies and categorizations of the field have impeded progress, I have been obliged to devise a new mesh of distinctions and classifications with which to work; and my neologisms and typographical innovations are the best way I can find of keeping the non-standardness of these distinctions and classifications before the reader's mind, and mine. The sacrifice of elegance and euphony I regret, but cannot avoid; the risk of unintelligibility I have tried to minimize by defining my new terminology as carefully as possible, and by indicating in the index where the definitions are to be found.

Because the complexity of the issues discussed, combined with the need for numerous neologisms, already sometimes pushes my arguments dangerously close to the threshold of what I can reasonably expect a reader to tolerate, I have not, except where the distinction is crucial to the argument at hand, distinguished used from mentioned sentence letters typographically, since what is intended is usually clear from context. Nor have I complicated my presentation by replacing the 'he' of standard English by 'he or she', nor restructured sentences so as to avoid the need for any pronoun. It should go without saying, however, that of course I think that women, no less than men, are knowing subjects.

But perhaps, these days, it does not go without saying that, unlike some proponents of 'feminist epistemology',[2] I do not think that women are capable of revolutionary insights into the theory of knowledge not available, or not easily available, to men. If I am sure of anything after the many years of work that have gone into this book, it is that the questions of epistemology are hard, very hard, for any philosopher, of either sex, to answer or even significantly to clarify.

No doubt, though, 'feminist epistemologists' will think this book wilfully politically obtuse. No doubt, also, foundationalists and coherentists of every stripe will think it too radical, while those who believe epistemology is misconceived will think it not nearly radical enough. And those who are more naturalistic, or more scientistic, than I will think it makes too little reference to the sciences of cognition, while those who are less naturalistic than I will think it makes too much.

But I hope there will be some who agree with me that the questions of epistemology are good, hard questions which have not been satisfactorily answered by the familiar (foundationalist, etc.) epistemological theories, and cannot be answered by science alone; and who will be, therefore, sympathetic to my conception of what it is that needs to be done. And those who share my respect for the epistemological work of the classical pragmatists, especially of Peirce (from whom I not only acquired my penchant for neologisms, but also learned much of epistemological substance), and also of James and, in smaller measure, of Dewey (from whom I borrowed '*Towards Reconstruction* . . .')[3] will, I hope, find some of my answers congenial – and, I trust, will share my distaste for the vulgarized caricature of pragmatism now in vogue.

At best, of course, I hope to have solved some epistemological problems. But I am well aware of lacunae in my arguments, of imprecisions in my categories and distinctions, of issues swept under the rug. So, recalling Peirce's observation that 'in storming the stronghold of truth one mounts upon the shoulders of another who has to ordinary apprehension failed, but has in truth succeeded in virtue of his failure',[4] I hope, at least, to have advanced the argument in ways that will help someone else solve those problems.

1
Foundationalism versus Coherentism: a Dichotomy Disclaimed

> One seems forced to choose between the picture of an elephant
> which rests on a tortoise (What supports the tortoise?) and the
> picture of a great Hegelian serpent of knowledge with its tail in its
> mouth (Where does it begin?). Neither will do.
>
> Sellars 'Empiricism and the Philosophy of Mind'[1]

Once upon a time – not so long ago, in fact – the legitimacy of epistemology was undisputed, the importance to epistemology of such concepts as evidence, reasons, warrant, justification was taken for granted,
and the question of the relative merits of foundationalist and coherentist
theories of justification was acknowledged as an important issue. Now,
however, it seems that disenchantment reigns. The most disenchanted
insist that the problems of epistemology are misconceived and should
be abandoned altogether, or else that they should be replaced by natural-
scientific questions about human cognition. The somewhat disenchanted,
though still willing to engage in epistemology, want to shift the focus
away from the concepts of evidence or justification and onto some
fresher concept: epistemic virtue, perhaps, or information. Even those
who still acknowledge that the concepts of evidence and justification
are too central to be ignored, are mostly disenchanted enough to want
to shift the focus away from the issues of foundationalism versus
coherentism and onto some fresher dimension: deontologism versus
consequentialism, perhaps, or explanationism versus reliabilism. A great
clamour of disenchantment fills the air, to the effect that the old epistemological pastures are exhausted and that we must move on to fresher
fields.

I disagree.

A full explanation of the now-fashionable disenchantment would no doubt be quite complex, and would require appeal to factors external to the philosophical arguments, as well as to those arguments themselves. I don't think it is unduly cynical to speculate that part of the explanation of the urge to move away from familiar epistemological issues towards questions more amenable to resolution by cognitive psychology or neurophysiology or AI, for example, lies in the prestige those disciplines now enjoy. But part of the explanation, and the part which concerns me here, lies in a widely-held conviction that the familiar epistemological issues have proved to be hopelessly recalcitrant, and, most particularly, that neither foundationalism nor coherentism will do.

I agree that neither foundationalism nor coherentism will do. Obviously, however, no radical conclusion follows about the bona fides of the concept of justification, let alone about the legitimacy of epistemology, unless foundationalism and coherentism exhaust the options. But, as I shall argue, they do not; and, as I shall also argue, there is an intermediate theory which can overcome the difficulties faced by the familiar rivals.

So my first moves 'towards reconstruction in epistemology' will take the old, familiar debates between foundationalism and coherentism as their starting point.

Lest I raise false expectations, I had better say right away that I can offer neither a fell swoop nor a full sweep. The former would require perfectly precise characterizations of foundationalism and coherentism and knock-down, drag-out arguments against both rivals, neither of which I am in a position to supply. The latter would require a comprehensive examination of all the variants of foundationalism and coherentism, which, again, is beyond my powers (and your tolerance). What I offer is a compromise, a hodgepodge of the two desirable but impossible strategies. In the present chapter I shall characterize foundationalism and coherentism as sharply as I can, and state the sturdiest arguments in the field as strongly as I can, hoping to show at least that there seem to be powerful arguments against each of the traditional rivals, which, however, the intermediate theory looks to be able to withstand; that, in other words, there is a pull towards the middle ground of foundherentism. In subsequent chapters I look in detail at specific foundationalist and coherentist theories, hoping to show not only that they fail, but that they fail in ways that point, again, towards the desirability of an intermediate theory.

One last preliminary: something should be said about how one should judge the correctness or incorrectness of a theory of justification. This task is surprisingly, but instructively, far from straightforward. In offering an explication of our criteria of justification the epistemologist is aiming to spell out with some precision and theoretical depth what is implicit in judgements that this person has excellent reasons for this belief, that that person has unjustifiably jumped to a conclusion, that another person has been the victim of wishful thinking . . . and so forth and so on. I call this project 'explication', rather than 'analysis', to indicate that the epistemologist will have to do more than faithfully describe the contours of usage of phrases like 'justified in believing' and its close relatives; since such usage is vague, shifting, and fuzzy at the edges, the task will involve a lot of filling in, extrapolation, and plain tidying up. But one way in which a theory of justification may be inadequate is by failing to conform, even in clear cases, to our pre-analytic judgements of justification.

But this is only part of the story. The concept of justification is an *evaluative* concept, one of a whole mesh of concepts for the *appraisal* of a person's epistemic state. To say that a person is justified in some belief of his, is, in so far forth, to make a favourable appraisal of his epistemic state. So the task of explication here calls for a *descriptive* account of an *evaluative* concept.

The evaluative character of the concept imposes a different kind of constraint on theories of justification. To believe that p is to accept p as true; and strong, or flimsy, evidence for a belief is strong, or flimsy, evidence for its truth. Our criteria of justification, in other words, are the standards by which we judge the likelihood that a belief is true; they are what we take to be indications of truth. Another way in which a theory of justification may be inadequate, then, is that the criteria it offers are such that no connection can be made between a belief's being justified, by those criteria, and the likelihood that things are as it says.

Satisfaction of both constraints would be the ideal. Not, of course, that there is any guarantee in advance that what we take to be indications of the truth of a belief really are such. But, if there is one, an account which satisfies both the descriptive and the evaluative constraints is what we are after.

The tricky part is to get the two kinds of constraint in the right perspective, neither excessively pollyannish nor excessively cynical. For now, let me just say that the epistemologist can be neither an uncritical participant in, nor a completely detached observer of, our pre-analytic standards of epistemic justification, but a reflective, and potentially a revisionary, participant. The epistemologist can't be a completely detached observer, because to do epistemology at all (or to undertake *any* kind of inquiry) one must employ some standards of evidence, of what counts as a reason for or against a belief – standards which one takes to be an indication of truth. But the epistemologist can't be a completely uncritical participant, because one has to allow for the possibility that what pre-analytic intuition judges strong, or flimsy, evidence, and what really is an indication of truth, may fail to correspond. In fact, however, I don't think this possibility is realized; I think pre-analytic intuition conforms, at least approximately, to criteria which are, at least in a weak sense, ratifiable as genuinely truth-indicative. Foundherentism, I shall argue, satisfies both constraints.

I

Before offering a characterization of the distinctive features of foundationalism and coherentism, I should explain my strategy for dealing with two initial difficulties which this enterprise faces. The main problem is that there is much variety and considerable vagueness in the way the terms 'foundationalism' and 'coherentism' are used in the literature. To protect myself, so far as this is possible, from the accusation that my characterization supports my thesis that foundationalism and coherentism do not exhaust the options simply as a matter of verbal stipulation, I can only do my best to ensure that my characterizations are in line with other attempts to go beyond the rather casual definitions sometimes assumed, and that they categorize as foundationalist those theories which are ordinarily and uncontroversially classified as foundationalist, and as coherentist those theories which are ordinarily and uncontroversially classified as coherentist.[2]

A minor complication is that both 'foundationalism' and 'coherentism' have other uses besides their use in the context of theories of justification. Sometimes they are used to refer to theories of knowledge rather than of justification specifically, but this is not a significant problem for the present enterprise. Nor is the fact that 'coherentism' has a distinct use as a term for a certain style of theory of truth. Potentially the most confusing ambiguity is that, besides referring to a certain style of theory of justification, and a corresponding style of theory of knowledge, 'foundationalism' also has two meta-epistemological uses: to refer to the idea that epistemic standards are objectively grounded or founded; and to refer to the idea that epistemology is an a priori discipline the goal of which is to legitimate or found our presumed empirical knowledge.[3] Later (chapter 9) it will be necessary to introduce typographical variants ('FOUNDATIONALISM', '*foundationalism*') to mark these other uses.

But here and throughout the book, 'foundationalism' will refer to theories of justification which require a distinction, among justified beliefs, between those which are basic and those which are derived, and a conception of justification as one-directional, i.e., as requiring basic to support derived beliefs, never vice versa. This, rough as it is, is sufficient to capture something of the metaphorical force of the term 'foundationalism'; the basic beliefs constitute the foundation on which the whole superstructure of justified belief rests. I shall say that a theory qualifies as foundationalist which subscribes to the theses:

> (FD1) Some justified beliefs are basic; a basic belief is justified independently of the support of any other belief;

and:

> (FD2) All other justified beliefs are derived; a derived belief is justified via the support, direct or indirect, of a basic belief or beliefs.

(FD1) is intended to represent the minimal claim about the requirements for a belief to qualify as basic. It is a claim about *how basic beliefs are (and how they are not) justified.* Many foundationalists have also held that basic beliefs are privileged in other ways: that they are certain, incorrigible, infallible . . . i.e., that it is impossible that they be falsely held.[4] 'Infallibilist foundationalism' will refer to theories which make this additional claim. (But theories which postulate certain or infallible beliefs, but do not take such beliefs to be required for the justification of all other beliefs, or do not require such beliefs to be justified independently of the support of any other beliefs, will not qualify as foundationalist.)

(FD1) admits of many and various variations. One dimension of variation concerns the material character of the beliefs claimed to be basic. Fundamental is the distinction between those foundationalist theories which take the basic beliefs to be empirical, and those which take them to be non-empirical. I distinguish:

> (FD1^{NE}) Some beliefs are basic; a basic belief is justified independently of the support of any other belief; basic beliefs are non-empirical in character.

Proponents of (FD1^{NE}) usually have in mind simple logical or mathematical truths, often thought of as 'self-evident', as basic.

(FD1^E) Some beliefs are basic; a basic belief is justified independently of the support of any other beliefs; basic beliefs are empirical in character.

'Empirical', here, should be understood as roughly equivalent to 'factual', not as necessarily restricted to beliefs about the external world. In fact, one style of empirical foundationalism takes beliefs about the subject's own, current, conscious states as basic, another takes simple beliefs about the external world as basic, and a third allows both.

I shall restrict my discussion, in what follows, to empirical foundationalism, leaving non-empirical foundationalism (and the possible variant which allows both empirical and non-empirical basic beliefs) out of account.

A different dimension of variation runs obliquely to this. It concerns the explanation given to the claim that a basic belief is 'justified, but not by the support of any other belief'. There seem to be three significantly different kinds of account: according to the experientialist version of empirical foundationalism, basic beliefs are justified, not by the support of other beliefs, but by the support of the subject's (sensory and/or introspective) experience; according to the extrinsic version of empirical foundationalism, basic beliefs are justified because of the existence of a causal or law-like connection between the subject's having the belief and the state of affairs that makes it true; and according to the intrinsic or self-justificatory version of empirical foundationalism, basic beliefs are justified because of their intrinsic character, their content is the guarantee of their justification. Thus:

(FD1$^E_{EXP}$) Some justified beliefs are basic; a basic belief is justified, not by the support of any other belief, but by the subject's experience

represents the first of these, while:

(FD1$^E_{EXT}$) Some justified beliefs are basic; a basic belief is justified, not by the support of any other belief, but because of a causal or law-like connection between the subject's belief and the state of affairs which makes it true

represents the second, and:

(FD1$^E_{SJ}$) Some justified beliefs are basic; a basic belief is justified, not by the support of any other belief, but in virtue of its content, its instrinsically self-justifying character

represents the third.

The intrinsic or self-justifying style of explanation of the justification of basic beliefs is, naturally, also attractive to those non-empirical foundationalists who would explain the justification of basic logical beliefs as resulting from their intrinsic character or content (or, more likely, their lack of content). But this need not be pursued here.

Experientialist empirical foundationalism may be restricted to relying on the subject's introspective experience, or may be restricted to relying on his sensory experience, or may allow both kinds; depending on which it does, it is likely to class as basic beliefs about the subject's own, current, conscious states, or simple perceptual beliefs, or both. Extrinsic foundationalism and self-justificatory foundationalism, likewise, cut across the sub-categories of empirical foundationalism with respect to the kinds of belief they take as basic.

The main reason I use the expression 'empirical foundationalism' rather than 'a posteriori foundationalism' should now be apparent. One reason, of course, is that 'a posteriori' versus 'a priori' does not lend itself to convenient abbreviation. The more substantial reason, however, is that, unlike the experientialist version, neither extrinsic nor self-justificatory foundationalism gives a justificatory role to the subject's experience. This leads to another significant point: that while experientialist foundationalism connects justification to the subject's experience, and extrinsic foundationalism connects justification to states of affairs in the world, self-justificatory foundationalism makes justification a matter solely of beliefs: their intrinsic character where the basis is concerned, and their support relations where the superstructure is concerned.

(FD1^E) also admits of variation with respect to the strength of the claim it makes about the justification of basic beliefs. The stronger version claims that basic beliefs are, simply, justified, independently of the support of any other beliefs; weaker versions, that they are justified prima facie but defeasibly, or to some degree but less than fully, independently of any other beliefs. As should be apparent, the weaker versions may, though they need not, require acknowledgement of degrees of justification. I distinguish:

> (FD1$_S$) Some justified beliefs are basic; a basic belief is (decisively, conclusively, completely) justified independently of the support of any other belief

and:

> (FD1$_W$) Some justified beliefs are basic; a basic belief is justified prima facie but defeasibly/to some degree but not completely, independently of the support of any other belief.

'Strong foundationalism' will refer to the first style, 'weak foundationalism' to the second.

(FD2) also admits of variations. According to the pure version, derived beliefs are always justified *wholly* by means of the support of basic beliefs; according to the impure version, derived beliefs are always justified *at least in part* by means of the support of basic beliefs, but the possibility is allowed that they may get part of their justification by means of mutual support among themselves. I distinguish:

> (FD2^P) All other justified beliefs are derived; a derived belief is justified wholly via the support, direct or indirect, of a basic belief or beliefs

and:

> (FD2^I) All other justified beliefs are derived; a derived belief is justified at least in part via the support, direct or indirect, of a basic belief or beliefs.

'Pure foundationalism' will refer to the first of these, 'impure foundationalism' to the second.

Like one variant of weak foundationalism, impure foundationalism is committed, at least implicitly, to recognizing degrees of justification.

The distinctions so far made permit a whole range of permutations. For example, the pair of distinctions strong/weak, pure/impure gives the fourfold classification: strong, pure, foundationalism; weak, pure, foundationalism; strong, impure, foundationalism; weak, impure, foundationalism.

The characteristic theses of coherentist theories of justification are that justification is exclusively a matter of relations among beliefs, and that it is the coherence of beliefs within a set which justifies the member beliefs. I shall say that a theory qualifies as coherentist if it subscribes to the following thesis:

> (CH) A belief is justified iff it belongs to a coherent set of beliefs.

Of course, there is room for variation as to just what set of beliefs is held to be relevant, and as to the exact content of the requirement that the set be coherent. It is usually agreed that consistency is necessary; most also require comprehensiveness; a more recently fashionable gloss is 'explanatory coherence'. But the most important distinction for present purposes is between those uncompromisingly egalitarian forms of coherentism which insist that all the beliefs in a coherent set are exactly on a par with respect to their justification, and those moderated, inegalitarian forms which do not. The uncompromising version disallows the possibilities both that any belief could have a distinguished initial status, independently of its relations to other beliefs, and that any belief could be more intimately interlocked in a set of beliefs than other members of the set. The moderated version comes in two styles. One results from allowing the first possibility, that some beliefs may have an initially distinguished status, independently of their relations to other beliefs, so that relations of mutual support must be weighted, with interconnections with initially distinguished beliefs counting for more than other interconnections. The other style of moderated coherentism results from allowing the second possibility, that, though no beliefs have any initial distinction, some may be more deeply embedded in a coherent set of beliefs than others. So I characterize 'uncompromising coherentism' thus:

(CH^U) A belief is justified iff it belongs to a coherent set of beliefs, no belief having a distinguished epistemic status and no belief having a distinguished place within a coherent set.

'Moderated coherentism' will refer to any theory which accepts the first part of (CH^U) but denies the second. 'Moderated, weighted coherentism' will be:

(CH^M_W) A belief is justified iff it belongs to a coherent set of beliefs, some beliefs having a distinguished initial status, and justification depending on weighted mutual support;

and 'moderated, degree-of-embedding coherentism' will refer to:

(CH^M_D) A belief is justified iff it belongs to a coherent set of beliefs, some beliefs being distinguished by being more deeply embedded in a coherent set than others.

Moderated coherentism, unlike the uncompromising kind, suggests an implicit acknowledgement of the possibility of degrees of justification.

With the various refinements, qualifications and modifications mentioned, the rival theories have come, in a way, closer together. Weighted coherentism and weak, self-justificatory foundationalism – especially impure, weak, self-justificatory foundationalism – bear more than a passing resemblance to each other. Self-justificatory foundationalism makes justification derive from relations among beliefs, as does coherentism in all its forms; weighted coherentism allows that some beliefs have an epistemic distinction not dependent on their relations to other beliefs, as does foundationalism in all its forms. But the theories remain distinct. Weighted coherentism allows for pervasive mutual support; even impure, weak, self-justificatory foundationalism insists on one-directionality, denying that a basic belief could receive any justification from the support of a non-basic belief.

From here, it will not take very elaborate argument to establish the main thesis of this section, that foundationalism and coherentism do not exhaust the options.[5] It is necessary, though, by way of preliminary, to make it clear that my thesis concerns foundationalism and coherentism *qua* rival theories of empirical justification. The idea that, for example, some form of coherentism might be correct as an account of a priori justification, and some form of foundationalism of an empirical stripe be correct as an account of empirical justification, is not presently at issue. Considered as theories of empirical justification, the point is, foundationalism and coherentism do not exhaust the options; there is logical space in between. At its simplest, the argument is this: foundationalism requires one-directionality, coherentism does not; coherentism requires justification to be exclusively a matter of relations among beliefs, foundationalism does not. (Matters are not perfectly symmetrical, since foundationalism only *allows*, but does not *require*, non-belief input; but this asymmetry does not affect the issue.) So: a theory which allows non-belief input cannot be coherentist; a theory which does not require one-directionality cannot be foundationalist. A theory such as the one I favour, which allows the relevance of experience to justification, but requires no class of privileged beliefs justified exclusively by experience with no support from other beliefs, is neither foundationalist nor coherentist, but is intermediate between the traditional rivals.

Foundherentism may be approximately characterized thus:

(FH1) A subject's experience is relevant to the justification of his empirical beliefs, but there need be no privileged class of empirical beliefs justified exclusively by the support of experience, independently of the support of other beliefs;

and:

(FH2) Justification is not exclusively one-directional, but involves pervasive relations of mutual support.

This is only a *very* rough first approximation; the task of working out the details and making this more precise is yet to be undertaken (chapter 4). But from even this very sketchy characterization it will be apparent that, since the subject's experience is to play a role, the account will be personal rather than impersonal, and that, since beliefs will be seen to be justified partially by experience and partially by other beliefs, the account will be gradational rather than categorical; the preferred *explicandum*, in short, will be: 'A is more/less justified in believing that p depending on . . .'.

Foundherentism is not, of course, the only 'third alternative' theory of justification to be suggested: contextualism is a more familiar third possibility. The characteristic feature of contextualist accounts is that they define justification in terms of conformity to the standards of some epistemic community. It is not unusual for contextualist accounts, once they go beyond this very general thesis, to have a two-level, one-directional structure reminiscent of foundationalism, but there is a very important difference: a contextualist may posit 'basic' beliefs by which all justified beliefs must be supported, but these will be construed, not as beliefs justified otherwise than by the support of other beliefs, but as beliefs which, in the epistemic community in question, *do not stand in need of justification.*

It is sometimes felt that contextualism does not really address the same question as the traditionally rival theories, a feeling sometimes expressed in the suggestion that contextualists are focused, not on the explication of 'A is justified in believing that p', but on the explication of 'A can justify his belief that p (to the members of C)', or, less charitably, that they have confused the two. The diagnosis of confusion of *explicanda* is not without merit, in my view, and there is indeed something about contextualism which sets it apart not only from foundationalism and coherentism but also from foundherentism: it leads in short order to the thesis that epistemic standards are not objective but conventional. And this means that contextualism is covertly anti-epistemological; it would undermine the legitimacy of the project of ratification. This is the first clue to why it has been thought – in my view, of course, wrongly – that, if neither foundationalism nor coherentism will do, the whole epistemological enterprise comes under threat.

That contextualism has radical consequences is no argument that it is mistaken. I think it *is* mistaken, but I shall not discuss it in any detail until much later (chapter 9). For the moment, since the purpose of the present chapter is to make a prima facie case for foundherentism, the point that needs emphasis is that the difficulties I shall identify in foundationalism and coherentism are clearly such as to point in the direction of foundherentism, not contextualism, as the most promising route to a successful resolution.

II

The goal, then, is to make a prima facie case for foundherentism. The strategy will be to examine the most significant arguments in the debate between foundationalism and coherentism with the aim of showing how they push one towards the middle ground of foundherentism.

Most, though not all, of the arguments to be considered are quite familiar; but I shall have to engage in a certain amount of rational reconstruction to get these familiar arguments into their strongest forms. Despite this, I can claim only to make a prima facie case, because the arguments under consideration are, even in their rationally reconstructed versions, seldom watertight; and it would be less than candid to disguise the fact that sometimes it is a matter of judgement whether a difficulty faced by the one style of theory, regarded by proponents of the other style as insuperable, is more reasonably regarded as a decisive objection or as a challenging, but superable, obstacle.

My meta-argument begins with a consideration of the **infinite regress argument**, which has often been supposed to show that some form of foundationalism must be accepted. The argument goes somewhat as follows: it is impossible that a belief should be justified by being supported by a further belief, that further belief being supported by a further belief . . . and so on, for unless this regress of reasons for a belief comes to an end, the first belief would not be justified; so there must be, as foundationalism holds, basic beliefs which are justified otherwise than by the support of other beliefs, and which serve as the ultimate justification of all other justified beliefs. There must be basic beliefs, in the foundationalist's sense, in other words, because there cannot be an infinite regress of reasons. Suppose it is granted that a person could not be justified in a belief if the chain of reasons for that belief never came to an end. The argument is still inconclusive as it stands, for it requires the assumption that the reasons for a belief form a chain which either ends with a basic belief, or doesn't end at all; and these are obviously not the only options. Perhaps the chain of reasons comes to an end with a belief which is not justified; perhaps the chain ends with the belief with which it begins, with the initial belief supported by further beliefs which it, in turn, supports . . .

Of course, the foundationalist would regard these options as no more palatable than an infinite regress. So a stronger version of the argument may be constructed – which, however, it no longer seems appropriate to call the 'infinite regress argument', since an infinite regress is only one of several possibilities it holds to be unacceptable. I will call this reconstructed argument the **no tolerable alternatives argument**. It would run like this:

> Suppose A believes that p. Is he justified in believing that p?
> Well, suppose he believes that p on the basis of his belief that q.
> Then he is not justified in believing that p unless he is justified in believing that q.
> Suppose he believes that q on the basis of his belief that r.
> Then he is not justified in believing that q, and hence not justified in believing that p, unless he is justified in believing that r.
> Suppose he believes that r on the basis of his belief that s.
> Then he is not justified in believing that r, and hence not justified in believing that q, and hence not justified in believing that p, unless . . .
> Now, either (1) this series goes on without end; or (2) it ends with a belief which is not justified; or (3) it goes round in a circle; or (4) it comes to an end with a belief which is justified, but not by the support of any further beliefs.
> If (1), if the chain of reasons never ends, A is not justified in believing that p.
> If (2), if the chain of reasons ends with a belief which is not justified, A is not justified in believing that p.
> If (3), if the chain goes round in a circle, with the belief that p depending on the belief that q, the belief that q depending on the belief that r . . . and the belief that z depending on the belief that p, A is not justified in believing that p.
> If (4), however, if the chain ends with a belief which is justified, but not by the support of any further beliefs, A is justified in believing that p.
> So, since (4) is precisely what foundationalism claims, only if foundationalism is true is anyone ever justified in any belief. (Foundationalism is the only tolerable – the only non-sceptical – alternative.)

This argument is still – though no longer, perhaps, obviously – inconclusive. I grant, once again, that a person would not be justified in a belief if the chain of reasons for that belief did not come to an end; I grant, also, that he would not be justified in a belief if the chain of reasons for that belief came to an end with a belief which was not justified. I even grant that if the chain of beliefs went round in a circle, with the further beliefs supporting the initial belief themselves ultimately supported by that very belief, he would not be justified in the initial belief. What I deny is that there need be a chain of reasons at all.

A significant clue to what has gone wrong is this: foundationalists suggest that 'going round in a circle' is the picture of justification that a coherentist must be offering, and that it is obviously unsatisfactory; coherentists are apt to respond by protesting that – though indeed they insist on the pervasiveness of relations of mutual support among beliefs – there is all the difference in the world between legitimate mutual support and a vicious circle of reasons. And here, I think, though rarely if ever do they manage to say just what this 'all the difference in the world' amounts to, the coherentists are in the right.

To repeat, there is a false assumption built into the no tolerable alternatives argument, but built in so integrally as to be almost invisible: that the reasons for a belief must constitute a chain – a series, that is, with the belief that p supported by the belief that q supported by the belief that r . . . and so on. *If* the reasons for a belief had to be a chain, a series, then mutual support would indeed have to be a circle, as in figure 1.1; and it is indeed impossible to accept that this kind of circle of reasons could be justifying.

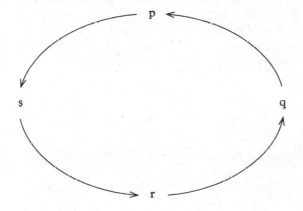

Figure 1.1

But the chain analogy is wrong even by the foundationalist's own lights. The appropriate picture for the structure the foundationalist envisages would be, not a chain, but a pyramid or inverted tree – as: belief that p based on beliefs q, r and s, belief that q based on beliefs t and u, belief that r based on belief that v . . . etc.;[6] as in figure 1.2; and it is *not* intuitively clear why it could not be the case that A is justified in believing that p even if part of A's justification for the belief that p is the belief that z, and part of A's justification for the belief that z is

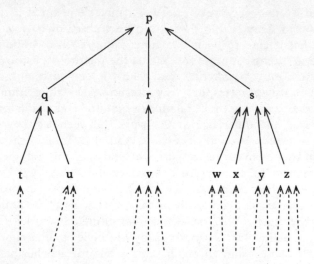

Figure 1.2

the belief that p – as in figure 1.3. It seems entirely plausible to suppose that the degree to which A is justified in a belief depends (at least) on how well his reasons support that belief, and on how justified he is, independently of that belief, in believing those reasons. If so, he can be justified, not completely but to however high a degree you like short of that, in the presence of such loops of justification.

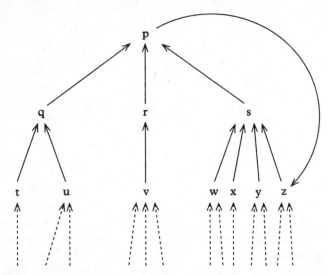

Figure 1.3

In fact, the impure form of foundationalism allows the possibility of just such loops of reasons; though, according to impure foundationalism, all justification rests at least in part on the support of basic beliefs, mutual support among derived beliefs can contribute to their justification. So even some foundationalists admit – as coherentists and foundherentists maintain – that there can be legitimate mutual support, that the interpenetration of beliefs need not necessarily involve a vicious circularity.

Other foundationalist arguments against coherentism are, I think, more damaging. I consider first the argument that consistency (which is assumed by coherentists to be a necessary condition of coherence) is too strong a requirement for justification. The point of this objection – I shall call it the **too much to ask objection** – is quite simple. Coherentism seems to entail that a subject who has inconsistent beliefs, and hence an incoherent belief-set, is not justified in any of his beliefs.[7] But this is excessively demanding; probably no one has a completely consistent set of beliefs, and in any case the mere fact that there is, say, a hidden contradiction within the corpus of my beliefs about the geography of Russia is, surely, no reason for saying that I am not justified in believing that snow is white, that there is a piece of paper before me, that my name is SH . . . Since it is hardly a serious option to discard consistency as a necessary condition of coherence, the only escape route open to the coherentist might be to rule that the set of beliefs coherence of which is to constitute justification, is to be, not the subject's whole belief-set, but some sub-set of that set. Indeed, the thought is plausible that even if (as I believe) a justified belief will always be one enmeshed in a whole complex of other beliefs, nevertheless not *all* of a person's beliefs are relevant to the justification of *every* belief of his.

A coherentist who subscribed to the idea that the best defence is a strong offence might point out that there is a certain awkwardness about the foundationalist picture which also relates, though in a slightly different way, to the matter of inconsistency among a subject's beliefs. Foundationalism, to be sure, does not imply (as the usual forms of coherentism do) that if a subject's beliefs are inconsistent, he is not justified in any of them. It focuses, not on the whole belief-set, but on the sub-set which plays a role in the tree of reasons for the particular belief the justificational status of which is at issue. So far, so good; foundationalism is not too high-minded about inconsistencies in a subject's belief-set. But it is a bit too low-minded about the possibility of inconsistencies in a person's reasons for a belief. All foundationalists, so far as I am aware, take it that if the reasons for a belief deductively imply it, they are conclusive; hence, since inconsistent propositions deductively imply any proposition whatsoever, inconsistent reasons for a belief must be deemed conclusive. Of course, the foundationalist doesn't have to say that if a person's reasons for a belief are inconsistent, and hence conclusive, he is thereby justified in the belief; on the contrary, one can confidently expect him to say that the subject is *not* justified in the belief, since he is not justified in believing the reasons for the belief. Still, the idea that reasons which are inconsistent are *eo ipso* conclusive is surely counter-intuitive, and should if possible be avoided.

To return, though, to the main thread of the discussion, which is presently focused on objections to coherentism: even if a restricted form of coherentism were possible which operated in terms of clumps of mutually relevant beliefs, it would still face other foundationalist objections. The too much to ask objection urges that consistency is too strong a requirement for justification; the next objection to be considered, which I shall call the **consistent fairy story objection**, urges that it is too weak. Coherentism cannot be correct, the argument goes, because the consistency of a set of beliefs is manifestly insufficient to guarantee, or to be an indication of, their truth. It might be thought that this is unfair, since coherentists usually require more than simple consistency of a coherent belief-set. But it is clear on very little reflection that adding a requirement of comprehensiveness doesn't make matters any better – at any rate, that a set of beliefs is consistent and large is no more a guarantee, or indication, of its truth than that it is, simply, consistent. Once again, however, as with the accusation that his conception of mutual support is a matter of 'going round in a circle', the coherentist is likely to protest that what he really proposes is not so simple-minded; perhaps he will insist that 'comprehensive' means not just 'large' but 'covering a significant range of topics', or perhaps he will claim that explanatory coherence, at any rate, is a more sophisticated conception which does not fall to any simple, easy objection along these lines. The foundationalist objector, on the other hand, is likely to be sceptical that elaboration of the concept of coherence will fix the problem. Are we, then, at a stalemate?

I think not; for what may lie behind the foundationalist's conviction that nothing like coherence, however sophisticated an elaboration of that concept is offered, can guarantee the required connection between justification and likely truth, is a further argument, and this time, to my mind, a pretty persuasive one. The fundamental problem with coherentism, according to this argument, lies precisely in the fact that it tries to make justification depend solely on relations among beliefs.

The point is expressed vaguely but vividly by C. I. Lewis when he protests that the coherentist's claim that empirical beliefs can be justified by *nothing but* relations of mutual support is as absurd as suggesting that two drunken sailors could support each other by leaning back to back – when neither was standing on anything!

To get this objection to coherentism in as strong a form as possible, it is desirable (though I shall continue to call it the **drunken sailors argument**) to spell it out literally. The fundamental objection is this: that because coherentism allows no non-belief input – no role to experience or the world – it cannot be satisfactory; that unless it is acknowledged that the justification of an empirical belief requires such input, it could not be supposed that a belief's being justified could be an indication of its truth, of its correctly representing how the world is.

In the end, I believe, this argument really is fatal to coherentism. A theory couched in terms exclusively of relations among a subject's beliefs faces an insuperable difficulty about the connection between the concepts of justification and truth. How could the fact that a set of beliefs is coherent, to whatever degree and in however sophisticated a sense of 'coherent', be a guarantee, or even an indication, of truth?

Well, coherentists, of course, think it *could*. On the face of it, at least, their most promising strategy is, while acknowledging that the objection may be fatal to uncompromising coherentism, to argue that a moderated, weighted form can avoid it. For the initial distinction accorded by this style of coherentism to a sub-class of beliefs, and the weighting of relations of mutual support, is intended precisely to make it plausible that justification is truth-indicative. But the appearance that this response solves the problem seems to be *mere* appearance. The objector will not fail to notice that weighted coherentism proposes to distinguish the very kinds of beliefs which foundationalism takes as basic, and will not fail to press the question: where, or how, do initially distinguished beliefs get their epistemic distinction? If the coherentist offers no answer, he is vulnerable to the objection that his initial distinctions among beliefs, and his weighting of support relations, is arbitrary; but if he answers, plausibly enough, that he distinguishes simple perceptual beliefs, say, because of their closeness to the subject's experience, then, while the objection that no place has been allowed for input from the world is met, the objection that he has covertly sacrificed the coherentist character of his theory is inevitable. In fact, moderated, weighted 'coherentism', when combined with this kind of rationale for its initial epistemic weightings, starts to look nearly indistinguishable from foundherentism.

Of course, even if this is sufficient to discredit the weighted coherentist

response to the drunken sailors argument, it is not sufficient to establish that *no* plausible response is available to the coherentist. I hope that
the arguments of chapter 3, against the defences offered by BonJour
and Davidson, will go some way towards making this deficiency good.
For now, however, I want to point out that *if* the drunken sailors
argument is a good argument against coherentism, which I think it is,
it is also a good argument against self-justificatory foundationalism; for
in that form foundationalism, just like coherentism, makes justification
exclusively a matter of relations among beliefs. One way of putting it
might be to say that self-justificatory foundationalism, like weighted
coherentism, is obliged to motivate the idea that some beliefs are
epistemically distinguished in virtue of their intrinsic character, their
content. *Perhaps*, in the case of some non-empirical beliefs, this is not
hopelessly implausible (what makes the belief that eggs are eggs self-
justifying, it might be said, is precisely its obvious lack of content); one
gloss on 'self-evident', after all, is 'such that failure to accept its truth
is an indication of failure to understand it'. But in the case of empirical
beliefs this recourse is not available. The basic beliefs of self-justificatory
empirical foundationalism will have to have *some* content. And it is not
clear how self-justificatory foundationalism is better equipped than
weighted coherentism to avoid the dilemma that, if the choice of initially distinguished beliefs is not arbitrary, it must be covertly motivated
by an assumed connection with experience or the world.

Extrinsic and experientialist versions of foundationalism, however,
are not, like self-justificatory versions, susceptible to the side-effects
(hangover?) of the drunken sailors argument. But they face other objections. The exact statement of the most important argument against
extrinsic foundationalism – I shall call it the **evidentialist objection** –
will depend on the exact formulation of the connection between the
subject's belief and the state of affairs that makes it true which the
extrinsic foundationalist is offering; but the main thrust is to the effect
that extrinsic foundationalism violates the intuition that what justifies a
belief should be something of which – as the etymology of 'evidence'
suggests - the subject is aware. In its strongest version, the evidentialist
objection is that extrinsic foundationalism violates intuition two ways,
being both too weak and too strong, allowing that a basic belief is
justified if there is an appropriate connection between the belief-state
and the state of affairs that makes it true, even when the subject has no
evidence for the belief or has evidence against it, and denying this if
there is no such connection, even when the subject has good evidence
for the belief. I note that the experientialist foundationalist is precluded

from using this objection – for it implicitly repudiates the one directionality on which, *qua* foundationalist, he insists. Though it would require further development to establish that no revised extrinsic formula would avoid it, my feeling is that the evidentialist objection is very damaging to extrinsic foundationalism.

This leads me to a familiar coherentist argument which, if it worked, would rule out experientialist as well as extrinsic foundationalism. For simplicity, and because I regard the evidentialist objection as already precluding extrinsic foundationalism, I state this argument in the form in which it applies to experientialist foundationalism. Experientialist foundationalism claims that basic beliefs are justified by the subject's experience. But while there can be *causal* relations, there cannot be *logical* relations between a person's experiences and his beliefs. Hence, since justification is a logical matter, it must be a matter exclusively of relations among beliefs.

The first premiss of the argument is true. A's seeing a dog may *cause him to believe* that there is a dog present, but it cannot *entail or confirm the proposition* that there is a dog present. But the argument that this shows that the subject's experiences are irrelevant to the justification of his beliefs – the **irrelevance of causation argument** – is inconclusive, because it requires the further premiss that justification is exclusively a logical matter, which is false. What justifies A in believing there is a dog present? – his seeing the dog, the fact that he sees the dog, is a natural answer. What this argument really shows is not that experience is irrelevant to justification, but that we stand in need of an account of how it is relevant, of the relations between the causal and the logical aspects of the concept of justification. And there is already a clue as to how one might go about constructing such an account in the coherentist's premiss that there can be only causal, not logical, relations between a subject's experiences and his beliefs. For in this premiss the term 'belief' is ambiguous (as my elaboration of the argument made apparent): there can be causal relations between a belief-*state*, *someone's believing something*, and that person's experiences; there can be logical relations between a belief-*content*, *a proposition, what someone believes*, and other belief-contents, other propositions. This suggests that an adequate account of how the fact that a person's having certain experiences contributed causally to his believing something could make it more or less likely that what he believes is true, will need to exploit the distinction between belief-states and belief-contents.

The most that has to be conceded by the experientialist in response to the irrelevance of causation argument is that only an account which combines logical and causal elements can allow the relevance of experience to justification. I say 'the most' because we have already, in the brief discussion of the mismatch between deductive consequence and conclusiveness in the presence of inconsistency, encountered one reason to doubt whether 'logical' is quite the right word for the non-causal, evaluative component of the concept of justification; and subsequently, when I come to argue the mismatch between 'inductive logic', so-called, and supportiveness of evidence, we shall encounter another. The appropriate response to the irrelevance of causation argument, therefore, is to insist on the 'double-aspect', or 'state-content' character of the concept of justification; acknowledging, of course, that an adequate account of how experience is relevant to justification will require an articulation of how the two aspects interrelate. Experientialist foundationalism usually leaves all this implicit; but it is not fatally damaged by the irrelevance of causation argument.

Foundherentism, as characterized in section I, is experientialist; so it too will require a double-aspect, state-content approach; when it comes to articulating the theory in detail (chapter 4), I shall make this as explicit as possible.

A second influential argument against foundationalism points out that it requires that basic beliefs be both secure (plausibly claimed to be justified independently of the support of any other beliefs) and rich (plausibly claimed to be capable of supporting a substantial body of other beliefs); and urges that no belief can fulfill both these requirements. For, the argument goes, these two requirements are in competition with each other; the first can be satisfied only by stripping down, the second only by beefing up, the content of the basic beliefs.

This argument seems to me extremely persuasive with respect to a restricted class of foundationalist theories, those, namely, which claim that the basic beliefs have to be certain or infallible, incapable of being false. But infallibilism is inessential to foundationalism, so the interesting question is what sort of force this argument has against other forms. A reasonable initial response is that while there is plausibility in the suggestion that the requirement of security is apt to compete with the requirement of richness (a plausibility vividly illustrated by the history of foundationalist programmes, which have indeed shown a marked tendency to swing back and forth between insisting on security at the expense of content, and insisting on content at the expense of security), it is unproven that the tension is irresoluble. Further reflection suggests that this argument – the **swings and roundabouts argument** – is the more plausible the more strongly privileged basic beliefs are required to be, and the more of the responsibility for the support of all other justified beliefs they are required to bear. This means that the argument is likely to be less effective against weak foundationalism than against strong foundationalism (since the former does not require basic beliefs to be absolutely justified independently of the support of other beliefs), and less effective against impure foundationalism than against pure foundationalism (since the former does not require basic beliefs to do all the work of supporting the superstructure of derived beliefs); least effective, therefore, against weak impure foundationalism. In fact, I am reasonably confident that this argument is quite *in*effective against weak impure foundationalism – and of course entirely confident that it has *no* force against foundherentism, which requires no privileged class of basic beliefs at all.

It remains to explain what persuades me that foundherentism is more plausible even than the modest forms of foundationalism which seem capable of withstanding the swings and roundabouts argument. Here I rely on an interlocking pair of arguments, not, so far as I am aware, previously deployed in the debate between foundationalism and coherentism. The first points to a lacuna in weak foundationalism which cannot be filled except by abandoning the one-directional character of justification; the second points to the lack of a cogent rationale for weakening one-directionality, as impure foundationalism does, without abandoning it altogether. I shall call these the **up and back all the way down arguments**.

According to weak foundationalism, a basic belief is justified prima facie but defeasibly, or to some degree but not completely, by something other than a belief. This sounds, at first blush, a sensible account of the following, common enough, kind of situation: suppose A believes that there is a dog present, and that he believes this because of his current sensory experience (his seeing what appears to be a dog); then A is justified prima facie, or justified to a considerable degree, in believing that there is a dog before him – but not indefeasibly justified, not fully justified, because appearances could be misleading. At second blush, however, an awkward question arises: would not A be *more* justified, or more securely justified, in believing that there is a dog before him if he also justifiedly believed that his eyes are working normally, that he is not under the influence of post-hypnotic suggestion, that there are no very lifelike toy dogs around, etc., etc.? Surely, he would. But the weak foundationalist cannot allow this, for his story is that basic beliefs get their justification exclusively from something other than the support of further beliefs; to allow that they get some justification from experience and some from the support of other beliefs would violate the one-directional character of justification, on which, *qua* foundationalist, he insists. And if this possibility were allowed, weak, experientialist foundationalism would be transmuted into a form of foundherentism.

The problem with impure foundationalism is, rather, that it lacks a cogent rationale. Unlike the pure foundationalist, who insists that justification always goes from basic to derived beliefs, the impure foundationalist maintains one-directionality only in the form of the negative thesis that justification never goes from derived to basic beliefs. But why, then, does he still insist that there must be a distinct, privileged class of basic beliefs which get their justification entirely without the support of any other beliefs, and which must contribute to the justification of all other beliefs? Perhaps the response will be: because there must be a role for input from outside the subject's beliefs. But this, though true, is obviously insufficient to establish that there must be a privileged class of basic beliefs which get *all* their justification from such input. And without this assumption, for which no reason has been given, impure experientialist foundationalism would be transmuted into a form of foundherentism.

The infinite regress argument for foundationalism is inconclusive, and so, too, is its stronger variant, the no tolerable alternatives argument. The too much to ask argument seriously damages the usual, holistic forms of coherentism, though it might possibly be avoided by retreat to a restricted, quasi-holistic version; it also suggests awkward questions about the foundationalist's own attitude to inconsistency. The drunken sailors argument, however, is decisive against coherentism; and the attempt to avoid it by a shift from the uncompromising, egalitarian form to a moderated, weighted variant turns out to amount, in the only form in which it has any prospect of success, to the adoption of a disguised form of foundherentism. So coherentism won't do.

The drunken sailors argument turns out to do as much damage to self-justificatory foundationalism as it does to coherentism. And the evidentialist objection is fatal to extrinsic foundationalism. But the irrelevance of causation argument is not fatal to experientialist foundationalism, but only points to the need for a double-aspect, state-content approach. The swings and roundabouts argument succeeds against infallibilist foundationalism and, probably, against strong and pure foundationalism. Weak and impure forms probably survive it. They succumb, however, to the up and back all the way down arguments. So foundationalism won't do.

So neither foundationalism nor coherentism will do.

Since it allows the relevance of non-belief input to justification, foundherentism survives the decisive argument against coherentism, the drunken sailors argument. It is untouched by the evidentialist objection to extrinsic foundationalism, and, like experientialist foundationalism, can survive the irrelevance of causation argument by adopting a double-aspect approach. Since it requires no privileged class of basic beliefs, it is under no threat from the swings and roundabouts argument. And its superiority to even weak and impure forms of experientialist foundationalism is exhibited by its ability, and their inability, to accommodate the up and back all the way down arguments. So foundherentism looks to be able to survive both the strongest arguments against foundationalism and the strongest arguments against coherentism.

This constitutes my prima facie case for foundherentism. The hope, of course, is that this prima facie case can be made even more convincing as the argument proceeds, first by way of detailed critical study of specific foundationalist and coherentist theories, and then by way of a detailed development and defence of the foundherentist alternative.

2
Foundationalism Undermined

... to deny that there are empirical certainties does not imply that
experience is a pure fiction, that it is without content, or even that
there is no given element ... That we have probable knowledge
... implies no certainty but only initial credibility.

Goodman 'Sense and Certainty'[1]

The present chapter is a case-study of the foundationalist theory offered
by C. I. Lewis in *An Analysis of Knowledge and Valuation*.[2] The goal is
in part, of course, to show that the theory fails; but also, more important,
to reveal tensions and ambiguities within Lewis's account which, I shall
argue, can be resolved only by moving – as Lewis himself sometimes
seems half-tempted to move – in a foundherentist direction.

The most striking feature of Lewis's theory, and the feature most
stressed by Lewis himself, is its infallibilist character. Understandably,
then, earlier critics – Goodman, Reichenbach, Firth and others[3] – mostly
concentrated their fire on this aspect. And, though their arguments
are not, I think, quite impeccable, their conclusion, that Lewis's infallibilism is indefensible, is quite correct. My target, however, is not
infallibilism, but foundationalism. Nevertheless, I shall offer some criticisms of Lewis's infallibilism on my own account; for Lewis himself insists that, where foundational beliefs are concerned, there is no distinction
to be made between their being immune from error and their being
immune from unjustifiedness; so it is necessary to deal with his reasons
for infallibilism because they are, from his point of view, also the reasons
for adopting a strong foundationalism.

But the position is far from straightforward, for there are deep tensions
at work in Lewis's book. One is surprised to find, for example, side by

side with Lewis's infallibilism, the shrewd observation that 'there is . . . no single and useful meaning of "knowledge" which wholly accords with the usual meaning of that term' (p. 29), that justification ('credibility' or 'probability' in Lewis's favoured terminology) comes in degrees, and that it is pointless to insist that only completely justified belief counts as knowledge. But, given all this, it is not so surprising to find that as the book proceeds there seem to be significant changes in the theory on offer.

Initially there seems to be no doubt that it is a strong foundationalist theory that is proposed. One's apprehensions of what is given to one in immediate experience are, according to Lewis, certain in the sense not only that they are immune from error but also in the sense that they are immune from unjustifiedness, and any other justified empirical beliefs one has are justified at least in part by their support. Later in the book, however, Lewis apparently shifts his ground. Only one's *present* experience is presently available to one in the peculiarly direct way which, according to Lewis, guarantees the complete justification of 'apprehensions of the given'; but most of one's empirical beliefs could be justified to a degree sufficient to constitute knowledge only by reference to *past* experiences – and these are presently available to one only through the fallible medium of memory. At this point, it seems that Lewis shifts to a weak foundationalism in which the basis includes, besides apprehensions of one's present sensory experience, still held to be completely justified, apprehensions, by means of memory, of past experiences, taken to be no more than initially credible. And then he takes what appears to be a step in a more radical direction: evidence about the circumstances in which memory is reliable is acknowledged as relevant to the credibility of these memory beliefs; and it looks, at least briefly, as if Lewis may be giving up the one-directional character of justification.

Throughout the book, even before the discussion of the role of memory seems to bring about a shift from strong to weak foundationalism and hints of a shift beyond foundationalism, the theory proposed is impure. Lewis allows that mutual support among derived beliefs is legitimate, and can raise the degree of justification they acquire from the support of basic beliefs. Lewis's preferred term for these relations of mutual support is 'congruence' – a significant choice, indicating the difference he wants to stress between his account, according to which, though congruence can raise the credibility of beliefs, it cannot confer credibility on them in the first instance, and coherentism.

And throughout the book, even after the discussion of the role of memory seems to bring about a shift from strong to weak foundationalism, and perhaps even beyond foundationalism, Lewis defends three key theses:

1 that one's apprehensions of what is given to one in immediate experience are certain;
2 that unless there were such absolutely certain apprehensions of experience, no empirical belief would be justified to any degree;
3 that the justification of all one's (justified) empirical beliefs depends ultimately at least in part on the support of these certain apprehensions of experience.

(Disambiguation will be necessary later, but for the moment 'certain' is to be understood as meaning both 'immune from error' and 'immune from unjustifiedness'.)

A main theme of my argument will be that Lewis's reasons for theses 1–3 are inconclusive, and that, in fact, all three are false. In each case, however, from Lewis's unsound argument for his strong conclusion, it is possible to reconstruct a sound argument for a weaker conclusion (one might say that Lewis succumbs to the 'fallacy of exaggeration'). My diagnosis will be, crudely, that Lewis's arguments run together the question of the epistemic status and role of a subject's experiences, and the question of the status and role of a subject's beliefs about his experiences – a diagnosis for which, I shall argue, the textual evidence speaks no less than its explanatory power. Lewis's three theses are false, but these are true:

1* that one has various sensory, introspective and memory experiences;
2* that unless one had such experiences, none of one's empirical beliefs would be justified to any degree;
3* that the justification of all one's (justified) empirical beliefs depends ultimately at least in part on these experiences.

My second main theme will be that the shifts in Lewis's position – from strong to weak foundationalism, his faltering steps in a foundherentist direction – are precisely such as to reveal that the sound arguments available to him, arguments which support the three true theses but not the three false theses, not only do not make the case for foundationalism, but in fact are most plausibly construed as contributing to the case for foundherentism.

The simplest strategy seems to be to consider each of Lewis's three key theses in turn, and to develop my two themes in the course of these discussions. At any rate, that is what I shall do.

I

'One's apprehensions of what is given to one in immediate experience are certain'. This thesis of Lewis's bristles with ambiguities: both about what 'apprehensions of the given' are supposed to be, and about what is meant by calling them 'certain'. My diagnosis will be that these ambiguities intersect in Lewis's argument in such a way as to disguise the fact that in any sense in which the thesis is epistemologically inter-esting, it is untrue.

The relevant ambiguities, in crude outline, are these. As I have already noted, according to Lewis the question of the truth of a belief and the question of its justification, though in most cases distinct, are not to be distinguished in the case of apprehensions of experience (p. 254). 'Certain', in this context, means both 'immune from error' and 'immune from unjustifiedness'. I will mark the distinction by speaking of 'T-certainty' ('T' for 'true') versus 'J-certainty' ('J' for 'justified'). There is also another, and as it turns out more consequential, ambiguity in Lewis's use of 'certain', which I shall mark by speaking of 'trivial' T- or J-certainty versus 'substantial' T- or J-certainty. An 'apprehension of the given' would be substantially T-certain if it *could not be false, because it is guaranteed to be true,* substantially J-certain if it *could not be unjus-tified, because it is guaranteed to be justified;* it would be trivially T-certain if it *could not be false, but also could not be true,* trivially J-certain if it *could not be unjustified, but also could not be justified.*[4] And, finally, Lewis's 'apprehensions of the given' refers sometimes to judgements about one's immediate sensory experiences, and sometimes to those experiences themselves.

The problem with Lewis's argument for his first thesis, still in rather crude outline, is this. That judgements about one's immediate sensory experience are substantially T- and/or J-certain is epistemologically interesting, but false; that one's sensory experiences are trivially T- and J-certain is true, but of no epistemological interest.

Of course, the equivocations I diagnose do not appear on the surface of Lewis's arguments; so it needs to be made plausible that they oper-ate, unseen, beneath the surface.

Identifying what Lewis means when he speaks of 'apprehensions of what is given in experience' is not made easier by the fact that, though he gives examples of statements intended to represent them, he is at pains to insist not only that such apprehensions are seldom, if ever, explicitly formulated (p. 182), but also that any linguistic formulation is likely to be inadequate (p. 172). Anyhow, Lewis's examples of the 'expressive statements' which best represent apprehensions of the given in experience take the form 'I now see what looks like a sheet of white paper', 'I now see what looks like a flight of granite steps', 'I now see what looks like a doorknob'. They are first person, present tense, indexical, and restricted in content to how things appear, rather than how they actually are. It is clear, however, that it is not *reports* of apprehensions of the given which Lewis takes to be certain; he acknowledges that such reports could be insincere or verbally mistaken. But it is not so clear whether it is *judgements about what is given in experience* (e.g., my judgement that I now see what looks like a doorknob) or *the experience itself* (e.g., my being aware of seeing what looks like a doorknob) that he takes to be certain. Phrases like 'presentations of sense', 'direct findings of sense' (p. 171), 'immediately presented . . . contents of experience' (p. 179), 'apprehended . . . facts of experience' (p. 182), might be taken either way.

And understanding what Lewis means by 'certain' is not made easier by the fact that he uses 'infallible', 'incorrigible', and 'indubitable' apparently interchangeably, when these have significantly different meanings ('incorrigible' suggesting immunity to correction, 'indubitable' immunity to doubt, 'certain' and 'infallible' immunity to error). It is clear enough, however, that Lewis's primary concern is with immunity to error, which he takes as equivalent, in the case of apprehensions of the given though not generally, to immunity to unjustifiedness.

For the moment, let us restrict our attention to T-certainty. That a person's sensory experiences are trivially T-certain goes almost without saying; for experiences are events, and therefore incapable of truth-value – hence, in particular, incapable of falsity. (An experience, as Goodman puts it, can no more be false than a desk can.) But this nearly trivial thesis is of no epistemological interest. The thesis Lewis must intend is not this, but the genuinely substantial thesis that *a person's judgements about his immediate sensory experience are substantially T-certain*. It seems, however, that Lewis's confidence that this substantial infallibilist thesis is true may derive in part (as Goodman suggests)[5] from his failure to distinguish it from the nearly trivial thesis.

Perhaps because he is convinced that there must be *some* substantially T-certain beliefs if *any* beliefs are to be justified, Lewis offers surprisingly little by way of specific argument that judgements about what is given to one in immediate experience *are* substantially T-certain. And what little he does offer sits cheek by jowl with discussion which tends rather to support the trivial thesis. Here is what seems to be the closest thing to an argument for the substantial infallibilist thesis:

Subtract, in what we say we see, or hear, or otherwise learn from direct experience, *all that conceivably could be mistaken*; the remainder is the given content of the experience inducing this belief. (pp. 182–3)

Only a paragraph later, Lewis seems to have retreated to the trivial thesis:

Apprehensions of the given which ... expressive statements formulate are not judgements, and they are not subject to any possible error. *Statement* of such apprehension is however true or false ... (p. 183, my italics)

Subtract, from Lewis's argument for the substantial infallibilist thesis, the illusion of support that may be lent it by confusion with the trivial infallibilist thesis; the remainder is the argument that judgements about one's immediate sensory experience are guaranteed to be true because they are so characterized as to exclude all possibility of error. And this argument is unconvincing. Indeed, it is potentially very misleading; for one cannot seriously suppose that Lewis thinks that the apprehensions in question are devoid of content. The judgement that I see what looks like a sheet of yellow paper is not empty; indeed, it is no weaker than the judgement that I see a sheet of yellow paper. (It is no harder to imagine a scenario in which the former is false and the latter true than it is to imagine a scenario in which the former is true and the latter false.) What is at stake must be not *type* but *token* certainty.[6] The point must be about *particular* judgements of how things sensorily appear to one at the time of making the judgement; and the argument must be that, since the characterization of the content of the judgement in question restricts it to how things presently appear to one, such a judgement, involving no element of interpretation, can involve no element of *mis*interpretation of the experience it represents. (Or in other words, that if a judgment-token concerns only what is sensorily given to the subject at the time of his making this judgement, and not how it is taken, there is no possibility of *mis*take.) But this is quite inconclusive in the absence of an argument to show that there *are* any judgements which simply report one's immediate experience and involve no element of interpretation.

If this is right, Lewis's only argument for the substantial infallibilist thesis fails; but of course this does not in itself have any tendency to show that the substantial infallibilist thesis is false. Nevertheless, I think

Figure 2.1

it is. Judgements about how things presently sensorily seem to one, on the rare occasions they are actually made, are no doubt usually true; but not, I think, invariably or necessarily so. Consider the ophthalmologist's test in which a patient is presented with a fan of lines of equal thickness, as in figure 2.1, and asked whether the lines look all of the same thickness, or whether the lines on the left, in the centre, or on the right look thicker. The question is not whether the patient is inclined to think that some of the lines *are* thicker – he may well be quite aware, as I was when subjected to this test, that they are all of the same thickness. The question is strictly about appearances, about whether any of the lines *look* thicker. (The purpose of the test is to detect astigmatism; if there is no astigmatism, the lines will look, as they are, of equal thickness; but if there is astigmatism, some lines will look thicker than others.) Now, it is common for patients to hesitate, to be unsure which, if any, lines look thicker; and it is standard routine for them to be asked this question more than once (looking through the same lens) *to allow for the possibility of mistake.* It is acknowledged that there is, for example, a possibility of wishful thinking – that the patient's judgement that the lines now look of the same thickness may be influenced by his hope that this is, at last, the right correction. Sometimes, looking at the same diagram through the same lens, the patient will give first one answer, and then, very shortly afterwards, another. It is acknowledged that it is possible that the way the lines look may change, even over a very short period, because of abnormal muscular adjustment; but if this is the case, other tests should confirm it.[7]

From what Lewis says in response to Goodman, it can be assumed that his reaction to this example would be to point out that it is compatible with all that has been said to insist that if the patient gives different answers (sincerely, of course, and without any verbal confusion) at however short an interval, then the way the lines look to him must have changed over that interval.[8] And, indeed, so it is. But this is not a decisive reply; for it is *also* compatible with all that has been said that one of the patient's judgements was mistaken. And Lewis's claim is that mistake is inconceivable – which, it seems to me, this example makes very implausible indeed.

If Lewis's identification of T-certainty and J-certainty in the case of apprehensions of the given is correct, the argument that apprehensions of the given are not T-certain is, equally, an argument that they are not J-certain. But since the identification is questionable (that if a judgement is T-certain it is J-certain seems plausible, but it is the converse implication which matters here) it will be as well to see how the argument may be modified to undermine the claim of J-certainty directly. Suppose, then, that the ophthalmologist's patient justifiedly believes that he is more than normally suggestible – he has recently seen the results of the psychological tests he has undergone, perhaps; and suppose that the ophthalmologist, who is anxious to get the examination over, has not been very careful about how he phrases his questions. 'There, that should do it, they all look the same thickness now, don't they?' he asks – and the patient duly agrees that they do. He has some justification for this judgement; but it is, surely, in view of his evidence that he may have been influenced by the ophthalmologist's 'question expecting the answer "yes"', far from complete.[9]

The conclusion I want to draw is that thesis 1 is false in any sense in which it is epistemologically interesting. But mightn't a defender of Lewis argue that this is premature, that the conclusion could be avoided if one took the argument of Lewis's considered earlier more seriously? If the judgement that I now see what looks like an array of lines of equal thickness is not substantially certain, the defender might argue, then that just shows that it is not, in the intended sense, an 'apprehension of what is given in immediate experience'. In response I would amplify my earlier observation, that Lewis's attempt to argue that apprehensions of what is given in immediate experience are substantially certain simply in virtue of how such apprehensions are characterized, fails for want of an argument that, once all that is conceivably false has been 'subtracted', anything that is capable of being true remains. My counter-example can be ruled out as not really an example, but only if the process of 'subtraction' is so radical as to leave 'apprehensions of experience' referring to the experiences themselves rather than to judgements about one's experience; and then the only certainty that is guaranteed is trivial, not substantial.

And this suggests the further conclusion that Lewis's unsuccessful argument for thesis 1 is most plausibly reconstrued as pointing out, simply, that we do have experiences, and that what experiences we have is not up to us. Lewis himself comes very close to acknowledging this, when he writes, immediately before he offers the infallibilist argument we have been considering, that '[the] point is simply that there is such a thing as experience, the content of which we do not invent' (p. 182). Thesis 1 is not established by Lewis's argument, and is false; thesis 1*, however, is a plausible conclusion from his premises, and is true.

II

'Unless there were absolutely certain apprehensions of experience, no empirical belief would be justified to any degree'. The first question that arises is: in what sense should 'certain' be understood here? The answer, I take it, is that it is substantial J-certainty that is at issue; that Lewis's thesis is that unless some empirical beliefs are fully justified independently of the support of any other beliefs, no empirical beliefs are justified to any degree.

Whereas Lewis offers very little explicit argument for thesis 1, he makes several elaborate arguments for this second thesis. But all these elaborate arguments are non sequiturs; in fact, they all fail for the same reason: they run together two senses of 'absolutely justified' – 'justified, and not relative to any further beliefs', and 'completely, not just partially, justified'.

Actually, Lewis himself rarely uses the word 'justification', preferring 'warrant', or more often 'credibility', and most often 'probability'. His preference has some significance, because it is indicative of his acknowledgement of the intuition (which of course I share) that justification comes in degrees. But though he acknowledges this intuition, Lewis does not always keep the gradational character of justification in full view as his argument develops; and it looks to be, indeed, in part because of this failure that he is vulnerable to the confusion of the two ways in which a belief might be 'absolutely justified' which I diagnose as fundamental to the failure of his arguments for thesis 2.

If what is to confirm the objective belief and thus show it probable, were itself an objective belief and thus no more than probable, the objective belief to be confirmed would only probably be rendered probable. Thus unless we distinguish the objective truth

belief in which experience may render probable, from those presentations of experience which provide this warrant, any citation of
evidence for a statement about objective reality, and any mention-
able corroboration of it, will become involved in an infinite regress
of the merely probable, or else it will go round in a circle – and
the probability will fail to be genuine. If anything is to be probable, then something must be certain. The data which eventually
support a genuine probability, must themselves be certain.
We . . . have such absolute certainties, in the sense-data initiating
beliefs. (p. 186)

'Objective' beliefs are beliefs about the external world, about how things
are (by contrast, that is, with 'expressive' judgements, which are solely
about how things appear to one).

This is Lewis's variant on the no tolerable alternatives argument.
What is being claimed is that an objective belief may be justified to
some degree, relative to some further beliefs which support it, but it
cannot be justified to any degree, non-relatively, unless, ultimately, the
series of beliefs comes to an end with some belief or beliefs which are
fully justified independently of the support of any other beliefs. For
present purposes neither my critique of the presupposition that the
reasons for a belief must constitute a series, a chain, nor my critique of
the presupposition that coherence is a matter of beliefs 'going round in
a circle', need be taken into account. For Lewis's version of the argument
is vulnerable to a less subtle objection. Even supposing (for the sake of
argument) that the reasons for a belief do constitute a chain, and even
supposing (for the sake of argument) that a coherentist account is ruled
out, still the argument is a non sequitur. Suppose A's belief that p is
justified to some degree relative to q, and q relative to r . . . and so on.
A's belief that p cannot be justified to any degree, non-relatively, unless, eventually, the chain ends with a belief or beliefs which is or are
justified to some degree *independently of any further beliefs*. But it is *not*
required that the basic belief or beliefs eventually reached be completely justified independently of any further belief.
    The same criticism applies to the following passage:

Proximate grounds of the probable or credible need not be certain;
it will be sufficient if they are themselves genuinely credible. If
'P' is credible on ground 'Q', then the credibility of 'Q' assures
a credibility of lesser degree than if 'Q' were certain. But if the
credibility of 'P' rests on the credibility of 'Q' and that of 'Q' on
that of 'R', and so on; and if in this regress we nowhere come to

rest with anything that is certain; then how can the credibilities spoken of be genuine; since each in turn is relative to a ground, and no ultimate ground is given? . . . Is it not, then, required that there be ultimate data . . . which are themselves certain? (p. 333)

If (again assuming the 'chain' picture for the sake of argument) the belief that p is justified to some degree relative to the belief that q, and the belief that q is justified to some degree relative to the belief that r, the belief that p will only be justified, *simpliciter*, to any degree, if at the end of the chain some belief is reached which is justified to some degree independently of any further beliefs. But once again it does not follow that this ultimate ground must be fully and completely justified independently of any further beliefs.

What is most remarkable about this is that just a few pages earlier Lewis himself had made precisely the point that undermines his argument:

> . . . that the ground of one belief, 'P', is another empirical belief, 'Q', which is less than certain, does not of itself invalidate the justification of 'P'. It is not the certainty, but only the genuine credibility of 'Q' that is called for; and if such genuine credibility can be assured for . . . 'Q', then the relation of 'P' to 'Q' will assure a similar credibility of 'P', even though the difference of credibility of 'Q' from certainty will be reflected in a correspondingly lower credibility which is thus assured to 'Q'. (p. 328)

But then why, if Lewis realizes that the grounds of a belief don't have to be certain, only 'credible', to transmit some degree of credibility to the target belief, does he lose sight of the point and insist that 'if anything is to be probable, something must be certain'? Perhaps he is impressed by what one might call the 'dilution of probabilities' argument. This argument does not seem to occur explicitly in *An Analysis of Knowledge and Valuation*, but it certainly comes into play in the discussion between Lewis and Reichenbach, who urges that the argument fails. Here is Lewis's comment:

> . . . the difficulty . . . then arises . . . [that] a statement justified as probable must have a ground; if the ground is only probable then there must be a ground of it; and so on. And to assess the probability of the original statement, its probability relative to its ground must be multiplied by the probability of its own ground, which in turn must be multiplied by the probability of its own ground, and

so on. Reichenbach denies that the regressive series of probability-values so arising must approach zero, and the probability of the original statement be thus finally whittled down to nothing . . . I disbelieve that [this] will serve his point . . . The supposition that the probability of anything whatever always depends on something else which is only probable in itself, is flatly incompatible with the justifiable assignment of any probability whatsoever.[10]

It is not necessary to make any elaborate argument in the theory of probabilities to see that the 'dilution' argument cannot rescue Lewis's thesis. Suppose it granted that, if p is justified to degree n (<1) relative to q, and q is justified to degree m (<1) relative to r . . . and so on, then, if this were to go on without end, the multiplication of degrees of justification less than 1 would converge towards 0. But all that follows is that *either* there must eventually be some fully and completely justified belief in the series (some probability of 1, in the less transparent terminology in which Lewis and Reichenbach conduct their debate) *or* the series must come to an end. It does not follow that *both* must be the case, that the series must *come to an end with a fully justified belief*.

Another part of the explanation of how Lewis fails to appreciate the equivocation may lie in the fact that he associates his inconclusive argument very closely with a better argument which, however, has a weaker conclusion. Reichenbach's position, he comments, strikes him as falsely presupposing that 'if enough probabilities can be got to lean against one another they can all be made to stand up'.[11] Already in *An Analysis of Knowledge and Valuation* Lewis had argued at length that coherence among one's beliefs could never, of itself, constitute a guarantee, or even an indication, of their truth; that there must be some non-belief input (pp. 339–40). And at one point he suggests that it is part of what is meant by calling a belief 'empirical' that its justification depends on experience.[12] I find the latter point appealing, but I think it must be resisted; though it is indeed part of the usual meaning of 'empirical' that an empirical belief depends on experience, one must allow a coherentist, or for that matter a foundationalist of a non-experientialist stripe, the possibility of modifying the usual meaning of 'empirical' so as to detach 'concerning how things are in the world' from 'depending on experience'. Even without the verbal wrinkle Lewis gives it, however, his version of the drunken sailors argument carries some weight. His conclusion, though, should be, not that there must be beliefs justified fully and completely by something other than a belief, but that there must be some non-belief input to empirical justification. It is not hard to see how Lewis might have been tempted, especially since he writes of the needed non-belief input as *'given data of sense'*, to think that this lends support to his thesis that empirical justification requires substantial J-certainty in the basis. But it doesn't.

This time there is little need for further argument, in addition to the considerations that show that Lewis's reasons for thesis 2 are inconclusive, to establish that thesis 2 is false. For, if my critique of Lewis's reasons is correct, it is already established that an objective belief could be justified to some degree provided only that the chain of reasons comes to an end with some belief or beliefs justified to some degree independently of any further beliefs – hence, that certainty is not required in the basis.

Nor is there much need for further elaboration to see that Lewis's argument for thesis 2 is a better argument for the weaker thesis I have called 2*: that unless one had experiences (the sensory and introspective experiences referred to in thesis 1*) one couldn't be justified, to any degree, in any of one's empirical beliefs. I trust it is clear how my strategy with respect to Lewis's thesis 2 parallels my strategy with respect to his thesis 1; in each case he offers what is in effect a plausible argument for an experientialist position, which, however, no doubt because he takes the exhaustiveness of the dichotomy of foundationalism and coherentism entirely for granted, he wrongly takes to be an argument for foundationalism. And Lewis's discussion usually indicates that – as my interpretation suggests – the apprehensions of the given which according to him constitute the foundations of empirical knowledge are justified by the experiences they represent.

There is just one passage which is hard to accommodate on this interpretation; a passage in which Lewis refers to these apprehensions of experience as 'self-justifying or self-evident' (p. 28). But not only is this passage isolated and uncharacteristic; it is also vulnerable to an argument Lewis himself develops in his reply to Reichenbach and Goodman – an argument about a difficulty faced by a moderated, weighted coherentism which is clearly also a difficulty for self-justificatory foundationalism:

> I see no hope for . . . a coherence theory which repudiated data of experience . . . – or no hope unless a postulate be added to the effect that *some* synthetic statements are probable a priori; . . . for example, that every perceptual belief has *some* probability just on account of being a perceptual belief.[13]

Like Lewis, I see such an idea as quite unacceptable.

III

'The justification of all one's (justified) empirical beliefs depends ultimately at least in part on the support of absolutely certain apprehensions of experience'. Lewis commits himself to this thesis both at the beginning of his chapter 7, 'The Bases of Empirical Knowledge':

> Our empirical knowledge rises as a structure of enormous complexity, most parts of which are stabilised by mutual support, but all of which rest, at bottom, on direct findings of sense (p. 171)

and near the close of his analysis of knowledge:

> ... the foundation stones which must support the whole edifice [of empirical knowledge] are still those items of truth which are disclosed in given experience. (p. 353)

And yet in between, in the context of his discussion of memory, he seems to repudiate it:

> ... any solution involving the suggestion that a belief is justified as probable on antecedent grounds which are either certain or, if only probable, then are such as have in turn their ... prior grounds ... until we come to final and sufficient grounds contained exclusively in direct empirical evidence – this solution by way of a finite linear regress ending in given data which are wholly certain – is quite impossible. (pp. 337–8)

It might be thought that the explanation is simple: that the last passage cited is no more than a reminder that the account offered is not purely linear, but involves an element of mutual support in the congruence of objective beliefs; but there is more to it than this, as becomes apparent when Lewis continues:

> What ... makes it impossible ... is the fact that the 'experience' looked to as the essential foundation of our whole pyramidal structure of empirical beliefs is mainly not given in sense experience, at the time when we appeal to it, but past experience, available to us only as remembered ... Hence no regressus of this sort can be brought to termination in empirical certainties. (p. 338)

It is important to understand why it is not open to Lewis to accommodate the problem about memory by sticking to his strong foundationalism and including, among the allegedly certain apprehensions of experience which constitute the basis, apprehensions of 'memorial' experience such as might be represented by expressive statements along the lines of 'It now seems to me that I remember seeing what looked like a doorknob'. Lewis might be able to maintain that such apprehensions of memorial experience are certain – this thesis would be, at any rate, no less (though also no more) plausible than the claim that apprehensions of sensory experience are certain; but the problem is that Lewis's account precludes such apprehensions of memorial experience serving as the basis for the rest of one's empirical beliefs.

To understand why, it is necessary to explore Lewis's account of the 'sense meaning' of objective judgements. According to Lewis's version of the pragmatic maxim, the sense meaning of an objective judgement is given by an infinite set of 'terminating judgements', judgements of the form 'If A (some action on the part of the subject) then E (some experiential upshot) would result'. The sense meaning of an objective judgement like 'There is a doorknob before me', for example, is given by way of its relation of mutual probabilification with a set of judgements along the lines of 'If I were to look directly ahead, I would see what looks like a doorknob', 'If I were to reach out my hand directly ahead, I would touch what feels like a doorknob', and so forth. Objective judgements are said to be 'non-terminating' because they cannot be decisively verified; 'terminating judgements' are so-called because, according to Lewis, they can. The problem for Lewis, then, is that the apprehensions of what is given in immediate experience on which he had up to this point insisted all one's justified empirical beliefs must ultimately rest are apprehensions of one's *current* experience, one's experience *at the time of making the judgement*; but that without the assistance of judgements about one's *past* experience such judgements would be, Lewis acknowledges, manifestly inadequate to support anything like what one ordinarily takes to be one's justified empirical beliefs. And – this is the crucial point for the present argument – the judgements about one's past experience that are required must be along the lines of 'I looked directly ahead and *saw what looked like a doorknob*'. It is not, in other words, *present apprehensions of memorial experience*, but *judgements of one's past sensory experience*, which are required (p. 264). And Lewis acknowledges that, since they depend on memory, these are *not* certain (p. 334). In effect, then, Lewis is being forced to retreat from strong to weak foundationalism by the pressure of something like the swings and roundabouts argument – apprehensions of one's present experience are, or so Lewis thinks, certain, but they are insufficient to form the basis, and while the addition of memorial judgements about past experience might provide a sufficient basis, it is at the price of the sacrifice of certainty.

Lewis's account of terminating judgements is deeply problematic: if the hypothetical action referred to in the antecedent of the conditional ('If A then E') is specified in objective terms ('If I were to do A'), the judgement can by no stretch of the imagination be classified as expressive, while if the action is specified in genuinely expressive terms ('If it were to appear to me that I did A'), Lewis's version of the pragmatic maxim would commit him to phenomenalism, which, however, he expressly disavows; and in any case it would still be hard to see how the whole conditional could be decisively verified by 'direct findings of sense', given Lewis's insistence that the 'If . . . , then . . .' be construed as subjunctive. At the same time, Lewis has missed a significant asymmetry here; for it seems clear that a single unfavourable instance could *falsify* a terminating judgement. But I shall not linger over these criticisms.[14]

The point that is important for present purposes is that Lewis himself is eventually forced to concede that thesis 3 is not true, that the justification of most empirical beliefs does not ultimately depend even in part on the support of supposedly certain apprehensions of what is presently given to one in experience; it depends, most often, on admittedly fallible memories of what was previously given to one in experience. Thesis 3, in short, is not shown to be true by any argument Lewis gives in support of it; and is in fact shown to be false by his argument about memory.

What is more, another argument of Lewis's points unmistakably towards the conclusion that it is really 3*, not 3, that is true. Lewis's initial reaction to the problem about memory seems to be to retreat to a weak impure foundationalism in which the basic beliefs include, besides apprehensions of one's present experience, taken to be completely justified by one's present sensory experience, judgements about one's past experience, taken to be justified prima facie by one's present memorial experience. But Lewis also acknowledges the force of a further argument, which, were this acknowledgement sustained, would push him away from foundationalism altogether, in a foundherentist direction. For he admits that:

> In addition to the present data of recollection, a generalization is required to the effect that when such data of memory are given, the seemingly remembered experiences may, with some degree of accuracy, be accepted as actual. (p. 336)

This further argument is in effect (though of course Lewis doesn't call it that) a version of the up and back all the way down argument against weak foundationalism. The credibility of judgements of past experience, Lewis here admits, depends in part on the support of generalizations about the reliability of memory. But obviously the latter can by no stretch of the imagination be held to be basic, justified by experience alone; and so the one-directional character of support relations is fatally compromised by this concession.

It is significant, in this regard, to recall that Lewis's argument against coherentism is not that mutual support is illegitimate, but that, without input from experience, it can only raise, not confer, credibility.

Lewis's acknowledgment of the pull towards foundherentism is faltering; less than twenty pages after he admits the relevance of generalizations about the reliability of memory to the justification of particular memory judgements – pages devoted to a discussion of congruence, of how mutual support relations can raise the credibility of non-basic beliefs beyond the initial credibility conferred on them by the support of basic beliefs – Lewis is repeating that 'the foundation stones which support the whole edifice [of empirical knowledge] are still those items of truth which are disclosed in given experience' (p. 353). Perhaps this is no wonder; for his faltering acknowledgement of the up and back all the way down argument is devastating to the whole foundationalist picture. If the justification of empirical beliefs derives in part from one's present memorial experience and in part from one's beliefs about the reliability of memory, justification goes up and back all the way down; and the strongest conclusion warranted is, not 3, but 3*: that the justification of all one's empirical beliefs depends ultimately, at least in part, on one's sensory and memorial experience.

Lewis's arguments fail to establish his strong foundationalist theses: 1 that one's apprehensions of what is given to one in immediate experience are certain, 2 that unless there were such absolutely certain apprehensions of experience, no empirical belief would be justified to any degree, and 3 that the justification of all one's empirical beliefs depends ultimately at least in part on the support of these certain apprehensions of experience. But, cleared of various confusions (between a subject's beliefs about his experiences, and those experiences themselves; between substantial and trivial certainty; between non-relative justification and complete justification; between present apprehension of memorial experience and present judgement of past apprehensions), Lewis's arguments make a good case for the theses: 1* that knowing subjects have (sensory, memorial, etc.) experiences, 2* that unless they had such experiences none of their empirical beliefs would be justified to any degree, and 3* that the justification of all a subject's justified empirical beliefs depends ultimately at least in part on those experiences. Unlike 1–3, 1*–3* are in no way distinctively foundationalist in tendency; they constitute, in fact, the core of *experientialism*. They could be accommodated at least as well by a foundherentist theory as by a foundationalist one.

In fact, that they can be *better* accommodated by a foundherentist theory than a foundationalist one is indicated – obliquely perhaps but unmistakably – by the arguments which lead Lewis first to retreat to weak foundationalism and then, though only falteringly, to acknowledge that justification goes, after all, up and back all the way down. The role of experience in justification is not, as experientialist foundationalism holds, as the sole means of support for some privileged class of beliefs, which in turn support the unprivileged remainder; it is rather, as foundherentism holds, to contribute its part to the justification of all justified empirical beliefs, all of which can also be, in varying degrees, justified in part by the support of other beliefs. The picture, in short, is as shown in figure 2.2.

Figure 2.2 (Black shading represents justification by experience, white shading represents justification by the support of other beliefs. No completely white square is presented, since no empirical belief can be justified independently of experience. The completely black square is bracketed, since foundherentism requires no beliefs justified solely and exclusively by experience.)

The goal of this chapter, I said at the outset, was not only to show that Lewis's foundationalist theory fails, but to show that it fails in ways which point us in a foundherentist direction. If this goal has by now, as I hope, been achieved, the next task is to make the parallel argument against coherentism. But since no single coherentist offers quite so convenient a target as Lewis, with his shift from strong to weak foundationalism, has done, this time I shall undertake not just one, but two detailed case-studies.

3
Coherentism Discomposed

Empirical knowledge – if there be any such thing – is distinguished by having as an essential factor . . . something disclosed in experience . . . There undoubtedly is some logical relation of facts . . . to which the name 'coherence' might aptly be given . . . But no logical relationship, by itself, can ever be sufficient to establish the truth, or the credibility even, of any synthetic judgement.

Lewis 'The Given Element in Empirical Knowledge'[1]

Lewis is quite right to hold that its inability to allow the relevance of experience to justification is an insuperable difficulty for coherentism. (This quotation, by the way, also seems to underscore one of the main themes of the previous chapter: that what Lewis really has a case for is experientialism, not foundationalism.) Coherentists, however, naturally enough, argue that the difficulty is superable. The present chapter is a case study of two attempts to overcome it: BonJour's in *The Structure of Empirical Knowledge*,[2] and Davidson's in 'A Coherence Theory of Truth and Knowledge'.[3] The goal is in part, of course, to show that these attempts fail; but also, and no less important, to show that the manner of their failure is not such as to force one back to a foundationalist position but, rather, such as to enhance the appeal of a move in the direction of foundherentism.

With BonJour, my argument is relatively straightforward. He attempts to accommodate experiential input within a coherentist framework by means of the imposition of an additional requirement, the 'Observation Requirement', on justification. This, however, turns out to be ambiguous: on one interpretation it is compatible with coherentism but fails to guarantee experiential input; on the other, it guarantees observational input all right but sacrifices the coherentist character of the theory

– resulting, however, not in a reversion to foundationalism, but rather, because of the retention of mutual support relations all the way down, in a quasi- or proto-foundherentist theory.

With Davidson, my strategy has to be less straightforward. He relies, positively, on an argument to the effect that it follows from a correct understanding of the attribution of propositional attitudes that most beliefs must be true. He relies, negatively, on the argument that a coherence theory is the only account of justification possible, since any account that supposes that a belief may be justified by something other than a belief falls to the objection that it confuses justification with causation. If his first line of argument is sound, it is not necessary that a theory of justification allow a role to experience; if his second is sound, it is not possible. The first stage of my critique will be to argue that the theory of interpretation on which Davidson's optimistic conclusion depends is unacceptable, and his conclusion, therefore, unproven. The second stage of my critique will be to argue that Davidson's version of the irrelevance of causation argument fails in a way that reveals particularly clearly that, rather than taking the heroic course of denying the relevance of experience to empirical justification, we need to devise a double-aspect, partly causal, partly evaluative theory to explain how causation is relevant; and that if, like Davidson, one repudiates the idea that there is a sharp distinction between observational and theoretical beliefs, there will then be, once again, a foundherentist pull.

I

To motivate his theory of justification, which he describes as an internalist coherentism, BonJour relies on an argument by elimination, an argument which presupposes that two dichotomies – foundationalism versus coherentism and internalism versus externalism – between them provide an adequate categorization of the alternatives available. I have already shown that the first of these dichotomies is not exhaustive; and the second, in my view, is not robust enough to carry any serious weight.[4] So naturally I think BonJour's strategy ill-chosen. Of course, BonJour might, for all that, have a successful theory to offer. In fact, as I shall argue, he does not; in the end his theory succumbs to the drunken sailors argument. But only in the end: BonJour is aware of the potential objection and develops quite a sophisticated manoeuvre to avoid it – a manoeuvre which, however, fails, and fails, perhaps, in ways which reflect the inadequacies of BonJour's map of the logical space of possible theories of justification.

BonJour's is a moderated, degree-of-embedding coherentism,

articulated by means of a distinction between local and global levels of justification. At the local level, where the concern is the justification of a single belief within the context of a cognitive system the justification of which is taken for granted, BonJour concedes that support relations look linear. But at the global level, where the concern extends to the justification of the overall system, they are seen to be essentially holistic. Even the justification of a single belief ultimately requires it to be supported by local, linear connections with other beliefs within an overall system which is justified holistically, by means of its coherence. Coherence, as BonJour conceives it, comes in degrees; and depends, not just on the logical consistency of the cognitive system, but also on its degree of probabilistic consistency, the pervasiveness and strength of its internal inferential connections, its degree of freedom from unexplained anomalies, etc.

BonJour's theory is internalist not only in the sense that it makes justification exclusively a matter of relations among a subject's beliefs (in this sense, *any* coherence theory is internalist), but also in the sense that it requires that the justification of a belief rely on premises, as BonJour puts it, 'possessed by' the subject himself.[5] This requirement leads BonJour to introduce a principle he calls the 'Doxastic Presumption' and describes as a presupposition of a subject's having any justified beliefs at all: that a believer 'must . . . have an adequate grasp of his total system of beliefs' (p. 102). This is all pretty vague, but fortunately this vagueness will not stand in the way of my critique.

BonJour acknowledges the force of the intuition that an adequate account of the justification of empirical beliefs must allow some role to experience ('observation' is his word – perhaps not the happiest choice, but it will do no harm to use his terminology in what follows). BonJour also acknowledges that there is reason to suspect that a coherence theory, which by definition holds that all justification is inferential, a matter of relations among beliefs, may be in principle incapable of satisfying this requirement. But he thinks that the apparent difficulty can be overcome.

There are two senses, he suggests, in which a belief may be said to be 'non-inferential': *with respect to its origin* and *with respect to its justification*. There are indeed, BonJour concedes, beliefs which are non-inferential in origin, i.e., beliefs such that what causes the subject to have them in the first place is not an inference from other beliefs of his, but something else – observation or introspection. But there are, he insists, no beliefs which are non-inferential with respect to justification, i.e., beliefs such that what justifies them is something other than their inferential relationships to other beliefs of the subject. One might reasonably feel some unease already; isn't inference, after all, one way of arriving at a belief? BonJour is not as clear as one could wish on this point, but his position seems to be that what matters where justification is concerned is not what prompted the belief originally but what sustains it at the time in question. He also remarks that it is not necessary that the subject should have gone explicitly through the inferential steps needed for justification; but neither is it enough, he adds, that the inference be 'available' – it must actually be the subject's reason for continuing to hold the belief. None of this is very satisfactory, but my strategy will be to work with it for the present. As the argument develops, it will become clear that BonJour himself cannot consistently maintain the distinction introduced here; but nothing is to be gained by crossing this bridge before we come to it.

Armed with this distinction, BonJour suggests that *beliefs which are non-inferential in origin may be justified, inferentially, by means of an argument which appeals to their non-inferential origin*; and this, he argues, will make it possible to allow a role to experience ('observation') while remaining faithful to the coherentist conception of justification as exclusively inferential.

At the local level, the justification of an observational belief, say, that there is a red book on the desk in front of me, might go, according to BonJour, like this (see pp. 118ff.):

1–O   I have a cognitively spontaneous belief of kind K that there is a red book on the desk in front of me;

2–O   conditions C obtain;

3–O   cognitively spontaneous beliefs of kind K in conditions C are likely to be true;

So:

4–O   [probably] there is a red book on the desk in front of me.

'Cognitively spontaneous' means, in effect, 'non-inferential in origin'. 'Kind K', in the present context, would be something like 'putatively visual', construed as saying something both about the content of the belief and about its etiology. 'Conditions C' might be, e.g., to the effect that lighting conditions are normal, that I am not under the influence of hallucinogenic drugs, etc.

The adequacy of such a local justification depends in turn on the justifiability of the premises. 2–O and 3–O, BonJour argues, being more or less straightforward empirical beliefs, will be justified in what according to his theory is the usual fashion, i.e., by being suitably embedded in a sufficiently coherent belief-set. 1–O, he suggests, is really a conjunction of three claims: (a) that the subject has the belief in question; (b) that it is of kind K; (c) that it is cognitively spontaneous. Sub-premiss (a), according to BonJour, is justified by means of the Doxastic Presumption; sub-premiss (b) is justified in part – where the content of the belief is concerned – again via the Doxastic Presumption, and in part – where its etiology is concerned – by introspection; and sub-premiss (c) is also justified by introspection.

This means that (in strikingly internalist fashion) the justification of observational beliefs always depends in part on the justification of introspective beliefs. At the local level, the justification of an introspective belief, say that I believe that there is a red book on the desk in front of me, might go, according to BonJour, like this (see pp. 133ff.):

> 1–I   I have a cognitively spontaneous belief of kind K′ that I believe that there is a red book on the desk in front of me;
> 3–I   cognitively spontaneous beliefs of kind K′ are usually true;

So:

> 4–I   [probably] I believe that there is a red book on the desk in front of me.

(No analogue of 2–O is needed, BonJour thinks, because the reliability of introspection, unlike the reliability of observation, is not normally sensitive to the conditions obtaining at the time.)

The adequacy of such a local justification is supposed to depend, again, on the justifiability of the premisses. 3–I, according to BonJour, is a more or less straightforward empirical claim, and hence justified in the same way as 3–O; and 1–I, he suggests, may be justified in the same way as 1–O.

BonJour realizes that this account of how it is *possible* for observation to play a role still doesn't establish that observational input is *necessary* for the justification of empirical beliefs. And it is here that his 'Observation Requirement' comes in. His statement of this requirement, which he describes as a 'regulative meta-principle' and admits is 'obviously quite vague', runs as follows:

> [I]n order for the beliefs in a cognitive system to be even candidates for empirical justification, that system must contain laws attributing a high degree of reliability to a reasonable variety of

cognitively spontaneous beliefs (including . . . those kinds of introspective beliefs which are required for the recognition of other cognitively spontaneous beliefs). (p. 141)

The Observation Requirement is crucial to what BonJour calls the 'meta-justification' (in my terminology, the ratification) of his theory of justification; his argument, that is, that his criteria of justification are truth-indicative. Since BonJour accepts a correspondence theory of truth, the thesis at which his meta-justification aims is that:

[A] system of beliefs which (a) remains coherent (and stable) over the long run and (b) continues to satisfy the Observation Require-ment is likely, to a degree which is proportional to this degree of coherence (and stability) and the longness of the run, to correspond closely to independent reality. (p. 171)

The role of the Observation Requirement in this meta-justification, according to BonJour, is that it 'guarantees that the system of beliefs will receive ongoing observational *input*', which 'provides the basic reason for thinking that a system of beliefs is likely to be true' (p. 170); for the best explanation of the continued coherence and stability of a system of beliefs in the face of ongoing observational input, he argues, is that the beliefs concerned correspond, at least approximately, to reality.

My target is not this meta-justificatory argument as such (though I have my doubts about whether it would withstand detailed critical scrutiny), but the claim that the Observation Requirement guarantees that a system satisfying it receives ongoing observational input, on which the meta-justificatory argument depends.

If one looks again at BonJour's statement of the Observation Re-quirement, an ambiguity reveals itself between what I shall call a doxastic and an experientialist interpretation. On the doxastic interpretation, the Observation Requirement requires that the subject *believe that he has* cognitively spontaneous beliefs, and that the subject believe that cog-nitively spontaneous beliefs are generally reliable. On an experientialist interpretation, it requires that the subject *have* cognitively spontaneous beliefs, and that he believe that cognitively spontaneous beliefs are generally reliable. (In either case, one assumes, since the Observation Requirement is called 'the Observation Requirement', the 'cognitively spontaneous beliefs' spoken of include beliefs prompted by the subject's sensory experience.) BonJour's statement is exactly ambiguous between these two interpretations: in saying that a system of beliefs 'must contain

laws attributing . . . reliability to . . . cognitively spontaneous beliefs'
(p. 141) BonJour might or might not be saying that the system must
actually contain cognitively spontaneous beliefs. Which interpretation
does BonJour really intend? I don't think there is a determinate answer.
It is not just that BonJour has expressed himself a bit ambiguously;
the ambiguity, presumably unconscious, is masking a serious difficulty
for his theory.

There is plenty of further textual evidence to support this diagnosis
of equivocation. Introducing his account of the inferential justification
of beliefs which are non-inferential in origin, BonJour writes as if the
subject's beliefs about the origin of his beliefs are *true* – but then immediately comments, in parenthesis, that he is doing this only for con-
venience of exposition:

> (It will be convenient to ignore the case in which the belief in
> question is not a cognitively spontaneous belief in the first
> place . . . I will also not trouble to distinguish between the actual
> facts of each situation and [the subject's] . . . conception there-
> of, but will simply assume that the latter is in accord with the
> former . . . [A]llowing for the opposite possibility would greatly
> complicate the discussion, but would not significantly affect the
> main issue.) (p. 119)

On the page immediately following the initial statement of the Observation Requirement, BonJour tells us that the Observation Requirement
'effectively guarantees that a cognitive system which satisfies it will
receive at least apparent input from the world' (p. 142). But by the
chapter following the one in which he introduced the Observation Requirement, where he is deploying it as a vital element of his meta-
justification, 'at least apparent' has conveniently been dropped, and
one finds BonJour claiming that '[t]he Observation Requirement . . .
guarantees that the system of beliefs will receive ongoing observational input' (p. 170).

It requires no very elaborate argument to back up my claim that in
its doxastic version the Observation Requirement (so-called: the term
now starts to look tendentious) does *not* guarantee observational input
(either at a time or 'ongoing'). Perhaps it might be suggested that if the
doxastic Observation Requirement is satisfied *and* the subject is justified in some beliefs which are observational in origin, then the subject
must not only believe, but believe *with justification*, that he has beliefs
which are observational in origin. This is true; but it is still clearly
insufficient to guarantee input from the world. Possibly BonJour is

covertly influenced by the apparently reassuring thought that his meta-justification establishes that if the subject believes with justification that he has beliefs which are observational in origin, then probably he does have beliefs which are observational in origin. But of course this makes matters no better; for BonJour's meta-justification itself relies on the assumption that input from the world is guaranteed if the Observation Requirement is satisfied, so this apparently reassuring thought really gives no reassurance at all.

The trickiest part of the argument is to show how, in its experientialist interpretation, the Observation Requirement radically alters the character of BonJour's theory. It will be useful to begin by offering two thumbnail sketches of the accounts of justification resulting from the two interpretations:

First (doxastic) interpretation:
  A is justified in believing that p iff:
    (local level)   1(i)   p is suitably embedded in A's belief-set;
    (global level)   1(ii)   A's belief-set is coherent and
                      1(iii)   (doxastic OR) includes beliefs to the effect that certain beliefs in the set are cognitively spontaneous.

Second (experientialist) interpretation:
  A is justified in believing that p iff:
    (local level)   2(i)   p is suitably embedded in A's belief-set;
    (global level)   2(ii)   A's belief-set is coherent and
                      2(iii)   (experientialist OR) includes cognitively spontaneous beliefs.

The first interpretation yields what BonJour purports to offer: a (strongly) internalist coherentism – which, however, does not guarantee experiential input. The second interpretation yields something which does guarantee experiential input – which, however, is no longer at all the kind of theory BonJour purported to be offering; no longer, in particular, a coherentist theory.

Clause 1(iii) is purely doxastic, couched purely in terms of relations among the subject's beliefs, and hence entirely consonant with coherentism. Clause 2(iii), however, is not purely doxastic, not couched purely in terms of relations among the subject's beliefs, and hence not compatible with coherentism. For what it says is that a requirement that some beliefs in a system are observational in origin is a necessary condition for any belief in the system to be justified. (I note, by the by, that this is of course quite inconsistent with BonJour's insistence on the distinctness of questions of origin and questions of justification.)

However, though on the second interpretation BonJour's account would not qualify as coherentist, it would not qualify as foundationalist either. I assume that it is not just required that the system include *some* cognitively spontaneous beliefs but in particular that *the beliefs the subject believes to be cognitively spontaneous be cognitively spontaneous.* (Unless one assumes this, it is hard to make any sense of the second account.) Then we would have, in effect, two classes of belief – those the justification of which depends on their being observational in origin, and those the justification of which does not so depend; but the distinction would not correspond to the foundationalists' distinction of basic and derived beliefs. For basic beliefs must be justified otherwise than by the support of further beliefs; whereas in this reconstructed version of BonJour's theory cognitively spontaneous beliefs would depend for their justification on the support of other beliefs as well as on their observational origin.

We see, in short, a shift towards foundherentism. Not that the theory reconstructed on the experientialist interpretation of BonJour's 'Observation Requirement' is exactly like the foundherentist theory I shall be offering; it is unlike it, in particular, in requiring a sharp distinction between beliefs which are observational and beliefs which are inferential in origin. But the reconstructed neither-coherentist-nor-foundationalist version of BonJour's theory, allowing, as it does, *both* a role to experience *and* pervasive mutual support, surely is recognizably foundherentist in tendency.

II

Though he entitles his influential paper 'A Coherence Theory of Truth and Knowledge', Davidson does not defend a coherence theory of truth; he claims, as BonJour does, that 'coherence [among beliefs] yields correspondence [with the facts]' (p. 120). Unlike BonJour, however, Davidson tries to make the connection not by means of an elaboration of the criteria of justification but by means of an exploration of the criteria for the attribution of beliefs; his positive strategy turns on the thesis that 'belief is in its nature veridical' (p. 128), and that therefore '[t]he question, How do I know my beliefs are generally true? answers itself, simply because beliefs are by nature generally true' (p. 133).

This might reasonably lead one to wonder what, if anything, is distinctively coherentist about Davidson's position. Less than advertised (as Davidson concedes, four years later, in his 'Afterthoughts' on this paper);[6] but more than so far meets the eye. Davidson is working with a very weak conception according to which a theory counts as coherentist provided only that it treats justification as a relation exclusively among beliefs. (By my lights this is necessary but not sufficient.) And the negative strategy of Davidson's paper turns on the thesis that the idea that a belief might be justified by something other than other beliefs rests on a confusion of justification with causation, so that there is no alternative to a coherence account. The positive and negative strategies interlock as Davidson concludes that, given that beliefs are mostly true, there is a presumption in favour of the truth of a belief which coheres with a substantial body of other beliefs.

The first part of my critique will be to show that Davidson's positive strategy fails; the second part, to suggest how his negative strategy may be avoided. Since Davidson's positive argument is conducted within the theory of interpretation, the first part of my argument will likewise fall within the philosophy of language; only when it comes to the second part will specifically epistemological issues come to the fore. Only then, also, will the pull towards a double-aspect theory, and ultimately towards foundherentism, become apparent.

In both the positive and the negative parts of his paper Davidson adopts the tactic of contrasting what he takes to be the advantages of his approach with what he takes to be the disadvantages of Quine's. I too will adopt the tactic of contrasting Davidson's approach with Quine's, but most often with the purpose of pointing out some advantage of Quine's approach over Davidson's.

'Beliefs are by nature generally true'. The natural reaction, surely, is that this sounds too good to be true. If this reaction is correct, as I believe it is, then Davidson's positive argument must be flawed; as I shall argue it is.

The key to Davidson's positive strategy is an argument to the effect that it is a consequence of a correct theory of belief-attribution – of radical interpretation, in Davidson's terminology – that an interpreter must so interpret his respondents' discourse as to attribute to them beliefs which are, by and large, true. This argument turns on Davidson's construal of the principle of charity; but this construal, I shall argue, makes the principle of charity too strong to be either plausible or realistic.

On its most modest construal, the principle of charity is conceived as a heuristic maxim to the effect that a translator has no option but to proceed on the basis of a defeasible presumption of *agreement* between himself and his respondents. Davidson, however, transmutes this into something much more ambitious, to the effect that 'an interpreter must so interpret as to make a speaker or agent largely *correct* about the world' (p. 133). Whatever the merits of the principle of maximizing agreement, the principle of maximizing truth is not defensible; but it is the latter principle which Davidson's theory of interpretation requires, and on which his epistemological argument depends.

Davidson describes himself as 'extending' Quine's principle of charity; he says this in part, apparently, because he applies the principle at the level of the interpretation of quantifiers as well as sentence connectives, and in part because, since he repudiates the distinction between observational and theoretical beliefs, he has no option but to apply the principle across the board (p. 130).[7] But this account of the matter is more than a little misleading. The difference is not (or not simply) a matter of the scope each gives to the principle, but a matter of the construals they give it. It would be more accurate to say that the character of Davidson's theory of interpretation obliges him to construe the principle of charity as requiring the maximization of truth, while it is consonant with Quine's theory of translation to construe it as requiring the maximization of agreement.

I should say right away, however, that neither Quine's nor Davidson's explicit remarks about how he understands the principle of charity make this very significant difference at all clear. Quine, indeed, might well give the impression that he is concerned with truth rather than agreement. In the context of his discussion of the translation of sentence connectives and his repudiation of the idea that there could be prelogical peoples, Quine observes that 'assertions startlingly false on the face of them are likely to turn on hidden differences of language', and comments that 'the commonsense behind the maxim is that one's interlocutor's silliness, beyond a certain point, is less likely than bad translation'.[8] Later in *Word and Object* Quine observes that something of the same kind applies at the level of analytical hypotheses, commenting that 'the more absurd or exotic the beliefs imputed to a people, the more suspicious we are entitled to be of the translations; the myth of the prelogical peoples marks only the extreme'.[9]

And Davidson shifts back and forth between explaining charity in terms of truth and explaining it in terms of agreement. In 'A Coherence Theory of Truth and Knowledge' he initially says that the principle of charity 'directs the interpreter to translate or interpret so as to read some of his own standards of truth into the pattern of sentences held true by the speaker'; on the next page, however, he writes that the interpreter is 'to interpret what the speaker says as true whenever he can'; but then further down the same page that, if his method is correct, 'most of the sentences a speaker holds to be true ... *are* true, at least in the opinion of the interpreter' (pp. 129–30).

These passages might give the impression that Davidson simply fails to distinguish the two versions of the principle of charity, but has been seduced by phrases like 'true, by the interpreter's lights' into running them together. But this would be an oversimplification; for both in 'A Coherence Theory of Truth and Knowledge' and most explicitly in an earlier paper, 'The Method of Truth in Metaphysics', Davidson acknowledges the distinction. His observations about the relations between the two versions of the principle hardly improve the situation. In 'The Method of Truth', after arguing at some length that 'I can interpret your words correctly only by interpreting so as to put us largely in agreement', and acknowledging that this 'leaves quite open the question whether what is agreed upon is true', Davidson remarks that this latter observation 'misses the point of the argument', since though 'the basic claim is that much community of belief is needed to provide a basis for communication ... the extended claim [is] ... that objective error can occur only in a setting of largely true belief'. The only argument offered for the 'extended claim' is that:

> ... massive error about the world is ... unintelligible, for to suppose it intelligible is to suppose that there could be [an omniscient interpreter] who correctly interpreted someone else as being massively mistaken, and this ... [is] impossible.[10]

The 'omniscient interpreter argument' alluded to here is spelled out in detail in 'A Coherence Theory of Truth and Knowledge':

> ... imagine for a moment an interpreter who is omniscient about the world, and about what does and would cause a speaker to assent to any sentence in his (potentially unlimited) repertoire. The omniscient interpreter, using the same method as the fallible interpreter, finds the fallible speaker largely consistent and correct. By his own standards, of course, but since these are objectively correct, the fallible speaker is seen to be largely correct and consistent by objective standards. We may also ... let the omniscient interpreter turn his attention to the fallible interpreter of the fallible speaker. It turns out that the fallible interpreter can be wrong about some things, but not in general; and so he cannot share universal error with the agent he is interpreting. Once we agree to the general method of interpretation I have sketched, it

becomes impossible correctly to hold that anyone could be mostly wrong about how things are. (p. 131)

This argument is so confusing that it is more apparent that it must go wrong somewhere than where the somewhere is. The core of the argument seems to be from 'imagine for a moment...' to '... by objective standards'. The trouble starts right at the beginning, when one is invited to imagine an omniscient interpreter proceeding in accordance with the principle of maximizing agreement. What is to be assumed, I take it, is that *there is an omniscient interpreter who, besides having true beliefs about the world, also interprets his respondents correctly, and who interprets conformably to the principle of maximizing agreement.* It does indeed follow from this assumption that people's beliefs are mostly true. For the omniscient interpreter attributes to his respondents beliefs which are mostly in accordance with his own; since his beliefs are all true, he will attribute to his respondents beliefs which are mostly true; and, since his attributions are all correct, the respondent's beliefs *are* mostly true. But this does not establish that people's beliefs are mostly true; only that *if there is an omniscient interpreter*, people's beliefs are mostly true. To establish that people's beliefs are mostly true, Davidson would need an argument that there is an omniscient interpreter. Of course, he has no such argument; his observation in 'The Method of Truth' that 'there is nothing absurd in the idea of an omniscient interpreter',[11] though no doubt correct, establishes at most that it is *possible* that there should be such an interpreter, not that there *is* one. How could Davidson have made such a slip? I think the explanation is to be found by re-examining the passage from 'The Method of Truth' in which he first hints at the argument under consideration. 'To suppose massive error intelligible', he urges, 'is to suppose that there *could be* [an omniscient interpreter] who correctly interprets someone else as massively mistaken, and this ... [is] impossible' (my italics). The 'could be' here invites just the slip Davidson makes. What is true is that 'there is an omniscient interpreter who interprets someone else conformably to the principle of maximising agreement but as massively mistaken' is impossible, i.e., that there could be no omniscient interpreter *unless* people's beliefs are mostly true. The 'could be' governs the conditional, not its antecedent. But Davidson's way of putting the point precisely encourages the idea that all that would be needed by way of discharging the assumption of an omniscient interpreter would be to show that there 'could be' such a thing. And this is *not* true.

But the shift from construing charity in terms of maximizing agreement to construing it in terms of maximizing truth is not simply a confusion on Davidson's part. There are good reasons in the character of his theory of interpretation which oblige him to adopt the construal in terms of truth,[12] and his resort to the question-begging argument just discussed is perhaps best seen as an abortive attempt to establish that the construal in terms of truth, which he is obliged to adopt anyway, is not significantly more demanding than the construal in terms of agreement.

'Meanings', according to Davidson, 'are given by objective truth-conditions' (p. 120); he proposes to construe meaning as Tarski-style truth-conditions, and to use T-theories for interpretation. Davidson's radical interpreter, that is, seeks, subject to certain empirical constraints, for each sentence of the respondent's language, a sentence of the form:

⌜p*⌝ is true in the respondent's language iff p

where the expression in quasi-quotes on the left names a sentence in the respondent's language, and the expression on the right is a translation of that sentence into the language of the interpreter.[13] Quine's radical translator, by contrast, seeks, again subject to certain empirical constraints, to correlate with each sentence of the respondent's language, a sentence of his own, as:

⌜p*⌝ is correlated with ⌜p⌝

where the expression in quasi-quotes on the left names a sentence in the respondent's language, and the expression in quasi-quotes on the right names a sentence in the translator's language. In line with this, the empirical constraints Quine imposes are to the effect that:

the respondent would assent to ⌜p*⌝ iff a speaker of my language would assent to ⌜p⌝,

so that *what matters is that there be agreement between the translator and the respondent in the perceived circumstances*. But in Davidson's theory of radical interpretation the sentence on the right is *used*, not mentioned, and this rules out anything like the Quinean kind of empirical constraints. Instead, in line with his emphasis on T-sentences, the empirical constraints Davidson imposes have to be, rather, to the effect that:

the respondent holds-true ⌜p*⌝ iff p,

so that *what matters is that the respondent be right*. It is not just that, as Davidson says, his interpreter 'takes the fact that speakers of a language hold a sentence true as prima-facie evidence that the sentence is true under those circumstances';[14] the important point for present purposes is that Davidson's interpreter must seek to translate sentences held true by speakers of a language by sentences which *are* true in the circumstances. Davidson's theory, to repeat, obliges him to construe charity as requiring an interpreter to make his respondents' beliefs mostly true; whereas Quine's theory encourages him to interpret the principle of charity as requiring a translator to make his respondents' beliefs mostly agree with his own.

Evidently Davidson himself does not fully appreciate this, for in 'On the Very Idea of a Conceptual Scheme' he writes that:

> . . . charity is not an option, but a condition of having a workable theory [of interpretation] . . . Until we have successfully established a systematic correlation of sentences held true with sentences held true, there are no mistakes to make. Charity is forced on us . . . [I]f we want to understand others, we must count them right in most matters.[15]

This exhibits the now-familiar shift from charity as maximizing agreement in the second sentence to charity as maximizing truth in the third. But the point I am concerned to highlight now is that Davidson is wrong to present his interpreter as seeking 'a correlation of sentences held true with sentences held true'. Unlike Quine's, Davidson's theory does *not* seek to correlate mentioned sentences in the speaker's language with mentioned sentences in the interpreter's language, or to match assent- with assent-conditions; it seeks to match assent- with *truth*-conditions by finding Tarski-style equivalences where, if the sentence mentioned on the left is held true by the speaker, the sentence used on the right is *true*.

Davidson himself suggests that the key difference between his theory of radical interpretation and Quine's theory of radical translation is that, whereas Quine characterizes assent/dissent conditions in terms of stimulations, he focuses, rather, on the physical objects and events which prompt beliefs (pp. 132–3). This is very misleading. It is not a matter of Quine's translator seeking to correlate sentences of the respondent's language with sentences of his own by matching assent/dissent conditions couched in terms of stimulations, and Davidson's interpreter doing the same thing but with assent/dissent conditions characterized in terms of physical objects and events; for Davidson's interpreter is, to repeat, not correlating mentioned sentences at all, but is concerned to match assent- with truth-conditions. Even if Quine's theory were modified to characterize assent/dissent conditions in terms of physical objects rather than stimulations, it would still not require that a translator attribute mostly true beliefs to his respondents, only that he maximize agreement between himself and them.

The key difference between Davidson's theory and Quine's is, on the contrary, precisely that Davidson is committed to the strong principle of charity, to maximizing truth, but Quine only to the weak principle of charity, to maximizing agreement.

It might indeed be doubted whether, even granted the principle of maximizing truth, Davidson's optimistic epistemological conclusion really follows. The move from 'an interpreter has no option but to proceed on the assumption that respondents' beliefs are mostly true' to 'people's beliefs must *be* mostly true' might be questioned. Compare the situation with other candidate maxims of translation. Perhaps, for example, it is true that a translator has no option but to proceed on the assumption that his respondents are not lying to him.[16] It is clear on a little reflection that it does not follow from this principle that it is impossible that respondents should systematically lie to the interpreter, only that, if they do, he may find it impossible to translate their utterances. In 'On the Very Idea of a Conceptual Scheme' Davidson claims that what is untranslatable into our language cannot be a language. But while perhaps there is a strong sense, 'untranslatable in principle', in which this might be defensible, there is surely no plausibility in supposing that just because we happen to be unable, in practice, to translate the utterance of certain people or creatures – if, for instance, they are too wary of anthropologists, or humans, to tell them the truth – it follows that they do not have a language.

There is also a significant gap between a presumption of truth and a requirement that the interpreter attribute to the speaker beliefs which are mostly true. Davidson himself admits that the difficulties of individuating beliefs stand in the way of giving a clear meaning to the idea that most of a person's beliefs must be true. But even aside from these difficulties, it is clear that it doesn't follow from there being a presumption that an F is a G that most Fs are Gs; from the presumption in law that a defendant is innocent until proven guilty, for example, it doesn't follow that most defendants are innocent.

But the point I want to stress is, simply, how very implausible the strong principle of charity is. A modest principle, in the form of a defeasible presumption of agreement between translator and respondent, has *some* claim to plausibility as a maxim of translational practice. But whatever claim to plausibility such a modest principle has, obviously, does not extend to the much more ambitious principle that an interpreter must attribute mostly true beliefs to his respondents.[17] Construed in this demanding fashion, the principle of charity is far too strong to be realistic; no ordinary, fallible interpreter could conform to it. For it directs the interpreter to interpret his respondents as holding-true ⌐p*⌐ just in case, in fact, p. A limited, fallible interpreter attempting to conform as closely as possible to this principle could do no better than to interpret his respondent as holding-true ⌐p*⌐ just in case, by his, the interpreter's, lights, p. (No wonder Davidson shifts between the agreement- and the truth-oriented version of the principle.) But, of course, if a limited, fallible interpreter happens to be mistaken about whether p, he will not have conformed to the truth-oriented principle of charity. To interpret correctly by Davidson's standards, an interpreter would have to be virtually omniscient. (No wonder Davidson doesn't realize that his 'omniscient interpreter' argument is question-begging.)

Davidson claims that Quine and Dummett, by '[t]rying to make meaning accessible', have 'made truth inaccessible' (p. 126). It is tempting to reply that, however that may be, by tying truth and meaning so tightly Davidson has not made truth accessible, but meaning inaccessible. Also apropos of Quine and Dummett, Davidson comments that '[t]here are common views of language that encourage bad epistemology' (p. 126). It is ironic, then, that it should turn out that Davidson's optimistic epistemological conclusion – 'beliefs are by nature generally true' – depends on an unacceptable theory of interpretation.

Even if Davidson's optimistic conclusion were true (and my argument, though it has, I hope, shown it unproven by Davidson's argument, has not shown it false) it would not, of itself, favour coherentism over other theories of justification; though it would overcome a significant objection to coherentism, the drunken sailors argument. To reach a coherentist conclusion, Davidson's negative strategy is also necessary.

The key to this negative strategy is an argument to the effect that the idea that justification might be anything other than a relation exclusively among beliefs rests on a confusion – a confusion of justification with causation. This is Davidson's version of what I called, in chapter 1, the irrelevance of causation argument; and, as I already suggested there and shall argue in detail here, it rests on a false assumption: that justification is a purely logical notion.

It will be convenient, by way of preliminary, to point out that Davidson's negative strategy is set against the backdrop of a classification of theories which is somewhat oblique to the one I am using, and to most familiar classifications. According to Davidson, '[w]hat distinguishes a coherence theory is simply the claim that nothing can count as a reason for a belief except another belief' (p. 123). As Davidson seems to be aware, by this definition not only all those theories which are ordinarily so classified but also what I have called self-justificatory foundationalist theories (according to which basic beliefs are self-justifying), as well as contextualist accounts, qualify as coherentist. In other words, as he concedes in 'Afterthoughts', Davidson's is really a distinction between theories which are purely doxastic and theories which are not. Coherentism (in my sense), self-justificatory foundationalism and contextualism are, to repeat, purely doxastic, hence coherentist in Davidson's sense; extrinsic foundationalism, experientialist foundationalism and foundherentism are not.

Theories which are *not* purely doxastic (which presumably represent the 'bad epistemology' Davidson thinks is encouraged by mistaken views of language) do not require justification to be a relation exclusively among beliefs; '[t]he attempts worth taking seriously' Davidson observes, 'attempt to ground belief in one way or another on the testimony of the senses' (p. 124). Davidson likes to describe such theories as requiring appeal to some kind of 'confrontation' (p. 120) between our beliefs and the world, and hence as requiring us to 'get outside our skins' (p. 125); it is worth noting, by way of a second preliminary, that these metaphors are notably prejudicial – for, of course, we cannot *literally* 'confront a belief with experience', or 'get outside our skins'. But this rhetoric, clever as it is, is no argument against a not-purely-doxastic (henceforth, for short, 'non-doxastic') approach to justification.

Davidson's case depends, rather, on the argument that such an approach represents a doomed attempt to 'transmut[e] a cause into a reason'. The argument is that:

[t]he relation between a sensation and a belief cannot be logical, since sensations are not beliefs or other propositional attitudes. What, then, is the relation? The answer is, I think, obvious: the relation is causal. Sensations can *cause* some beliefs, and in *this* sense are the basis or grounds of those beliefs. But a causal explanation of a belief does not show how or why the belief is justified. (p. 125)

Davidson thinks that this shows that justification must be purely doxastic. Quine, he suggests, with such remarks as '. . . our only source of information is through the impact of light rays and molecules upon our sensory surfaces',[18] betrays that he has fallen victim to exactly the kind of confusion of justification with causation which, according to this argument, inevitably vitiates non-doxastic theories.

I note first that to deny that a subject's experiences could count as *reasons* for his beliefs is not *eo ipso* to deny that they could count as *evidence* for his beliefs – the idiom is, after all, 'the evidence of the senses' – nor, therefore, in and of itself, to deny that experience could be relevant to justification. And to assume that all the evidence for a belief must consist of reasons for the belief would of course beg precisely the question at issue.

This paves the way for the point I want to stress: that Davidson's argument is simply a non sequitur. For it runs: there can be only causal, not logical, relations between beliefs and experiences; therefore, experience is irrelevant to justification. The conclusion does not follow without the further premiss that justification is a purely logical matter. And it is not at all obvious that this is true. Perhaps it might seem so, if one takes for granted that justification must be *either* a purely logical *or* a purely causal concept; but why should one take this for granted? It is certainly possible, and seems prima facie plausible, to hold that the concept of justification, though not purely causal, is not purely logical either. This, certainly, is the picture suggested by what seems to me a very sturdy intuition: that whether, or to what degree, someone is justified in some belief depends both on *what* he believes and on *why* he believes it.

It is plausible, furthermore, to construe Quine's talk of 'sensory evidence', etc., as an indication that he is working, implicitly, on the assumption that justification is just such a two-faced, double-aspect concept as this intuition suggests.[19] The accusation that he confuses justification with causation is, at the least, premature.

So Davidson's argument does not establish that a non-doxastic account is necessarily based on a confusion. What it does do, I think, is to reveal particularly clearly that a theory which is not purely doxastic – including foundherentism as well as experientialist foundationalism – will have to be a double-aspect theory, and will need to articulate the relations between the causal and the logical aspects of the concept of justification. (Actually, for reasons which will only be fully articulated in chapter 5, I think 'logical' not the ideal term; 'evaluative' is better. But this matter need not detain us now.)

Ironically enough, Davidson himself recognizes something of the double-aspect character of the concept of justification. Early in 'A Coherence Theory' he concedes that a coherence theory couched in terms simply of sets of sentences would not be plausible (in effect, because of the consistent fairy story objection). His theory, he says, is to explain justification not in terms of the coherence of sets of *sentences, simpliciter,* but in terms of the coherence of sets of *beliefs.* In the course of this one paragraph, however, he gives – apparently unaware of the shift – two quite different accounts of what beliefs are: first, 'sentences held true by someone'; then, 'states of people . . . that are caused by, and cause, events inside and outside the bodies of their entertainers' (p. 121). Initially, then, Davidson is talking about belief-*contents* (which are capable of evaluation as, e.g., coherent or incoherent with one another); subsequently, about belief-*states* (which can be causally related to each other and to other states or events, e.g., sensory experiences).[20] But if it is only belief-contents, not belief-states, which can cohere or fail to, and if belief-contents are just sentences, why does Davidson regard this as better than the coherence-of-sentences account? I take it this is because *which* sets of sentences are at issue is narrowed down by the requirement that they be sets of sentences held true by some subject, i.e., the *contents* of some subject's belief-*states*. But it is not, in general, the case that a coherence theory is more plausible with respect to narrower than to broader sets of sentences (in fact, the popularity of 'comprehensiveness' as a component of coherence suggests, if anything, the reverse). So how does Davidson think this improves the situation? The reply that suggests itself is this: some of a person's belief-states are prompted, at least partly, by his experiences, his sensory interactions with the world; so sets of sentences which are the contents of such states are a better choice than sets of sentences, *simpliciter*, because this anchoring is, as it were, built in. But if this is what Davidson is thinking – and I think that, at some level of awareness, it must be – he is implicitly acknowledging that justification is not after all purely logical, and that a satisfactory account of justification would have to have a causal as well as an evaluative element.

That there is an implicit acknowledgement of the double-aspect character of the concept of justification to be found in Davidson's paper despite his official endorsement of the irrelevance of causation argument indicates something of the strength of the pull towards experientialism. I claimed, however, that we would also feel a pull, more specifically, towards foundherentism; and this requires an additional step. The additional step is this: foundationalist experientialism requires a distinction between beliefs justified by the subject's experience and beliefs justified by the support of his other beliefs; but this is precluded if, like Davidson, and myself, one repudiates a sharp distinction between purely perceptual and other empirical beliefs.

BonJour's strategy of saving coherentism from the drunken sailors argument by imposing the 'Observation Requirement' fails because, in the only interpretation in which it really guarantees experiential input, it has sacrificed the coherentist character of the theory in favour of a kind of proto-foundherentism. Davidson's strategy of saving coherentism from the drunken sailors argument by establishing that 'beliefs are by nature generally true' fails because it requires as premiss a version of the principle of charity too demanding to be acceptable. And Davidson's development of the irrelevance of causation argument against experientialist theories not only fails, but fails in a way which points up the need for a double-aspect theory: a double-aspect theory which, in the absence of a sharp distinction of observational versus theoretical beliefs, would be foundherentist in character.

The case-studies presented in this and the previous chapter, in short, pull in the same direction as the general arguments presented in chapter 1. The task which now faces me is to articulate in detail the kind of theory to which the arguments thus far point: double-aspect foundherentism.

4
Foundherentism Articulated

The stimulation of his sensory receptors is all the evidence anybody has had to go on, ultimately, in arriving at his picture of the
world.

Quine 'Epistemology Naturalized'[1]

. . . there can be mutual reinforcement between an explanation
and what it explains. Not only does a supposed truth gain credibility if we can think of something that would explain it, but also
conversely: an explanation gains credibility if it accounts for
something we suppose to be true.

Quine and Ullian *The Web of Belief*[2]

The goal is an explication of epistemic justification which conforms to
the desiderata which emerged from the arguments of the previous chapters: to allow the relevance of experience to empirical justification (which
will require an articulation of the interplay of causal and evaluative
aspects); and to allow pervasive mutual support among beliefs (which
will require an account of the difference between legitimate mutual
support and objectionable circularity).

The *explicandum* is: A is more/less justified, at time t, in believing that
p, depending on . . . This choice of *explicandum* already indicates some
substantial presuppositions: that it is a personal locution, not an impersonal locution like 'the belief that p is justified' which is primitive;
that justification comes in degrees; that whether or to what degree a
person is justified in believing something may vary with time. The
rationale for these assumptions will become clearer as the articulation
proceeds.

My procedure might be called a 'method of successive approximation'.

I begin with a formulation which seems intuitively very plausible but is (not surprisingly) also very vague, and attempt gradually to articulate more precisely what is implicit in the initial, vague formula. The initial, very approximate, first approximation is: A is more/less justified, at t, in believing that p, depending on how good his evidence is. I am inclined to regard this initial formulation as close to trivial (indeed, to think of 'justified' as in effect epistemologists' portmanteau word for what in ordinary parlance would most often be expressed in the less technical vocabulary of strong or flimsy reasons, a weak or overwhelming case, good or tenuous evidence, etc.). In the context of current debate in epistemology, however, it must be conceded that even this innocuous-seeming formula is not entirely innocent of presuppositions; it is, in particular, an indication of a preference for an evidentialist over an extrinsic approach.[3] For the present I shall offer no rationale for this preference over and above its intuitive plausibility. Later, however, this prima facie consideration will be buttressed by arguments against extrinsic theories (chapter 7).

Successive elaborations of the initial formula will depend on articulating the relations between the causal and the evaluative aspects of the concept of justification. Fundamental to this articulation will be the distinction between the state and the content senses of 'belief', between someone's believing something and what they believe; a distinction marked in what follows as 'S-belief' versus 'C-belief'[4] (henceforth, if I speak of 'beliefs', *simpliciter*, the ambiguity will be intended). How justified A is in believing that p depends, according to the first approximation, on how good his evidence is. Elaboration of this first approximation will require three stages. The first stage, couched in terms of causal relations between A's S-beliefs and other, including perceptual, states of A, will be an attempt to characterize 'A's S-evidence with respect to p'. The second, intermediate stage will be a manoeuvre by means of which to arrive, on the basis of the characterization of 'A's S-evidence with respect to p' (which consists of certain states of A) at a characterization of 'A's C-evidence with respect to p' (which consists of certain sentences or propositions). The third, evaluative stage will complete the explication of 'A is more/less justified in believing that p' by characterizing 'how good A's C-evidence with respect to p is'.

What is on offer will be at best a sketch of a theory – a sketch, furthermore, more than somewhat uneven in its level of detail. The reason, of course, is that this is, for the present at least, the best I can do. In hopes that I, or someone else, may find it possible eventually to improve the articulation of the theory, I shall try to identify where the chief difficulties lie, and to discern which of those difficulties are peculiar to a foundherentist approach and which shared by more familiar theories of justification; though I shan't make light of any of the difficulties, even when the problems seem peculiar to my approach I shall take the attitude that those which arise only because my account is in some respects more detailed than its rivals should be regarded rather as challenges than as grounds for abandoning ship. I shall also try to be as clear as possible which parts of the formulation offered here are capable of standing independently, and may be usable, therefore, even if other parts fail.

I

How justified a person is in believing something depends not just on *what* he believes, but on *why* he believes it; 'why he believes it' being a matter not simply of what else he believes, or of what else he believes and perceives, introspects or remembers, but of what it is, in his S-beliefs and experiences, on which his having the S-belief in question depends. (Consider two people both of whom believe that the accused is innocent, one because he saw her himself, a hundred miles away, at the time of the crime, the other because he thinks she has an honest face. The former is more justified than the latter.) Suppose, then, that A believes that p; how justified A is in believing that p depends in some fashion on what it is that causes him to have that S-belief.

As a first step towards spelling out 'depends *in some fashion* on what it is that causes him to have that S-belief' it is necessary to distinguish the *initiating* causes of A's S-belief that p – whatever it was that was involved in his coming to believe that p originally – and the causes *operative at the time in question*, i.e., at the time at which his degree of justification is at issue. These may be the same, but they may be different; and when they are different, it is on the causes operative at the time in question that justification depends. (Suppose that initially, at t_1, A comes to believe that the accused is innocent for no better reason than that she has, he thinks, an honest face; but that later, at t_2, A learns that she has a watertight alibi, and it is this which, at that time, causes him to continue to believe she is innocent. He is more justified at t_2 than at t_1.) That is why the *explicandum* includes the condition, 'at t'; this should, henceforth, be understood if it is not stated.

As a second step, it is necessary to recognize that what causes someone to believe something, at a time, is often a matter of a balance of forces: some factors, that is, incline him towards believing that p, others incline him against it, with the former outweighing the latter. (Suppose that Prof. Smith believes that Tom Grabit stole the book, and that his

S-belief is sustained by his remembering having seen Grabit leave the library surreptitiously with a guilty expression and a suspicious bulge under his sweater, and that this outweighs his desire not to believe ill of his students and his belief that it is possible, for all he knows, that Grabit has a light-fingered identical twin.) So in considering what causes A to have such-and-such an S-belief, at t, it is necessary to distinguish sustaining from inhibiting causes. Both, however, are relevant to an assessment of degree of justification.

The third step is to distinguish those sustaining or inhibiting factors which are states of the person concerned from those which are not. (For example, A's S-belief that there is a dog in the room might be sustained in part by his being in a certain perceptual state, and that state in turn be caused by there being a dog in the room.) Only causes of A's S-belief which are states of A will figure in the characterization of his S-evidence.

'The causal nexus, at t, of A's S-belief that p' will refer to those states of A which are operative at t, whether sustaining or inhibiting, in the vector of forces resulting in A's believing that p. 'Nexus' is meant to suggest a mesh of S-beliefs interconnected with each other, with the subject's perceptual experience, with his desires and fears, and so forth. The causal nexus of an S-belief is to include the states which directly sustain or inhibit that S-belief, the states which sustain or inhibit those states . . . and so on. The idea is that our criteria of justification are neither simply atomistic nor unqualifiedly holistic: they focus on those elements of the whole constellation of A's states at t which bear a causal relation, sustaining or inhibiting, to the particular S-belief in question.

Before even an initial explication of 'A's evidence with respect to p' is possible, a distinction is needed between evidential and non-evidential components within the causal nexus of an S-belief. Belief states, perceptual states, introspective states, memory traces, will count as evidential; other states, such as the subject's desires and fears, his being under the influence of alcohol or panic, etc., will not. That such states contribute to sustaining/inhibiting A's S-belief that p may have a bearing on the likelihood that p is true. (For instance, someone who is terribly afraid that p may turn out to be the case may greatly exaggerate the significance of his evidence that p *is* the case; 'fearful thinking', one might call this; someone who is under the influence of LSD is subject to extreme disorder of his senses; and so on.) Nevertheless, such components of the causal nexus of A's S-belief that p are not counted as part of A's evidence, because they are intuitively regarded as factors affecting a person's reaction to, or judgement of, his evidence, not as themselves part of his evidence. That such non-evidential states belong to the causal nexus of an S-belief may well form a necessary part of an explanation of how it is that the subject believes something despite the flimsiness of his evidence; it will not, however, form part of the calculation of the degree to which he is justified.

We now have the necessary apparatus for a preliminary conception of 'A's evidence', called, in an obvious extension of the state/content distinction, 'A's S-evidence with respect to p'.[5] 'A's S-reasons for believing that p' will refer to those S-beliefs which sustain A's S-belief that p; 'A's current sensory S-evidence for believing that p' to the perceptual states which sustain A's S-belief that p; 'A's past sensory evidence for believing that p' to the perceptual traces which sustain A's S-belief that p; 'A's sensory S-evidence for believing that p' to A's current and past sensory S-evidence for believing that p; 'A's current introspective S-evidence for believing that p' to the introspective states which sustain A's S-belief that p; 'A's past introspective S-evidence for believing that p' to the introspective traces which sustain A's S-belief that p; 'A's introspective S-evidence for believing that p' to A's current and past introspective S-evidence for believing that p; 'A's experiential S-evidence for believing that p' to A's sensory and introspective S-evidence for believing that p; and 'A's S-evidence for believing that p' to A's S-reasons and experiential S-evidence for believing that p. 'A's S-evidence against believing that p' will be characterized like 'A's S-evidence for believing that p', but with 'inhibit' for 'sustain'; and 'A's S-evidence with respect to p' will refer to A's S-evidence for believing that p and A's S-evidence against believing that p. 'A's direct S-evidence with respect to p' will refer to those evidential states which directly sustain/inhibit his S-belief that p, 'A's indirect$_1$ S-evidence with respect to p' will refer to those which directly sustain/inhibit his direct S-evidence with respect to p . . . and so on.

A's S-reasons with respect to p are themselves S-beliefs of A's, with respect to which A may have further S-evidence (which will be part of his S-evidence with respect to p). But A's experiential S-evidence with respect to p consists of non-belief states of A, not the kind of thing with respect to which A has, or needs, evidence. Experiential S-evidence evidentially sustains/inhibits S-beliefs, but not vice versa. A's experiential S-evidence is, one might say, his *ultimate* S-evidence. (This is the important truth that experientialist foundationalism tries to accommodate – but in a forced and unnatural way.)

The pre-analytic notion of 'the evidence of the senses' is not innocent of theory. Human beings, according to the commonsense picture, perceive things and events in the world around them; one interacts, by means of one's senses, with the things in one's surroundings; these interactions are what 'sensory experience' refers to. Our senses are, by and large, good at detecting what goes on around us; but in unfavourable circumstances one may be unable to see or hear clearly, and may misperceive, and in extremely unfavourable circumstances where one's senses are grossly disordered one may even 'perceive' what is not there at all.

The previous sentence with its scare quotes indicates that the commonsense conception takes for granted that ordinarily a subject's perceptual states are the result of his sensory interactions with things around him, but that in extraordinary circumstances the subject could be in a state which is indistinguishable by him from the states resulting from his sensory interactions with the world, which are however *not* the result of such interactions, but the product of some disorder in himself. The intention is to represent both the positive and the negative aspects of this picture. In what follows, 'perceptual state' will be given a somewhat lax interpretation, to include states phenomenologically indistinguishable from perceptual states in the stricter sense. When it comes to the transition from the causal to the evaluative stage of the explication, however, the commonsense assumption that perceptual states are ordinarily the result of one's sensory interactions with things and events in the world will be built in.

'Introspective S-evidence' has been included as a kind of experiential S-evidence in the belief that it is also part of the commonsense picture underlying our pre-analytic conception of justification that a human being has some means of awareness of (some of) his own mental states and processes, as well as senses for scanning things and events in the world. But nothing will be said about introspection here beyond the observation that sensory S-evidence and introspective S-evidence are treated as distinct with the intention of avoiding any confusion of the two, any elision of perception into introspective awareness of one's own mental states. Such an elision would betray the commonsense presumption that what we perceive are the things around us – which I wish, on the contrary, to preserve.

As the role played by perceptual states locates the relevance of current sensory experience to justification, the role played by perceptual [and introspective] traces locates the role of memory, in the sense represented by the locution 'A remembers seeing/ hearing/ etc . . .'. Here again the terminology will be used with deliberate laxity. 'Perceptual [introspective] traces' will be allowed possibly to include states which are indistinguishable by the subject from those which are the present traces of past perceptual [introspective] states.

The distinction of perceptual state/perceptual trace, of current/past sensory S-evidence, is very crude – probably cruder than the pre-analytic ideas it represents. Perception isn't instantaneous, but an ongoing process. But degree of justification can change in the course of the process, when, for instance, one gets a better look at a thing ('It looked just as if someone was standing at the front door, until I got closer and saw it was only the shadow of the hydrangea bush'). To mitigate the crudeness of the distinction of current/past sensory S-evidence somewhat, 'perceptual state' should be construed not as instantaneous, but as having some unspecified, gerrymanderable duration.

Past sensory S-evidence represents one of the ways in which memory fits into the picture. Memory also crops up in a second form: to say 'A remembers that p' is to say that he earlier came to believe that p and now still believes it, he has not forgotten it (and, of course, that p is true). How justified A is in such a 'persisting' S-belief will depend, as with all beliefs, on how good his evidence – his evidence at the time in question – is. (This needn't mean that it has to be said that I am not justified, for instance, in believing that my high-school English teacher's name was 'Miss Wright'; this persisting belief is now sustained by past experiential S-evidence – of seeing and hearing the name used by myself and others, and so forth.)

A person's S-beliefs are often maintained, in whole or part, by his hearing, seeing, or remembering hearing or seeing, what someone else says or writes. Such testimonial evidence, as one might call it in an obvious extension of the usual sense, enters the picture by way of the role played by A's sensory S-evidence; as when A's S-belief that p is sustained by his remembering hearing B say that p, and his S-beliefs that B is well-informed and that B has no strong motive for deceit or concealment on this matter. (It is assumed that if A doesn't understand B's language, if he has the S-belief that p, his hearing B say ⌜p⌝ will not form part of its causal nexus.)

II

A's S-evidence with respect to p consists of a gerrymandered collection of states of A. But in the evaluative stage of the explication 'evidence' will have to mean 'C-evidence', for it is sentences or propositions, not states of a person, which can support or undermine each other, probabilify or disconfirm each other, be consistent or inconsistent with each other, cohere or fail to cohere as an explanatory story. So a bridge is needed from S- to C-evidence. 'A's C-reasons for believing that p' will refer to the C-beliefs A's believing which constitute A's S-reasons for believing that p; 'A's experiential C-evidence for believing that p' to sentences or propositions to the effect that A is in a certain state or states – the state(s) which constitute(s) A's experiential S-evidence for believing that p; 'A's C-evidence for believing that p' will refer to A's C-reasons for believing that p and A's experiential C-evidence for believing that p; 'A's C-evidence against believing that p' will be characterized like 'A's C-evidence for believing that p', but with 'against' for 'for'; and 'A's C-evidence with respect to p' will refer to A's C-evidence for believing that p and A's C-evidence against believing that p. A's direct, indirect$_1$, indirect$_2$, etc., C-evidence with respect to p is distinguished in parallel to the corresponding distinctions for A's S-evidence.

This was couched with deliberate vagueness in terms of 'sentences or propositions'. The main advantage of this deliberate vagueness is that, because of the lack of clear criteria of identity for propositions, it temporarily puts off some hard questions, e.g., about what sorts of characterization of perceptual (etc.) states might be appropriate here. Our ordinary ways of describing 'the evidence of the senses' offer some clues. What justifies me in believing that there's a woodpecker in the oak tree? – 'my seeing it, the fact that I can see it', is a natural answer; an answer, however, often enough qualified or hedged, as: 'but I only got a glimpse', or 'but it's against the light', or 'but it's too dark to see the markings clearly', and so forth, and possibly revised to 'well, it looked just as if there was a bird there'. It seems desirable to tie 'A's sensory evidence' at least loosely to 'how it looks (etc.) to A'; and at the same time to respect the commonsense distinction of more and less favourable circumstances – a good look is better evidence than a glimpse or glance, seeing a thing in full view and good light better evidence than a look at it partly hidden and at dusk . . . and so on. For these (and other) reasons I am inclined to favour characterizations along the lines of 'A is in the sort of perceptual state a normal subject would be in, in normal circumstances, when looking at a rabbit three feet away and in good light', 'in the sort of perceptual state a normal subject would be in, in normal circumstances, when getting a brief glimpse of a fast-moving rabbit at dusk' . . . and so on. This is how, though 'perceptual state' has been allowed to include states phenomenologically indistinguishable from those resulting from one's sensory interactions with the world, the presupposition that normal perception *is* the result of such interactions is retained.

There is another significant asymmetry built in, this time at the level of C-evidence, between A's reasons and his experiential evidence. A's C-reasons with respect to p will consist of propositions which may be true or may be false. His experiential C-evidence, however, will consist of sentences or propositions *all of which are true*. This is no reinstatement of any sort of infallibilism with respect to perceptual or introspective *beliefs*; it is just that the propositions concerned are to the effect that A is in such-and-such a perceptual (etc.) state, and they are all true because, *ex hypothesi*, A *is* in that perceptual (etc.) state. This feature guarantees what may be called the 'experiential anchoring' of justified empirical beliefs.

How justified someone is in believing something, then, according to the second approximation, depends on how good his C-evidence is. The remaining problem is to explicate 'how good'. Before turning to that task, however, lest anyone, struck by the fact that the second approximation is couched entirely in terms of C-evidence, should suspect that the causal aspect of the theory was redundant after all, it should be re-emphasized that the characterization of 'A's C-evidence with respect to p' is dependent on the characterization of 'A's S-evidence with respect to p', which the causal part of the theory supplied. Which sentences or propositions constitute A's C-evidence with respect to p depends on what states feature in the vector of forces maintaining A's S-belief that p.

III

That justification comes in degrees is attested by numerous familiar locutions: 'he has *some* justification for thinking that . . .'; 'he would be *more* justified in thinking that . . . if . . .'; 'his evidence is quite strong/at best flimsy/somewhat partial/one-sided'; 'his grounds are reasonable/ quite reasonable/overwhelming'; 'his evidence gives colour to/gives some credence to . . .' – Roget's *Thesaurus* has an entire section entitled 'Degrees of Evidence'. The explication being articulated here aspires to respect the gradational character of justification; not, however, to offer anything like a numerical scale of degrees of justification, or even anything as ambitious as criteria for a linear ordering, but only to say what factors raise, and what factors lower, the degree to which someone is justified in believing something.

The model is not, as a foundationalist's might be, how one determines the soundness or otherwise of a mathematical proof; it is, rather, how one determines the reasonableness or otherwise of entries in a crossword puzzle.[6] This model is more hospitable to a gradational account. But the main motivation is that the crossword model permits pervasive mutual support, rather than, like the model of a mathematical proof, encouraging an essentially one-directional conception. The clues are the analogues of the subject's experiential evidence; already filled-in entries, the analogue of his reasons. The clues don't depend on the entries, but the entries are, in variable degree, interdependent; these are the analogues of the asymmetries already noted between experiential evidence and reasons.

How reasonable one's confidence is that a certain entry in a cross-word puzzle is correct depends on: how much support is given to this entry by the clue and any intersecting entries that have already been filled in; how reasonable, independently of the entry in question, one's confidence is that those other already filled-in entries are correct; and how many of the intersecting entries have been filled in. Analogously, how good A's C-evidence with respect to p is would depend on:

1 how *favourable* A's direct C-evidence with respect to p is;
2 how *secure* A's direct C-reasons with respect to p are, *independently of the C-belief that p*;
3 how *comprehensive* A's C-evidence with respect to p is.

It should be noted that, although clause 2 mentions explicitly only A's direct C-reasons with respect to p, its application takes one progressively outward, to the appraisal of A's indirect$_1$, indirect$_2$ . . . etc., C-evidence with respect to p. For in considering how independently secure A's direct C-reasons are, it will be necessary to consider how well his indirect$_1$ C-evidence supports them, and how independently secure his indirect$_1$ C-reasons are . . . and so on.

C-evidence may be favourable or unfavourable with respect to a C-belief, with its being conclusive representing one extreme, and its pre-cluding the truth of the proposition in question representing the other. C-evidence may be favourable but not conclusive, supportive to a greater or lesser degree; or unfavourable but not fatal, undermining to a greater or lesser degree. One might say that at the upper limit evidence E makes it certain that p, at the lower limit E makes it certain that not-p; and that E is more supportive the more likely it makes it that p, the more undermining the more unlikely it makes it that not-p. But this, though true enough, is not very helpful, since 'E makes it certain that p', 'E makes it likely that p', and so forth are little more than verbal variants on the locutions in need of explication. One might say, a little more helpfully, that if E is conclusive it leaves no room for alternatives to p, and if it is favourable but not conclusive it is the more supportive the less room it leaves for alternatives to p. I can't resist calling this 'the Petrocelli Principle'.

With respect to the limit cases, I suggest the following rather straight-forward characterization. E is conclusive with respect to p just in case its p-extrapolation (the result of adding p to it) is consistent, and its not-p-extrapolation inconsistent; E is fatal with respect to p just in case its not-p-extrapolation is consistent, and its p-extrapolation consistent.

The characterization of degrees of supportiveness less than conclusiveness presents more difficulty. The Petrocelli Principle offers some clues, but not enough, I think, to determine a unique solution. It directs us, at any rate, to look at the success of p relative to its competitors. So here is a tentative first move. A proposition C[p] is a competitor of p iff (i) given E, it precludes p, and (ii) the C[p]-extrapolation of E is better explanatorily integrated than E is. A strong characterization of supportiveness might run somewhat as follows: E is supportive to some degree with respect to p just in case the addition of p to it improves its explanatory integration more than the addition of any of its competitors does. A weaker characterization would go, rather, along these lines. E is supportive to some degree with respect to p just in case the addition of p to it improves its explanatory integration; E is the more supportive with respect to p the more the addition of p to it improves its explanatory integration more than the more of its competitors do. The crossword analogy pulls one somewhat in the direction of the weaker characterization, which I am therefore inclined to favour – though not by a very large margin.

I had formerly favoured the conjecture that E is supportive with respect to p just in case its p-extrapolation is better explanatorily integrated than its not-p-extrapolation, and the more supportive the more its p-extrapolation is better explanatorily integrated than its not-p-extrapolation. But I no longer think this can be correct; the problem is that, if p is potentially explanatory of E or some component of E, it is not to be expected that not-p will be a rival potential *explanans*. (For this reason, the conjecture was also not well motivated by the crossword analogy.) This now-rejected characterization of supportiveness was prompted in part by its isomorphism with the characterization of conclusiveness. With either of the characterizations now on the table, I note, at least an analogy of structure can be sustained: conclusiveness is a matter of the superiority of p over its *negation* with respect to *consistency* with E; supportiveness is a matter of the superiority of p over its *competitors* with respect to the *explanatory integration* of E.

The proposed characterization is not equivalent to more familiar accounts appealing to deductive implication and inductive support of p by E; and where it differs it has certain advantages. Although, if E is conclusive with respect to p, it deductively implies it, the converse is not true without exception. If E is itself inconsistent, E deductively implies p, but it does not qualify as conclusive with respect to p. If E is inconsistent, not only its not-p-extrapolation but also its p-extrapolation is inconsistent. This upshot, that inconsistent evidence with respect to p is, as I shall say, indifferent, is surely more plausible than the foundationalist line that it is conclusive; and it is achieved without succumbing to the excessively strenuous coherentist thesis that if there is any inconsistency in A's belief-set, he is not justified in any of his beliefs.

The intuition is much stronger that there is such a thing as favourable-but-not-conclusive evidence than it is that there is such as thing as 'inductive implication' or 'inductive logic' – certainly if 'inductive logic' is taken to indicate relations susceptible of a purely syntactic characterization. My approach to 'E is supportive (favourable but not conclusive) with respect to p' has, from this point of view, at least the negative advantage of requiring no appeal to an 'inductive logic' which is prone to paradox at best, perhaps mythical at worst.[7]

Perhaps it also has a positive advantage. At least, by appealing to the notion of explanatory integration in the explication of supportiveness, foundherentism borrows some of the intuitive appeal of the notions of (on the foundationalist side) inference to the best explanation and (on the coherentist side) explanatory coherence. Like these more familiar notions, it should be construed as undemanding with respect to truth; i.e., as requiring the truth neither of *explicantia* nor of *explicanda*. The notion of inference to the best explanation is both *one-directional* and *optimizing* in character; the notion of explanatory coherence has neither characteristic.[8] So the explication tentatively proposed here is closer to the latter, coherentist notion, since, first, explanatory integration is taken to be a property possessed in varying degrees by sets of propositions; and, second, because of my weak preference for the weaker characterization of supportiveness, the p-extrapolation of E does not have to be better explanatorily integrated than all C[p]-extrapolations for E to count as supportive with respect to p.

How favourable E is with respect to p is not sufficient by itself to determine degree of justification. If A's direct C-evidence with respect to p includes other beliefs of his, the degree to which he is justified in believing that p will also depend on the degree to which he is justified in believing those C-reasons. The possibility of mutual dependence is not precluded; it could be that A's C-reasons with respect to p include some C-belief, say the C-belief that z, one of A's C-reasons with respect to which is the C-belief that p. The point of the qualification 'independently of the C-belief that p' in clause 2 is to avoid the danger of circularity this would otherwise present.

The idea of independent security is easiest to grasp in the context of the crossword analogy, so I shall discuss it with reference to the small,

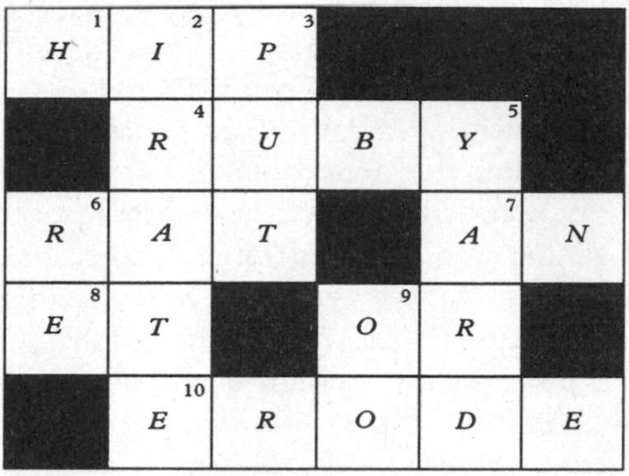

	1 H	2 I	3 P		
		4 R	U	B	Y 5
6 R	A	T		7 A	N
8 E	T		9 O	R	
	10 E	R	O	D	E

ACROSS	DOWN

ACROSS

1 A cheerful start (3)
4 She's a jewel (4)
6 No, it's Polonius (3)
7 An article (2)
8 A visitor from outside fills this space (2)
9 What's the alternative? (2)
10 Dick Turpin did this to York; it wore 'im out (5)

DOWN

2 Angry Irish rebels (5)
3 Have a shot at an Olympic event (3)
5 A measure of one's back garden (4)
6 What's this all about? (2)
9 The printer hasn't got my number (2)

Consider 4 across – RUBY

How reasonable it is to think this is correct depends on:
(1) the clue
(2) how likely it is that IRATE is correct
(3) how likely it is that PUT is correct
(4) how likely it is that YARD is correct

How reasonable it is to think that IRATE is correct depends on:
(i)   the clue
(ii) how likely it is that HIP is correct (which also depends on IRATE and PUT)
(iii) how likely it is that RAT is correct (which also depends on IRATE and RE)
(iv) how likely it is that ET is correct (which also depends on IRATE and RE)
(v)   how likely it is that ERODE is correct (which also depends on IRATE, OO, and YARD)
(vi) how likely it is that RUBY is correct

How reasonable it is to think that PUT is correct depends on:
(a) the clue
(b) how likely it is that HIP is correct (which also depends on IRATE and PUT)
(c) how likely it is that RAT is correct (which also depends on IRATE and RE)
(d) how likely it is that RUBY is correct

How reasonable it is to think that YARD is correct depends on:
(a) the clue
(b) how likely it is that AN is correct (which also depends on YARD)
(c) how likely it is that OR is correct (which also depends on YARD and OO)
(d) how likely it is that ERODE is correct (which also depends on YARD, IRATE, and OO)
(e) how likely it is that RUBY is correct.

Figure 4.1

one-spade crossword puzzle in figure 4.1. How reasonable one's confidence is that 4 across is correct depends, *inter alia*, on how reasonable one's confidence is that 2 down is correct. True, how reasonable one's confidence is that 2 down is correct in turn depends, *inter alia*, on how reasonable one's confidence is that 4 across is correct. But in judging how reasonable one's confidence is that 4 across is correct one need not, for fear of getting into a vicious circle, ignore the support given it by 2 down; it is enough that one judge how reasonable one's confidence is that 2 down is correct *leaving aside the support given it by 4 across*. And this is just how my account of the independent security of A's C-reasons with respect to p avoids vicious circularity.

The crossword analogy also shows the way around another potential objection. The degree of independent security of A's C-reasons with respect to p has been explained in terms of the degree to which A is justified, independently of the C-belief that p, in believing his C-reasons with respect to p. So, since 'justified' occurs on the right-hand side, won't the explication be ineliminable? No – but the explanation is a bit tricky, and again easier to see in the case of the crossword puzzle. In figuring out how reasonable one's confidence in some entry is, one will eventually reach a point where the issue is not how well some entry is supported by others, but how well it is supported by its clue. Analogously, in appraising how justified A is, independently of the C-belief that p, in believing his C-reasons with respect to that belief, one will eventually reach a point where the issue is not how well some belief is supported by other C-beliefs, but how well it is supported by experiential C-evidence. And the question of justification doesn't arise with respect to experiential C-evidence.[9] But doesn't this mean that the account is lapsing into a kind of foundationalism? No. What it means is that 'justified' eventually drops out of the *explicans* as one reaches the question, how well some belief(s) is (are) supported by experiential C-evidence; this does not require that any beliefs be justified exclusively by experiential C-evidence, nor, *a fortiori*, that all other justified beliefs be justified by the support of such beliefs. (Recall the foundherentist interpretation of 'the ultimate evidence for empirical beliefs is experience'.)

There is an asymmetry to be noted between the role of A's C-reasons for believing that p and the role of A's C-reasons against believing that p. A is more [less] justified in believing that p the more [less] justified he is, independently of the C-belief that p, in believing his C-reasons for believing that p; but the less [more] justified in believing that p the more [less] justified he is, independently of the C-belief that p, in believing his C-reasons against believing that p.

Degree of supportiveness and degree of independent security together are still insufficient to determine degree of justification; there remains the dimension of comprehensiveness. The comprehensiveness condition is the nearest analogue, in my account, of the more familiar total evidence requirement on inductions. Unlike this requirement, however, and like the comprehensiveness condition imposed by some coherentists, it is not a factor determining degree of supportiveness of evidence, but a separate criterion entering into the determination of degree of justification.

Comprehensiveness promises to be tougher to spell out even than supportiveness and independent security; the crossword analogy isn't much help here, and the characterization of 'A's evidence' cannot be extrapolated in any easy way to 'evidence', *simpliciter*. Perhaps fortunately, the role of the comprehensiveness clause is most apparent negatively, when one judges someone unjustified or little justified in a belief because of their failure to take account of some relevant evidence. It is worth noting that 'failure to take some relevant evidence into account' includes failure to take a closer look, to check how the thing looks from the back, etc., etc.; so the comprehensiveness condition must be construed to include experiential evidence.

Even in advance of any further analysis, it is pretty clear that the dimension of comprehensiveness is not likely to yield a linear ordering. And there is a further complication because the relevance of evidence is itself a matter of degree: an indeterminacy about how to weigh failure to take a lot of marginally relevant evidence into account relative to failure to take just a bit of more centrally relevant evidence into account.[10] Relevance of evidence is being taken to be an objective matter. What evidence *appears to A to be* relevant depends on various background beliefs, which may be true or may be false. What evidence *is* relevant, however, coincides with what evidence appears to A to be relevant only if A's background beliefs are *true*.

It can now be seen that inconsistency in one's belief-set does carry a price, though a lesser price than the coherentist exacts. Inconsistency in one's C-evidence with respect to some belief has the consequence that one is not justified in that belief. To avoid this a subject whose beliefs are inconsistent will have to keep the incompatible parts of his belief-set apart from each other; and this can be achieved only at the price of sometimes failing to take relevant evidence into account – which itself lowers the degree of justification of the beliefs it affects.

'A is more justified in believing that p the more supportive his direct C-evidence with respect to p is, the more [less] independently secure his direct C-reasons for [against] believing that p are, and the more comprehensive his C-evidence with respect to p is'. This is a bit more specific than the first and second attempts, but it still leaves the question, what the minimal conditions are for A's being justified to *any* degree in believing that p.

One necessary condition is, simply, that there *be* such a thing as A's C-evidence with respect to p; if his belief were the result of a blow to the head, for example, or of one of those pills philosophers are fond of imagining, he would not be justified at all. Furthermore, since it is the justification of empirical beliefs which is at issue, it is necessary that A's C-evidence include some experiential C-evidence. (This is my analogue of BonJour's Observation Requirement – note, however, that while his requirement was quite out of place in BonJour's coherentist theory, mine is precisely *in* place in my experientialist foundherentism.) Another necessary condition has already been suggested, in the context of the discussion of supportiveness: A's C-evidence must be favourable with respect to p. Presumably also some minimal standard of comprehensiveness is necessary; it is tempting to suggest that A's C-evidence must at least include all the relevant evidence A possesses – but this is unfortunately too demanding. Given A's other beliefs, some of the relevant evidence he possesses may not appear relevant to A; worse, this suggestion would have the undesired consequence that, after all, any inconsistency in A's belief-set precludes his being justified in any belief. With respect, finally, to the question of the minimal standards of independent security, the obvious suggestion is that A must be justified to some degree in believing his direct C-reasons for believing that p; but the asymmetry between A's C-reasons for believing that p and his C-reasons against believing that p means that no such obvious suggestion offers itself on the negative side.

What about the upper end of the scale? Our ordinary talk of someone's being 'completely justified' in believing something is highly context-dependent; it means something like: 'in the circumstances – including such matters as how important it is to be right about whether p, whether it is A's particular business to know whether p, etc., etc. – A's evidence is good enough (supportive enough, comprehensive enough, secure enough) that he doesn't count as having been epistemically negligent, or as epistemically blameworthy, in believing that p'. This may be represented by 'A is *completely* justified in believing that p', which will refer to a context-dependent area somewhere vaguely in the upper range of the scale of justification. Its vagueness and context-dependence is what makes this ordinary conception useful for practical purposes (and for the statement of Gettier-type paradoxes). But philosophical talk of 'complete justification' is best construed in a more demanding, context-neutralized fashion. This may be represented by 'A is COMPLETELY justified in believing that p', which would require A's C-evidence to be conclusive and maximally comprehensive, and his C-reasons to be maximally independently secure.

Now for some extrapolations and applications.

IV

The explication taken as primitive here, 'A is more/less justified in believing that p', presupposes that A believes that p; but what of 'A would be more/less justified in believing that p', which presupposes that A doesn't believe that p? The degree to which A would be justified, presumably, depends on how good the evidence is that A has with respect to p. So an explication of this locution would refer to those beliefs and experiences of A's which are relevant to p, and to how justified A is in believing that p on the assumption that those beliefs and experiences are his evidence with respect to p, in the sense explained above.

What about the possibility of speaking of the degree to which, not an individual, but a group of people, is justified in believing that p? (I am thinking, for instance, of the kind of case where a group of scientists produces a report of work which is joint in the sense that different members of the group have done different but related parts of it, in more or less complete awareness of the others' work.)[11] It might be feasible to make some kind of sense of this by starting with the degree to which a hypothetical subject whose evidence includes all the evidence of each member of the group would be justified in believing that p, and then discounting this by some index of the average degree to which members of the group are justified in believing that the other members are reliable. If the result of pooling the evidence of the various members of the group were inconsistent, this would have the consequence that the group, *qua* group, is not justified to any degree, even if some or even all its members were, in believing that p. This consequence seems correct.

As for the impersonal locution, 'the belief that p is more/less justified', though I would not go so far as to say that no sense can be made of it, I have to say that I have no explication to offer. The problem may be in part that the locution works differently in different contexts; in some, perhaps, it may mean 'someone is or would be more/less justified in believing that p', but this doesn't seem plausible as an all-purpose explication. The obstacle, of course, is that since empirical justification depends ultimately on experience, and since it is persons who have experience, an impersonal locution is prima facie out of place.

It is possible to adapt the account suggested so as to accommodate the idea that belief, as well as justification, comes in degrees. (A gradational conception of belief is not obligatory, since there is the alternative of allowing degrees of approximation to belief construed categorically; but it is one way, and quite a useful one, of acknowledging that a person's acceptance of a proposition as true may be more or less complete.) The basic principle of adaptation is simple: that degree of justification is inversely related to degree of belief – i.e., assuming A's evidence held constant, the less strongly A believes that p, the more justified he is in this (weak) belief. This principle is the nearest analogue, in my account, of Hume's injunction that one proportion one's beliefs to the strength of one's evidence.[12] It may look, however, as if there is an awkward complication concerning A's reasons with respect to a belief: how is the possibility that A believes his reasons less than fully to be accommodated? It turns out, however, that one can let the degree to which A is justified in believing that p depend, *inter alia*, on the degree to which he would be justified in *fully* believing his reasons with respect to p (even if, in fact, he only partially believes them). If A less-than-fully believes his reasons for believing that p, either this will be reflected in a lowering of his degree of belief that p, or not. If so, the inverse relation between degree of belief and degree of justification already suggested will raise the degree to which he is justified in his (properly weak) belief that p. If not, it will lower the degree to which he is justified in his (improperly strong) belief that p. And this – plus the usual asymmetrical *mutatis mutandis* clause for his reasons against believing that p – seems to be all that is needed.

Let me close this section by seeing how my account fares with regard to the lottery paradox – a challenge for any theory of justification, and one which it is plausible to think a gradational account might have some advantages in meeting.

Suppose A believes that ticket no. 1 won't win, and that his evidence is: that there are 1 million tickets, that exactly one ticket will win, that the chance that ticket no. 1 will win is 1/1 million, that the chance that ticket no. 2 will win is 1/1 million . . . etc. [E]. Suppose also that his evidence is comprehensive, and his reasons perfectly secure. E is highly supportive but not conclusive with respect to the belief that ticket no. 1 won't win. That it is not conclusive follows from the explication given. It would take more articulation of the explication of supportiveness to establish conclusively that it is highly supportive, but this is precisely in line with the Petrocelli Principle, which is intended as a guide to

further articulation. So A is justified to a high degree, but not COM-
PLETELY, in believing that ticket no. 1 won't win. The same argument applies if we suppose that A believes that ticket no. 2 won't win,
and that his evidence is, again, E; . . . and so on for the belief that ticket
no. 3 won't win . . . and the belief that ticket no. 1 million won't win.

Now suppose that A believes that neither ticket no. 1 nor ticket no.
2 will win. If his evidence is, again, E, then it is, again, not conclusive;
it is still highly supportive, but less supportive than it is of 'ticket no.
1 won't win' or of 'ticket no. 2 won't win'. So he would be justified,
not COMPLETELY, but to a high degree, though lower than the
degree to which he would be justified in believing that ticket no. 1
won't win or in believing that ticket no. 2 won't win, in believing that
neither ticket will win. If, now, one supposes that A believes that none
of tickets nos 1–3 will win, again on evidence E, the same line of
argument shows that he would be justified in believing this, but to a
degree lower than that to which he would be justified in believing that
neither ticket no. 1 nor ticket no. 2 will win.

As more conjuncts are added, A's degree of justification would fall;
he would be less justified in believing that none of tickets nos 1–100
will win, less justified again in believing that none of tickets nos 1–
1,000 will win . . . and so on. In due course, E will cease to be supportive and become undermining; A would not be justified in believing that
none of tickets nos 1–500,001 will win.

Now suppose that A believes that no ticket will win. If his evidence
is E, it is not just not conclusive, not just not supportive, but fatal; for
it includes: some ticket will win. So A would not be justified in believing
that no ticket will win.

But this, it may be said, misses the point. By assuming, throughout,
that A's evidence is just E, I have evaded the problem, which arises
from the intuition that A would be justified in believing that ticket no.
1 won't win, justified in believing that ticket no. 2 won't win . . . and
justified in believing that ticket no. 1 million won't win, but *not* justified
in believing their conjunction, i.e., that *no* ticket will win.

Very well. Go back to the case where A believes that neither ticket
no. 1 nor ticket no. 2 will win, but now assume that his evidence is E,
plus the C-belief that ticket no. 1 won't win, *plus* the C-belief that ticket
no. 2 won't win. Call this E'. E' is conclusive with respect to the C-
belief that neither ticket no. 1 nor ticket no. 2 will win. But though *ex
hypothesi* A is COMPLETELY justified in believing E, he is not COM-
PLETELY justified in believing that ticket no. 1 won't win, nor in
believing that ticket no. 2 won't win. So now, though his reasons are
conclusive, they are not fully independently secure. It seems reasonable

to assume (though this goes beyond what the explication of independent security is precise enough decisively to entail) that though he would be justified to a high degree in believing that neither ticket no. 1 nor ticket no. 2 will win, he would be justified to a lesser degree in believing the conjunction than he would be in believing either conjunct. And if so, then, as before, as more conjuncts are added, his degree of justification would fall.

Finally, suppose that A believes that no ticket will win, and now that his evidence is E, *plus* the C-belief that ticket no. 1. won't win, *plus* the C-belief that ticket no. 2 won't win . . . *plus* the C-belief that ticket no. 1 million won't win [E*]. E* deductively implies that no ticket will win. But this is not sufficient to make it conclusive. In fact, E* is inconsistent (for it includes E, which includes the C-belief that exactly one ticket will win), and hence, by my account, indifferent. So, once again, A is not justified to any degree in believing that no ticket will win.

I hope this draws the sting of the paradox. It is more oblique than more familiar proposed solutions, but this is not necessarily a disadvantage. Instead of simply requiring us to drop the principle that, if A is justified in believing that p and justified in believing that q, then he is justified in believing that p and q, it supplies the beginnings of an explanation of what is wrong with it. Briefly and roughly: it shows how it can be that A is justified to some degree but not COMPLETELY in believing that p, and justified to some degree but not COMPLETELY in believing that q, and his evidence with respect to p and q can be less good than his evidence with respect to p or his evidence with respect to q, or, indeed, no good at all.

It may be helpful to back up this rather abstract observation with a homely and non-paradoxical example which points in the same direction. Suppose that A is justified to a high degree, but not COMPLETELY, in believing that colleague number 1 will be at tomorrow's departmental meeting (his direct C-evidence being, say, that colleague number 1 is reliable and conscientious and has never missed a meeting yet); and that A is justified to a high degree, but not COMPLETELY, in believing that colleague number 2 will be at the meeting (his direct C-evidence being, say, that colleague number 2 has repeatedly said that he is very keen to see that a certain item on the agenda is passed, and would not except in the direst emergency fail to turn up to vote for it). It seems intuitively clear that A is *less* justified in believing that colleague number 1 will turn up *and* colleague number 2 will turn up. Why? Well, still speaking intuitively, it is because there is more to go wrong, more of a gap between his C-evidence and the truth of the conjunction. His C-evidence with respect to the belief that colleague number 1 will be there is not conclusive – A doesn't know, e.g., that there won't be a domestic emergency or car breakdown preventing him from showing up; and neither is his C-evidence with respect to the belief that colleague number 2 will turn up – A doesn't know, e.g., that colleague number 2 hasn't realized, overnight, that the proposed changes would involve a significant increase in teaching loads, and decided that the least embarrassing course of action is to invent an excuse for not showing up after all. And if *any* of these gaps in A's C-evidence should turn out differently, *one* of the two colleagues would be absent.

Complex as this has been, it is very far from complete. I have helped myself to a whole slew of concepts, some of which have been left completely unexplicated, and of none of which a fully satisfactory account has been given. This cannot be excused by appeal to the fact that the pre-analytic conception of justification is itself vague; for one purpose of explication is to improve precision. Nor can it be excused by appeal to the fact that any explication must come to an end somewhere; for the concepts on which I am relying are hardly so transparent as to be prime candidates for this status. In partial mitigation, however, it may be observed that close relatives of some of the concepts needed (explanatory integration, comprehensiveness) are already current in the literature, and that the foundherentist is free to borrow the best efforts of rival theorists to spell them out.

The successive approximations by means of which the explication has been presented mean that it would be possible to follow me through some steps without following me all the way. This is reassuring, since the successive steps get dicier as, and to the extent that, they get more specific. It would also be possible to borrow the double-aspect approach without subscribing to the foundherentist structure offered; to adapt the crossword model of the structure of evidential support without adopting the double-aspect approach; or to follow me with regard to the double-aspect approach and the crossword model without accepting my explication of supportiveness in terms of explanatory integration; and so on.

But my hope is that this explication, imperfect as it is, represents at least approximately the kind of theory which, as I argued in chapters 1–3, is required to overcome the difficulties faced, on the one hand, by foundationalism and, on the other, by coherentism. Still, there is quite a way yet to go.

Since a prime motivation for seeking a 'third alternative' theory was, from the beginning, that a coherentist account cannot allow the relevance of experience to justification at all, while a foundationalist account can allow it only in a forced and unnatural fashion, it will certainly be necessary to say more than I have so far about the role of experience in the foundherentist account. It will be not only convenient, but also, I hope, illuminating, to combine this task with a critique of Popperian 'epistemology without a knowing subject', which throws the problem of the role of experience into particularly sharp relief.

5

The Evidence of the Senses:
Refutations and Conjectures

It is the external world that we directly observe ...
[The perceptive judgement] is plainly nothing but the extremest
case of the Abductive Judgement.

Peirce Collected Papers[1]

The goal of this chapter is to contribute to the development of, and the
motivation for, double-aspect foundherentism by focusing in more detail
on the question of the role of experience in justification. Up to now
the case for foundherentism has been made using foundationalism and
coherentism as a foil; now, however, against the danger that it may be
thought that, by working within this fairly restricted set of parameters,
I have avoided the false dichotomy of foundationalism versus coherentism only to succumb to a false trichotomy of foundationalism versus
coherentism versus foundherentism, I take the opportunity to develop
the foundherentist account by contrast with the radical 'epistemology
without a knowing subject' championed by Popper.

The key theses of the chapter will be, negatively, that Popperian
'epistemology without a knowing subject' is indefensible, because what
Popper calls 'the problem of the empirical basis' is not only unsolved
by him but in principle insoluble within the Popperian constraints of
strict deductivism and uncompromising anti-psychologism; and, positively, that the foundherentist account not only solves the problem, but
also supplies the theoretical backbone for an explanation of how the
Popperian constraints should be modified, and how the arguments for
these constraints should be answered.

Stated thus briefly and roughly, the goal sounds simple enough; but the strategy will have to be somewhat tortuous. This is in the first instance because a detour is necessary to look at a recent book in which Watkins purports to offer a solution to the problem of the empirical basis within the Popperian constraints; for if Watkins succeeds, of course, my diagnosis and critique of what I regard as the inevitable Popperian impasse must be mistaken. But it turns out not only that – on the only interpretation in which it has any claim to be more plausible than Popper's own – Watkins' account covertly compromises the Popperian constraints; but also that on that interpretation it differs only verbally from a familiar style of infallibilist foundationalism. The detour turns out to be fruitful. Watkins' theory is vulnerable to the familiar objections to infallibilist foundationalism; it is also dependent on a conception of perception as of sense-data rather than of external objects and events which provides the perfect foil for the development and defence of the more realist theory of perception embedded in foundherentism.

And this leads to another, luckily also another fruitful, complication. Watkins defends his account of perception by appeal to psychology; not only does the work he appeals to fall short of establishing his claims, however, but also, within the context of Watkins' project – the familiar Popperian project of establishing the rationality of science – it is quite improper for Watkins to appeal to psychology at all. The conclusion is not that appeals to psychology are either irrelevant or illegitimate; I shall make them myself, as an indirect source of support for the foundherentist conception of the evidence of the senses. It is, rather, that their legitimacy depends on a meta-epistemological stance quite foreign to the Popperian – a modestly naturalistic stance with which, as I shall suggest, foundherentism has a special affinity.

I

Some background needs to be sketched by way of initial orientation. At first blush, it might seem that Popper's enterprise is so different from mine that it is perverse to choose it for a comparative case-study. Popper's attitude to the epistemological mainstream to which the present work belongs is frankly scornful ('belief philosophies'). But the superficial appearance of simple divergence of interests is more than somewhat misleading; the divergence is less, and much less simple, than it seems.

Popper's focus is not, as mine is, on empirical knowledge in general, but on scientific knowledge specifically. He is preoccupied with the problem of demarcating science from non-science – a problem which is (and by no accident, as will become apparent in due course) no preoccupation of mine. But scientific knowledge, one might assume, is part of empirical knowledge; isn't this enough to show that there is a large area of overlap? Not really; this is still too simple.

What is most distinctive about Popper's philosophy of science is that it is falsificationist, holding, that is, that scientific theories can never be verified, confirmed, or justified, but only falsified, refuted, or, at best, corroborated – i.e., tested but *not* falsified; and that it is, in a distinctively Popperian sense, 'objectivist', i.e., concerned solely with the objective contents of theories, etc., and their logical relations. Scientists neither do, nor should, *believe* their theories; what is important is not scientists' beliefs – that is a subjective matter – but abstract theories, propositions, problems. That is what 'objective, scientific knowledge', as Popper uses the phrase, refers to.[2]

From the point of view of the epistemological mainstream, in fact, Popper might be described as a closet sceptic: in any sense in which justified, true belief is required for knowledge, at any rate, he denies that we *have* any knowledge. 'Objective, scientific knowledge', in his sense, is never justified, should not be believed, and may not be true. It would be true to say that Popper is not interested in the concept of justified belief; but more illuminating, in the interests of locating his projects relative to more traditional approaches to epistemology, to say that he is not interested in the concept because he thinks there *are no* justified beliefs.

It would be true to say that Popper denies that we have knowledge, in the usual sense; but more illuminating, in the interests of locating the point of intersection of our projects where my critique will get its purchase, to say that he denies that we can have knowledge, in the usual sense, while holding that, for all that, science is a rational enterprise – not because scientists are ever justified in believing their theories, but because genuinely scientific theories are subject to rational criticism. The first moment of Popperian epistemology is the demarcation of science from non-science, and its fundamental project is to establish that science is, though only in a negative sense, rational. This project depends on establishing that it is possible, not indeed to show that a true scientific theory is true, but to show that a false scientific theory is false; and that depends on the solution to the 'problem of the empirical basis', i.e., the problem of the role of experience in falsification.

By arguing, at the epistemological level, that Popper has, and can have, no credible solution to the problem of the empirical basis, and urging the superiority of the foundherentist account of the evidence of the senses, I aim of course to take the case for foundherentism a step further. At the same time, at the meta-epistemological level, I aim, first, to emphasize the strength of the case for an epistemology *with* a knowing subject, and, second, to delineate the initial stages of an argument for an acknowledgement of the contributory relevance to epistemology of the sciences of cognition, for a modest naturalism – and, in the process, of an articulation of my gradualist conception of the relation of philosophy and science.

II

The title of section 5 of *The Logic of Scientific Discovery*,[3] 'Experience as a Method', suggests that Popper believes that its sensitivity to experience is characteristic of empirical science. When he asks, 'How is the system that represents our world of experience to be distinguished?' and answers, 'by the fact that it has been submitted to . . . and has stood up to tests', one might be led to suppose that he thinks that scientific theories are tested against experience. Sections 25–30, however, make it clear that this is not his view: scientific theories are to be tested, not against experience, but against 'basic statements' – singular statements reporting the occurrence of an observable event at a specified place and time. And – this is the crucial point – though Popper characterizes basic statements as observational in content, and though he concedes that scientists' decision to accept a basic statement may be causally prompted by their experience, he insists categorically that *basic statements cannot be justified or supported by experience*:

> . . . the decision to accept a basic statement . . . is causally connected with our experiences . . . But we do not attempt to *justify* basic statements by these experiences. Experiences can *motivate a decision,* and hence an acceptance or rejection of a statement, but a basic statement cannot be *justified* by them – no more than by thumping the table. (p. 105)

Though they are not clearly distinguished in the text, with a certain amount of rational reconstruction one can identify two arguments at work here, both leading to the startling negative thesis that experience cannot justify the acceptance of basic statements.

The first runs as follows. Basic statements are theory-impregnated. The content of a statement like 'Here is a glass of water' goes beyond what is immediately observable; for the use of general terms like 'glass' and 'water' implies that the container and the contained substance would behave thus and so in these or those hypothetical circumstances. So basic statements could be justified by experience only if some kind of ampliative inference, from a thing's present, observable character to its future and hypothetical behaviour, could support them. But induction is unjustifiable; only deductive arguments are in any sense valid; only evidence which deductively implies a statement can support it. Hence, basic statements cannot be justified by experience (pp. 94–5). Since its crucial premiss is that there is no supportive evidence which is not, so to speak, 'deductively conclusive', I shall refer to this as the 'anti-inductivist argument'.

The second argument is a version of the by now familiar irrelevance of causation argument. There can be causal relations between a person's experiences and his acceptance or rejection of a basic statement. A's seeing a black swan, for instance, may cause him to reject the statement 'All swans are white'. But there cannot be logical relations between experiences and statements. 'Here is a black swan' logically implies 'There is at least one black swan' and is logically incompatible with 'All swans are white'; but it makes no sense to speak of A's seeing a black swan as implying 'There is at least one black swan' or as incompatible with 'All swans are white'. And justification is not a causal or psychological notion, but a logical one. Hence, basic statements cannot be justified by experience (pp. 93–4). In the present context I shall mark the reliance of this argument on a fundamental Popperian theme by referring to it as the 'anti-psychologistic argument'.

Both arguments are valid.

Their conclusion, however, is simply incredible: scientists' acceptance of a basic statement like 'The needle on the dial points to 7' is in no epistemologically relevant way supported or justified by their seeing the needle on the dial point to 7; scientists' perceptual experiences are, in fact, *completely irrelevant* to epistemological issues. This is bad enough. But recall that a scientific theory is said to be 'refuted' or 'falsified' if it is incompatible with an accepted basic statement. Since the acceptance of a basic statement is in no epistemologically relevant way supported or justified by scientists' experience, *there is no reason to suppose that accepted basic statements are true, nor, consequently, that a 'refuted' or 'falsified' theory* (the terms are now seen to be tendentious) *is false.* Science is not, after all, even negatively under the control of experience.

And what Popper has to offer by way of an alternative to the idea that basic statements are supported by experience serves less to mitigate one's incredulity than to aggravate it. The acceptance and rejection of basic statements, he asserts, is a matter for 'decision' or 'convention' on the part of the scientific community; he even notes that his view has affinities with the conventionalism espoused by Poincaré, but for its being focused not at the theoretical but at the observational level – where, I may add, it is obviously much less plausible. True, Popper insists that the acceptance/rejection of basic statements (though always a matter for decision maybe prompted but never justified by experience) is not arbitrary. Acceptance or rejection of a basic statement, he says, is conjectural and revisable; if there is disagreement about whether a basic statement should be accepted, it can be tested against other basic statements, with the process resting, temporarily and provisionally, with basic statements *which are readily testable* (pp. 104, 108–11). But 'testable' is itself tendentious in this context; and Popper's account offers no reassurance whatever that science rests, at some point, on something besides unjustified and unjustifiable decisions, but only postpones the point at which unjustified and unjustifiable decisions are reached.

I am not the first to take Popper to task on this point. Quinton holds, as I do, that Popper's conventionalism about basic statements undermines his whole theory of empirical knowledge.[4] And Ayer protests, as I have done, that Popper's account is incredible, and insists, as I do, that the acceptance of basic statements surely *can* be justified, albeit not fully or incorrigibly justified, by experience.[5] Popper's reply to Ayer is completely unconvincing – but very revealing. He presents himself as defending, without compromise, the account he gave in *The Logic of Scientific Discovery*. He insists that Ayer has misunderstood his position, and stresses that he always denied that the decision to accept or reject a basic statement is 'arbitrary or unmotivated'. But he goes on to concede that 'our experiences are not only motives for accepting or rejecting observational statements, but they may even be described as *inconclusive reasons*', and amplifies by explaining that 'they are reasons because of the generally reliable character of our observations' but that 'they are inconclusive because of our fallibility'.[6] But this is not to defend, but to abandon, the radical position adopted in *The Logic of Scientific Discovery*; Popper admits that experiences can after all constitute reasons for, not just causes of, the acceptance or rejection of basic statements, and that there can be reasons which fall short of deductive conclusiveness. Popper disguises – perhaps from himself more successfully than from the reader – how radical a concession he is making, by using the term 'motivated' in a shifting way: if 'motivated' means 'causally prompted' and is contrasted with 'justified', then it would be true that he had never suggested that the decision to accept/reject a basic statement is unmotivated, but reiteration of this point would constitute no reply to Ayer's objection; if, on the other hand, it is used equivalently to 'justified' or 'supported by reasons', it constitutes a capitulation to the objection, and is not a defence of, but flatly inconsistent with, Popper's earlier position. Ayer clearly wins this round.

But matters cannot be left at that. Popper's early, radical position was supported by two powerful arguments, but Ayer offers no reply to those arguments, and neither, though he at least half-concedes that their conclusion is false, does Popper himself. These arguments are valid; so, since their conclusion is false, they must each have at least one false premiss. It should be clear from the work of earlier chapters which, according to me, those premisses are.

The premisses of the anti-psychologistic argument are that there can be only causal, not logical, relations between a subject's experience and his acceptance or rejection of a basic statement, and that only logical relations are relevant to the rationality of the acceptance/rejection of statements. The first is true; the second false. The premisses of the anti-inductivist argument are that basic statements are theory-laden, and that there are no non-deductive, ampliative support relations. The first is true; the second false.

It is now apparent, by the way, why Popper does not sharply distinguish these two arguments, but treats them as interlocking, seeing psychologism and inductivism as two sides of the same (verificationist) coin: the anti-psychologistic assumption has it that only logical relations are epistemologically relevant, the anti-inductivist assumption has it that the only logical relations are deductive; together, therefore, they imply that only relations of deductive logic are epistemologically relevant.

The assumptions on which these two arguments rest are very deeply rooted in Popper's philosophy. That, since induction is unjustifiable, scientific method must be exclusively deductive in character, is the fundamental idea behind Popper's falsificationism. That questions of justification are logical rather than causal in character is the fundamental idea behind the importance Popper attaches to the discovery/justification distinction, his relegation of all questions of discovery to the sphere of sociology or psychology, his denigration of psychological concepts and issues as 'subjective', and, ultimately, his championship of an 'epistemology without a knowing subject' concerned solely with world 3, with propositions and their logical relations; it even underlies the peculiar character of Popper's allegiance to an evolutionary epistemology couched, not in terms of the evolution of human beings and their cognitive capacities, but of the evolution of theories and problem-situations.[7]

If this diagnosis is correct, there can be no solution to the 'problem of the empirical basis' within the Popperian constraints of anti-inductivism and anti-psychologism – and no escape, within those constraints, from the profound scepticism to which, via the conclusion that science is not even negatively under the control of experience, and that scientific theories can no more be shown false than they can be shown true, it leads. This profound failure reinforces my conviction, first, that the notion of justified belief is not after all beyond redemption, and, second, that the best prospects for explicating this notion lie in the articulation of an experientialist epistemology in which the human subject plays a central role.

My diagnosis seems to be threatened, however, by an optimistic Popperian book, Watkins' *Science and Scepticism*,[8] which purports to offer an account of when, and why, it is rational to accept a basic statement which both avoids scepticism and conforms to the Popperian constraints. It will be worth a detour to show how, and why, it fails.

III

Watkins interprets Popper's position on the problem of the empirical basis much as I do, and thinks, as I do, that it is quite unsatisfactory. In response to Popper's suggestion that the process of settling disputed basic statements be handled by stopping, provisionally, with basic statements which are easily testable, he comments that, having arrived at some basic statement which is especially easy to test, scientists surely ought, before they accept it, 'to make one last effort and actually *test* it' (p. 53). Quite so.

Watkins' attempt to do better involves introducing another class of statements, more basic than Popper's 'basic statements'. Watkins' 'level-1' statements are characterized as 'singular statements about observable things and events' (e.g., 'There's a new moon tonight'); these correspond to Popper's basic statements. Watkins' 'level-0' statements are characterized as 'perceptual reports of a first-person, here-and-now type' (e.g., 'In my visual field there is now a silvery crescent on a dark blue background'). Level-0 statements, Watkins claims, are certain; the subject can infallibly know them to be true. Level-0 statements cannot deductively imply level-1 statements. However, level-1 statements may, together with other hypotheses, e.g., about the conditions of perception, constitute explanations of the truth of level-0 statements. Perception, as Watkins puts it, 'grows spontaneously into perceptual judgements'; this involves, he suggests, a good deal of interpretation, processing, but processing of which the subject is not normally aware. A hypothetical subject who was fully aware of this usually-unnoticed mental processing, Johnny Wideawake, would go through some such reasoning process as: 'In my visual field there is now a silvery crescent on a dark blue background. What could explain this? Ah – maybe there is a new moon tonight'. Johnny Wideawake's acceptance of this level-1 statement, according to Watkins, would be rationally justified. And since ordinary mortals go *un*consciously through the mental processing through which, *ex hypothesi*, Johnny Wideawake goes consciously, their acceptance of level-1 statements can be quasi-rationally justified (pp. 79–80 and 254–62).

The first part of my critique is to the effect that Watkins' account has no chance of success unless it is interpreted as compromising the Popperian constraints of anti-psychologism and anti-inductivism.

That Watkins' account needs to be understood as, after all, giving a significant role to the knowing subject is too obvious to require argument. What requires work is to get clearer about what psychologism amounts to; for there is a significant ambiguity in the dichotomy of psychologism versus anti-psychologism. At one extreme, we have:

> full-blooded psychologism, according to which justification or rational acceptability is a wholly psychological concept;

and at the other:

> extreme anti-psychologism, according to which psychological factors are wholly irrelevant to questions of justification/rational acceptability.

But there is also (an intermediate position):

> 'moderate [anti-]psychologism', according to which psychological factors do not exhaust, but have contributory relevance to, questions of justification/rational acceptability.

Watkins' account has no prospect of improving on Popper's unless it is interpreted as conceding at least the intermediate position, i.e., as no longer anti-psychologistic in the strong sense. It has two components: how level-0 statements get to be certain, and how their relations to level-0 statements may make level-1 statements rationally acceptable. I take these in turn.

Level-0 statements are not empty tautologies; the claim that they are certain is most plausible if interpreted as: some level-0 *judgements*, those made in appropriate circumstances, are certain; for such judgements are epistemically fully secure when fully supported by the perceptual experience which prompts them. But this kind of explanation is available only on the assumption that what causes the subject to accept a level-0 statement – his sensory experience – is relevant to justification; hence, it is incompatible with extreme anti-psychologism.

If Watkins seems blithely unaware of this, there is, I think, a plausible explanation. First, his policy is to use the term 'psychologism' to mean 'holding psychological factors to be relevant *where they are not*' – and hence to regard the danger that *he* might be guilty of psychologism as negligible. Second, he shifts from describing *level-0* statements as 'perceptual reports' to referring to *level-1* statements as 'perceptual judgements', and from construing 'perceptions' as the *explananda* of which 'perceptual judgements' are potential explanations to construing judgements about one's experience as *explananda* of which judgements about physical objects are the potential explanations (pp. 79, 258–9). If the threefold distinction between one's perceptual experiences, statements about one's perceptual experiences, and statements about observable characteristics of physical objects were clearly acknowledged, the choice between an account which does and an account which does not allow the relevance of experience to the justification of level-0 statements would have had to be squarely faced; Watkins manages to avoid it by fudging the distinction.

Since acceptance of a level-1 statement is supposed to be quasi-rationally justified if it is brought about by unconscious mental processing analogous to Johnny Wideawake's conscious processing, it is clear enough that the second component of Watkins' account, like the first, has no hope of working under the Popperian constraint of extreme anti-psychologism.

The argument that Watkins is best interpreted as also compromising the Popperian constraint of anti-inductivism is simple with respect to the first component of his account: if the explanation of the certainty of level-0 statements must appeal to the subject's experiences, since there cannot be logical relations between experiences and statements, it follows that the explanation of the certainty of level-0 statements cannot be purely logical, and so *a fortiori* cannot be purely deductivist.

The argument with respect to the second component is more tangled, because it reveals a significant ambiguity in the dichotomy of inductivism versus deductivism. The thesis Watkins explicitly calls 'deductivism' is: only deductive derivations are valid. But he also contrasts deductivism and inductivism, as if they were incompatible theses; and he takes the idea that a subject's experiences might constitute inconclusive reasons for accepting basic statements to amount to a capitulation to inductivism.[9] But 'experiences may constitute inconclusive reasons for accepting basic statements' is not incompatible with 'only deductive derivations are valid' (though it is with 'only deductive derivations are valid, and only valid derivations can constitute reasons for accepting statements'). So it is necessary to distinguish:

extreme deductivism (or 'extreme anti-inductivism'), according to which only deductive derivations are valid, and only valid derivations can constitute reasons for accepting statements;

full-blooded inductivism, according to which inductive as well as deductive derivations are in some sense valid, and can constitute reasons for accepting statements;

and an intermediate position:

'supportive evidentialism', according to which only deductive derivations are valid, but valid derivations are not the only reasons for accepting a statement.

Watkins' account of the quasi-rational acceptability of level-1 statements has no chance of working unless it is interpreted as conceding at least the intermediate position, i.e., as no longer anti-inductivist in the strong, Popperian sense.

By way of preliminary it is necessary to say something about what Watkins means by speaking of the '[quasi-]rational acceptability' of a statement. This locution reflects a characteristically Popperian aversion to talk of 'justification' or 'belief'. It also interlocks with Watkins' account of the goal of science, which he characterizes as having an explanation-oriented and a truth-oriented component, the latter being construed in studiedly modest fashion: science aspires to truth, but not to 'proven' truth, only to 'possible' truth. So when Watkins speaks of its being rational 'to accept' some statement, he means 'to accept it as possibly true'. This in turn interlocks with his falsificationist methodology, in which 'possibly true' is explicated like this:

The system of scientific hypotheses adopted by a person . . . at any one time should be possibly true for him, in the sense that, despite his best endeavours, he has not found any inconsistencies in it or between it and the evidence available to him. (pp. 155–6)

The prominence of the knowing subject in this passage is worthy of note; so is the way the notorious problems about the connection between corroboration and verisimilitude are evaded as, in effect, Watkins characterizes the goal of science as: to find well-corroborated hypotheses. But the present issue is the question of the compatibility of Watkins' account with extreme deductivism.

Arguably, even Watkins' account of the grounds for rational

acceptability of a level-2 statement (an empirical generalization) requires some compromise of extreme deductivism. What is supposed to make it rational to accept a level-2 statement is not that it is deductively derivable from some statement itself rationally acceptable, but that, together with auxiliary assumptions, it deductively implies the negations of certain level-1 statements, and that these consequences have been tested without any falsifying instances being found. The schema is: $[S_2 \& A] \vdash$ not-S_1; S_1 has not been found to be rationally acceptable; so S_2 is rationally acceptable. So it is not the level-2 statement itself, but *the statement that the level-2 statement has been tested but not falsified*, which is deductively derivable from rationally acceptable statements.

Watkins' account of the rational acceptability of level-1 statements is even more clearly incompatible with extreme deductivism. What is supposed to make it rational to accept a level-1 statement is that the truth of the level-1 statement, along with auxiliary assumptions, would explain the truth of some level-0 statement, and that the level-0 statement is certainly true. Watkins stresses (p. 225) that the conjunction of the level-1 statement and the auxiliary hypotheses must deductively imply the level-0 statement; but this does not mean that what makes it rational to accept a level-1 statement is that it is deductively derivable from some level-0 statement which is certainly true, but that a level-0 statement *which is deductively derivable from the level-1 statement and the auxiliary hypotheses* is certainly true. The schema is: $[S_1 \& A] \vdash S_0$; S_0 is certainly true; So, S_1 is rationally acceptable. This can by no stretch of the imagination be squared with extreme deductivism.

Watkins has to allow that it is rational to accept a statement as possibly true if that statement constitutes part of a possible explanation of something known to be true. For all his verbal ingenuity in transmuting 'inconclusive reasons for thinking a statement to be true' into 'grounds for the rational acceptability of accepting a statement as possibly true', this does not (as advertised) really avoid scepticism while remaining within the confines of strict deductivism. *Really* it represents a shift to an intermediate position which acknowledges, as supportive-but-not-conclusive reasons, what philosophers less inhibited by Popperian scruples have called 'inference to the best explanation'.

Briefly and bluntly, then: unless Watkins' account is interpreted as compromising Popperian anti-psychologism and anti-inductivism, it has no better chance of success with respect to the problem of the empirical basis than Popper's own account. This confirms the diagnosis of the Popperian impasse offered in section II.

But even on its more promising, less Popperian, interpretation Watkins' account faces many objections. The objections are familiar ones, for on this interpretation Watkins' account is in important respects virtually identical with a familiar, infallibilist style of experientialist foundationalism. The vocabulary is different, but the essential themes are shared: the certainty of level-0 statements parallels the supposed infallibility of basic beliefs; the dependence of the rational acceptability of higher level statements on their relations to lower-level statements and ultimately to level-0 statements parallels the ultimate dependence of derived beliefs on the support of basic beliefs. The difference of vocabulary, the insistence on talking of the rational acceptability of statements rather than the justifiedness of beliefs, looks less and less important as one reflects on the fact that Watkins' un-Popperian theory really is an infallibilist, experientialist foundationalist 'epistemology with a knowing subject'.

It is not necessary to recapitulate the objections to infallibilist foundationalism spelled out in previous chapters. It will be more productive to concentrate on a related set of issues more specific to an understanding of the evidence of the senses. These issues may be introduced by way of asking how, exactly, Watkins' level-0 statements are to be identified. One passage, in which Watkins alludes to Descartes's observation that 'it is at least quite certain that *it seems to me* that I *see light*, that I *hear noise* . . . (p. 259), suggests at once that what is special about level-0 statements may be their cautious, hedged character ('It seems to me') and at the same time that it might be their nearly trivial grammatical character ('I see light, I hear noise'). But Watkins' examples (the 'silvery crescent', p. 78, and the 'white, pencil-like shape', p. 258), favour a third interpretation: that level-0 statements describe the arrangement of colour patches in one's visual field (and, presumably, the order of heard sounds, and whatever the analogues would be for the other senses). And this indicates a conception of perception according to which what we see is patterns of colour patches (etc.), to explain which we conjecture (in Johnny Wideawake's case, consciously, but, in the usual case, unconsciously) the presence of physical objects and events.

This conception is not intuitively plausible. It is doubtful, to say the least, whether subjects more than very rarely *have* beliefs about the arrangement of colour patches in their visual fields. Watkins' example is cleverly chosen, but hard to extrapolate. Just before I wrote this paragraph I was looking out of my study window at the front garden, the gate, the street beyond, passing pedestrians, cars, etc.; I find myself entirely at a loss to describe the arrangement of colour patches in my visual field, and I think it strongly counter-intuitive to say that it is patches of colour, rather than a holly tree, a rose bush, a passing Volvo, my next-door neighbour, etc., that I saw. *Perhaps*, in a certain frame of mind, artists or photographers see colour patches. But the statements or judgements Watkins takes as basic are nothing like as ubiquitous as his account would apparently require if we are more than very rarely to be rational in accepting any level-1 (or, therefore, any higher-level) statement. Watkins may reply that for quasi-rational acceptance only *unconscious* inference is required. It is not clear whether this should or should not be taken to imply that one need only unconsciously accept the level-0 statement that serves as premiss. If so, it has to be said that it is more than somewhat obscure what 'unconsciously accepting a statement about the arrangement of colour patches in one's visual field' could amount to over and above *having* that arrangement in one's visual field. And if not, the reply does not answer the objection. Furthermore, it is more than somewhat implausible to suppose that one's judgements about the arrangements of colour patches in one's visual field are certain or infallible; and it obviously doesn't follow from the fact that perceptual processing is more complex or active than the subject ordinarily realizes that this process always, or ever, involves an unconscious conjecture as to the possible explanation of a level-0 statement. In short, this whole conception of perception – which both encourages and is encouraged by infallibilist (and, for that matter, by strong) foundationalist styles of experientialism – seems forced and counter-intuitive.

It remains to be seen whether the quite different conception implicit in the very sketchy picture so far offered of the foundherentist understanding of 'sensory evidence' can be filled out into a clearly preferable alternative account.

IV

One moral of the previous sections is that any plausible account of the epistemic relevance of experience will have to throw off the Popperian constraints of extreme deductivism and extreme anti-psychologism. This is no radical proposal, for those constraints are thoroughly counter-intuitive.

The crucial premiss of Popper's anti-psychologistic argument is that psychological factors are wholly irrelevant to questions of justification. But two people may believe the same thing, and one of them be justified in believing it and the other not, or one justified to a high degree and the other only to a very modest degree. Suppose A (a patient) and B (his doctor) both believe that A's symptoms are psychosomatic, and not indicative of serious heart disease; and suppose further that A's belief is the result of wishful thinking (he exaggerates the significance of the fact that in 10 per cent of cases, he has heard, such symptoms are not serious), whereas B's is sustained by his having studied the results of the numerous reliable tests to which A has been submitted. One is strongly inclined to say, surely, that A is not justified in his belief, but B is; hence, that why the subject believes what he does is epistemically relevant.

The crucial premiss of Popper's anti-inductivist argument is that evidence can support a belief only in virtue of deductively implying it. But A's evidence may support the belief that p better than B's evidence, even though neither A's evidence nor B's evidence deductively implies p. Suppose A (a tourist holidaying in Africa) and B (a zoologist) both believe that the rock-rabbit is the closest surviving relative of the elephant; and suppose that A's evidence is that a fellow tourist told him he read this somewhere, while B's is that rock-rabbits and elephants both have such-and-such skeletal structure, digestive system, etc., etc., and that these and those intermediate species between the rock-rabbit and the elephant were to be found in such-and-such locations but are now extinct because of these and those geological upheavals and climatic changes, and so on. One is strongly inclined to say, surely, that B's evidence is much more supportive than A's; hence that evidence may be highly supportive without being deductively conclusive.

It is already apparent how my account accommodates these intuitions, and throws off the Popperian constraints: the characterization of A's S-evidence with respect to p as a sub-nexus of the causal nexus of that S-belief, and the characterization of A's C-evidence with respect to p by reference to his S-evidence, allows the relevance of the causes maintaining his S-belief, and the sub-categories of sensory S- and C-evidence allow, specifically, for the relevance of his sensory experience; while the notion of supportiveness, explicated in terms of the explanatory integration of p relative to its competitors, allows for supportive-but-not-conclusive evidential support.

A second moral of the previous sections is that a plausible account of the evidence of the senses should not require either the infallibilist foundationalism, or the atomistic sensationalism, to which Watkins resorts in his attempt to avoid the Popperian impasse. It is already abundantly, perhaps even painfully, clear that the account on offer here is not infallibilist, nor foundationalist. It is also apparent, though only at a fairly crude level, that the account of perception presupposed here is very different from Watkins'.

Fundamental to the commonsense conception I have tried to build into my explication is the idea that the senses are the means by which we perceive things and events around us, and (pardon the pun) its mirror-image, that perception is a matter of interacting, by means of one's senses, with those things and events. One might describe this as a kind of epistemological realism. It is hardly naive, however, for it recognizes that we cannot always perceive clearly, that we sometimes misperceive, that our senses can be fooled by well-camouflaged insects and birds, by magicians and illusionists, artists and psychologists, and that in seriously disordered conditions people may even 'perceive' what is not there at all (hear voices, see pink rats, and so forth); also that we may, if inattentive or flustered, fail to see what is before us, that we may not recognize, or may mis-identify, what we see, hear, etc., that it can take training to learn to make some kinds of perceptual discrimination (to identify a wine or perfume blindfold, say, or to make sense of what one sees in an X-ray photograph or a rear-view mirror).

My picture also acknowledges a partnership of perception with background belief, in the sense that our *beliefs about* what we see, hear etc., are affected not only by what we see and hear, but also by already-embedded beliefs about how things are. Expecting a friend to meet me at the airport, the briefest glimpse of red hair is enough to lead me to believe that is she in the crowd at the gate; seeing you go to the tap, fill a glass and drink, given my belief that it is water, not gin or vodka, that is piped to taps in people's houses, I believe that you are drinking a glass of water. It even acknowledges that in some circumstances one may infer what is there from the splodges of colour one sees ('look, over there, that brown patch under the tree – must be the cat').

Implicit in what I have said so far is a point that ought to be made as explicit as possible, for it is often, perhaps usually, disguised in discussions of 'realist' versus 'anti-realist' or 'direct' versus 'indirect' theories of perception. The account I offer makes perception of things and events around one, not of sense-data, colour patches, or whatever. But at the same time it allows for the pervasive interpenetration of background beliefs into our beliefs about what we see, hear, etc. It combines, in other words, what might be described as realist with anti-realist, or direct with indirect, elements. I hope I have already dispelled the idea that there is anything inconsistent about this, but, in case not, let me try one more time: that our beliefs even about 'observable' things and events around us depend in part on other beliefs does not imply that they must be inferences, conscious or otherwise, from judgements about arrangements of colour patches, sounds, and so forth.

My position is not new. As is rather well known, Peirce thinks of perceptual judgements as like abductions (as potentially explanatory hypotheses); as is less well known, he also holds that perception is direct, in the sense that its objects are the objects and events around us.[10] In my account the realist face of the commonsense picture is represented in the suggested characterizations of sensory C-evidence, which presuppose that normal perception is of things and events around one, and which also accommodate something like the commonsense distinction of more and less favourable circumstances of perception, of glimpses and glances versus good looks. Its less realist face is represented both in the decision to use 'perceptual state' loosely enough to include states phenomenologically indistinguishable from those caused, in the normal way, by sensory interactions with the world, and, most important, in the pervasive interpenetration envisaged of background beliefs even with those beliefs closest to perception.

The last phrase indicates my intention to avoid the whole idea of a class of propositions or C-beliefs properly labelled 'observational'. This is in part, but only in part, a matter of reservations about the robustness of an observational/theoretical distinction. The less familiar, and more important, part is that *the very same sentence* may represent sometimes the content of an S-belief largely supported by the subject's sensory evidence, and sometimes the content of an S-belief supported relatively much less by his sensory evidence, largely by background beliefs. Consider the belief that there's a cat around, first in circumstances where I get a good look at the thing in full view and good light three feet away, then in circumstances where I get a glimpse, at dusk, of a fast-moving creature at the far end of the garden, then in circumstances where I see my horribly-allergic friend break suddenly into tears, wheezes and blotches . . .

According to the theory sketched in chapter 4, a subject's being in a certain perceptual state can contribute to the justification of a belief of his which it causally sustains, by virtue of its contribution to the explanatory integration of a set of propositions including the C-belief in question and the proposition that he is in that perceptual state. Suppose for instance that A believes that there is a dog in the room, and that this S-belief of his is sustained by his being in a certain perceptual state – the kind of state a normal observer would be in when looking at a dog in full view and good light. A's sensory S-evidence, then, is this perceptual state, and his sensory C-evidence, the proposition that he is in this state. And this C-evidence is pretty supportive with respect to the C-belief in question; for there being a dog in the room before him is a pretty good explanation of his being in that perceptual state. Or, to stick a little closer to the definitions of chapter 4, the p-extrapolation of his C-evidence with respect to p (he is in the sort of perceptual state a normal observer would be in when looking at a dog in full view and good light, and there is a dog in the room before him) is better explanatorily integrated than its competitors (he is in the sort of perceptual state a normal observer would be in when looking at a dog in full view and good light, but there is no dog in the room). He would be even better justified if, for instance, his C-evidence also included the C-belief that there are no *trompe l'oeil* pictures of dogs or very lifelike dog-artifices in the vicinity, that he is not under the influence of post-hypnotic suggestion, etc., and if these beliefs were reasonably secure independently of the belief that there is a dog before him. And he would surely be less justified if, for instance, his C-evidence also included the C-belief that the local psychologists have recently been trying out experiments with holograms on (they think, unsuspecting) colleagues, and this belief was reasonably secure independently of the belief that there is a dog before him. Or again, suppose that A believes that a dog is slinking by at the far end of the street, and that this S-belief of his is sustained by his being in a certain perceptual state – the kind of state a normal observer would be in when getting a vague glimpse of a small, dark-coloured dog moving quickly at a distance of 100 yards and at dusk. A's sensory S-evidence, then, is this perceptual state, and his sensory C-evidence, the proposition that he is in this perceptual state. This C-evidence is appreciably less supportive with respect to the belief in question; the p-extrapolation of his sensory C-evidence in this case is not much better explanatorily integrated than its competitors. His being in *that* perceptual state might almost as well be explained by there being no animal in the street, only a paper bag blowing in the wind, or a large cat slinking by . . . and so on.

In view of the Popperian preoccupation with objectivity (and, one might add, the lack of subtlety in the Popperian conception of what objectivity is) it may be worth stressing that the approach offered here – though it puts the knowing subject centre stage, and makes the personal locution, 'A is more/less justified' primary – avoids the need to make beliefs about the content of one's own visual field, etc., in any sense more basic than, epistemologically prior to, beliefs about things and events in the world around one. It can, however, comfortably accommodate the fact that ordinarily we take many of a person's beliefs about the things and events around him – things and events which he perceives, and which others can perceive too – to be *completely* justified by the evidence of his senses.

V

The argument of section IV was premised on the assumption that our criteria for appraising whether, or to what degree, someone is justified in believing something *presuppose certain claims about human cognitive capacities and limitations*. Is it not, then, proper to ask whether the theory (or proto-theory) of perception presupposed in my explication of those criteria is sustained by psychology? And, in particular, since part of what is at issue between Watkins and myself is whether his or my conception of perception is the more plausible, should we not be looking to psychology for an answer?

These questions are much trickier than they superficially appear – but, first things first. Watkins cites the work of various psychologists and philosophers of psychology in support of his account; so the first order of business is to assess the merits of his evidence. It is hardly comprehensive; but that is not the main problem, for, selective as it is, it does not clearly support the thesis Watkins claims it does. That thesis, remember, is that level-1 judgements, judgements about 'observable' things and events, are (often enough) arrived at by an unconscious process of devising an hypothesis potentially explanatory of a level-0 judgement, e.g., a judgement about the arrangement of colour patches in one's visual field, which is itself certain – presumably, in virtue of its representing only what is available to the subject in experience.

Watkins first cites a philosopher of psychology, Wilkes, describing the scanning movements of the eye. He continues by quoting N. F. Dixon to the effect that perception involves processing of which the subject is unaware. He then observes: that the wall of a normal room will look, as it is, rectangular, but if one looks at a corner where it meets the ceiling one 'will observe' (he here cites Moritz Schlick) 'three angles, each greater than a right angle'; that we see things 'in their true colours, offsetting the distorting effects of sunglasses, dark shadows, etc.'; that if commissurotomized patients are shown a picture of a whole face, but in such a way that only half of the picture can be transmitted to the primary visual cortex, they will report seeing a whole face; that there are visual illusions (Gregory's inverted mask, the Penroses' 'impossible' figures) which persist even when we are well aware that we are seeing what is not there; and (to take care of non-visual perception) that the conversation at a cocktail party will sound like a 'collective buzz' – until someone mentions one's name. There is also an appeal to authority, when Richard Gregory is cited as explaining our perception of ambiguous figures as 'a process of hypothesis-testing' (pp. 255ff.).[11]

What *does* this miscellany show? That perception is active, in the sense that it involves movements of the eyes, etc.; that the subject may not be aware of some of the activity involved – but this is not in dispute. That what one notices is affected by salience – but this is not in dispute. That a subject's reports of what colour or shape something is will not necessarily correspond to a correct description of a photograph of the thing taken from the subject's perspective – but this is not in dispute. That, presented with a puzzle picture – an artifact designed precisely to supply too little information to determine what it is a picture of, or to supply too much information for it to be a picture of any actual object – a subject will report that he sees now a picture of a young girl, now a picture of an old woman . . . etc. – but this is not in dispute.

To repeat, what is at issue is *not* that one's beliefs about things and events around one may be justified in virtue of their potentially explaining what one sees, hears, etc. – on this, Watkins and I agree – but that 'what one sees, hears, etc.' must be construed as referring to the arrangements of colour patches in one's visual field, the order and pitch of sounds, etc., and that all rationally acceptable judgements must be consciously or unconsciously arrived at as potentially explanatory of judgements about such arrangements, etc.

The realist aspects of the picture of perception which, if I am right, is implicit in our pre-analytic conception of the evidence of the senses, and which I therefore tried to build into my explication, are strongly consonant with the theory of 'direct perception' central to the 'ecological psychology' of J. J. Gibson and his followers.[12] Fundamental to Gibson's approach is the idea that the senses of human beings and other animals are to be conceived as 'perceptual systems', i.e., as systems for the detection of information afforded by the things and events in their environment. From this perspective, the study of perception in its natural habitat – active, exploring animals or persons finding their way around the world, seeking food, shelter, a mate – is expected to be more revealing than laboratory studies in which subjects are given artificially-restricted, static, controlled glimpses of puzzle pictures and trick artifacts; the theory of normal, successful perception is seen as central, not as something to be devised after a model suggested by the study of *mis*perception; the perception of natural objects and events looks more fundamental than the perception of images, and *a fortiori* of deliberately misleading images. The elaborations offered of how the senses detect the information afforded by objects in the environment (a matter, according to Gibson, of 'detecting significant invariants in the stimulus flux'), the ingenious empirical studies of how this detection works, and how, in the various kinds of misperception, it fails to work; and the embedding of Gibson's theory of perception in a thoroughly evolutionary conception of the aptness of organisms' perceptual systems for coping with their environmental niche, all speak strongly in its favour.

But it is not a simple matter of my arguing, against Watkins, that his account of perception is at odds with commonsense and the best psychological work, while mine comports with both. For one thing, I am concerned to maintain not only (1) that perception is of things and events around us, but also (2) that our beliefs about things and events around us are justified, *inter alia*, to the extent that they explain our sensory experiences – and, while Gibson's work supports the first of these, it is neutral with respect to the second. Indeed, Gibson himself – being intensely preoccupied with arguing against 'sensationalism', i.e., the idea that the objects of perception are sense-data – sometimes encourages the false dichotomy which it is part of my point to avoid.

For another, it is certainly not the case that this issue between Watkins and myself can or should simply be handed over to psychology to adjudicate. The question, what the objects of perception are, is synthetic, empirical; but it is clearly not the kind of question for which a philosopher can simply disclaim responsibility. It couldn't be decisively settled by any imaginable experiment (which is why the gap between the psychological work Watkins cites, and the conclusion he draws from it, is so substantial); it is, rather, the sort of question one's attitude to which determines which experiments seem most significant. Gibson is under no illusions about this; he not only acknowledges the influence of Thomas Reid, philosopher of commonsense par excellence, but also is keen to pin the blame for the sensationalist approach on such philosophical works as Berkeley's *New Theory of Vision*.[13] He recognises, that is, that the issue lies in the border territory between philosophy and psychology.

And there is much more at stake here than whether Watkins' or my picture is better supported by more plausible psychological work. The fact of the matter is that Watkins has no business appealing to psychology at all. Why so? Because his project presupposes a sharp demarcation between philosophy and the natural sciences, psychology included, and imposes a meta-epistemological ordering according to which it is the task of the philosophical theory of knowledge to legitimize the sciences. From Watkins' meta-epistemological perspective, it is both literally and metaphorically *out of order* for the philosophical theory of knowledge to depend on assumptions taken from the natural sciences; for the legitimacy of the sciences waits upon the philosophical theory of knowledge.

Watkins gets the worst of both worlds. By restoring the knowing subject to a central position, he is committed to accepting the relevance of psychology; by retaining the Popperian conception of the relation of epistemology to the sciences, he is committed to denying the legitimacy of using the psychological material to the relevance of which he is committed.

Like Watkins, I am committed to admitting the relevance (I should say, the contributory relevance) of psychology. Unlike Watkins, happily, I can also acknowledge the legitimacy of using relevant evidence from psychology. For, instead of insisting on a sharp demarcation, I hold that philosophy differs from the natural sciences rather in degree of abstraction and generality. And, instead of seeing epistemology as epistemically prior to the sciences, I see epistemology and the sciences as parts of a whole web of more or less mutually supportive beliefs. The foundherentist criteria of justification, as I conceive the matter, apply to the justification of one's epistemological as of one's other beliefs; so it is agreeable to find that the assumptions about perception presupposed in my epistemological theory are also embedded in a plausible psychological theory which is itself consonant with an evolutionary approach. To a degree depending on the plausibility of the theory and the intimacy of the embedding, this lends support to those assumptions and to my epistemological theory.

Looking backwards, one could summarize the argument thus: the so-called 'problem of the empirical basis' ('so-called' because 'basis' is tendentious) is absolutely insoluble within a Popperian epistemology without a knowing subject. Nor is it solved by Watkins' disguisedly foundationalist, pseudo-Popperian epistemology with a knowing subject. And Watkins loses not only the epistemological argument, but the meta-epistemological argument as well; his account of the role of experience is not plausible, and his appeal to psychology in support of this account is illegitimate from his meta-epistemological perspective.

But the meta-epistemological argument has led to a whole new set of questions. With the knowing subject occupying a central place, epistemology is seen to depend, in part, on presuppositions about human cognitive capacities and limitations. In other words, the first step has been taken towards a modest kind of meta-epistemological naturalism. But the way ahead is far from smooth or straight: it will be necessary to get a good deal clearer just what naturalism in meta-epistemology amounts to, just how close its connection with foundherentism might be, just what approach to the question of the epistemic status of science it suggests . . . and so on.

It is likely, at this point, that it is beginning to look to some readers as if the theory offered here is little more than an elaboration of Quine's naturalistic 'epistemology with a knowing subject'. As the quotations introducing chapter 4 were intended to indicate, my account is, indeed, in part a development of some themes learned from Quine. But only of some; for Quine's naturalism is profoundly equivocal, as mine, I trust, is not. It is fortunate, then, that the desirability of locating my views relative to Quine's coincides with the necessity of exploring some of the ambiguities of 'epistemology naturalized'. This is the task to which I now turn.

6
Naturalism Disambiguated

There is not any superfine brand of knowledge, obtainable by the philosopher, which can give us a standpoint from which to criticize the whole of the knowledge of everyday life. The most that can be done is to examine and purify our common knowledge by an internal scrutiny.

Russell Our Knowledge of the External World[1]

Among the significantly different (and in some instances incompatible) conceptions which fall under the seductively ambiguous rubric 'naturalistic epistemology' are at least the following:

1 an extension of the term 'epistemology' to refer not only to the philosophical theory of knowledge, but also to natural-scientific studies of cognition;

2 the proposal that epistemology be reconstrued as the philosophical component of a joint enterprise with the sciences of cognition, in which the questions about human knowledge tackled by philosophy will be extended to include new problem areas suggested by natural-scientific work;

3 the thesis that traditional problems of epistemology can be resolved a posteriori, within the web of empirical belief;
3' the thesis that results from the sciences of cognition may be relevant to, and may legitimately be used in the resolution of, traditional epistemological problems;
  [(a) – all the traditional problems;
  (b) – some of the traditional problems];

4 the thesis that traditional problems of epistemology can be resolved by the natural sciences of cognition;
   [(a) – all the traditional problems;
   (b) – some of the traditional problems];

5 the thesis that traditional problems of epistemology are illegitimate or misconceived, and should be abandoned, to be replaced
by natural-scientific questions about human cognition;
   [(a) – all the traditional problems;
   (b) – some of the traditional problems].

These have been ordered from the least to the most radical.

Since both 1 and 2 involve an extension of the scope of 'epistemology', they may be classified as forms of expansionist naturalism. Since
both 3 and 4 allow the legitimacy of traditional epistemological problems,
but propose to tackle them in a novel, 'naturalistic' fashion, while 5
denies their legitimacy and proposes to replace them by more 'naturalistic' projects, one might classify 3 and 4 as reformist and 5 as revolutionary naturalism. Since, on the other hand, both 4 and 5 make
epistemology an enterprise internal to the natural sciences, while 3 does
not, one might classify 4 and 5 as scientistic and 3 as aposteriorist
naturalism. The obvious compromise is to label 3 'reformist, aposteriorist
naturalism'; 4 'reformist, scientistic naturalism'; and 5 'revolutionary,
scientistic naturalism'. A label is also needed to distinguish version (a)
from version (b) of positions 3, 4 and 5; I shall call the former 'narrow'
and the latter 'broad'. In what follows I shall sometimes change the
order of my labels, speaking of 'scientistic reformist naturalism', for
example, when contrasting this position with aposteriorist reformist
naturalism, but of 'reformist scientistic naturalism' when contrasting it
with revolutionary scientistic naturalism.

I mention expansionist naturalism only to put it, for the present,
aside;[2] my focus will be on positions 3, 4 and 5. All these repudiate, in
a more or less dramatic way, the apriorist conception of the philosophical theory of knowledge as wholly disparate from the scientific study of
human cognition. But from the perspective of the present work the
differences among them are more important than their commonalities.
Most obviously, the distinction of revolutionary versus reformist naturalism is crucial; for revolutionary naturalism denies the legitimacy of
the very projects in which I am engaged. And the distinction of scientistic
versus aposteriorist naturalism is also crucial; for scientistic naturalism
would have the projects in which I am engaged turned over to the
natural sciences of cognition.

I called the rubric 'naturalistic epistemology' *seductively* ambiguous because most of those who would describe themselves as engaged in naturalistic epistemology seem to be ambivalent between two or more of these quite different positions. But the theory offered in this book will be, unambiguously, a narrow, reformist, aposteriorist naturalism – it represents, in fact, the most modest naturalistic departure from what may be called, for short, 'traditionalist apriorism'. And so, though it is, indeed, in part a development of some themes learned from Quine, it is not in any straightforward sense 'just an elaboration of Quine's "Epistemology Naturalized"'. For Quine's naturalism is not unambiguously of an aposteriorist (rather than a scientistic) or even unambiguously of a reformist (rather than a revolutionary) stripe.

My modestly naturalistic position lies between traditionalist apriorism on the one hand and more ambitious forms of naturalism on the other. The argument against traditionalist apriorism was begun at the end of chapter 4 and continued in chapter 5, with the thesis that manifestly synthetic, and hence a posteriori, presuppositions about human cognitive capacities and limitations are built into our criteria of evidence. The argument against scientistic reformist naturalism was just barely begun at the end of chapter 5, with the thesis that the presuppositions about perception built into our criteria of evidence are of such abstraction and generality as to belong to the border territory between psychology and philosophy, rather than being the proper business of psychology exclusively. But most of the case against more ambitious forms of naturalism than mine remains to be made.

The purpose of the present chapter is twofold: first, to diagnose and explain the ambiguities and shifts in Quine's conception of naturalism; and second, picking up some clues from that diagnostic work, to put in place one more piece of the argument against the more ambitious kinds of naturalism – specifically, against both forms (reformist and revolutionary) of broad scientism.

I

Quine characterizes naturalism thus:

> . . . naturalism: abandonment of the goal of a first philosophy . . . The naturalistic philosopher begins his reasoning within the inherited world theory as a going concern. He tentatively believes all of it, but believes also that some unidentified portions are wrong. He tries to improve, clarify, and understand the system from within. He is the busy sailor adrift on Neurath's boat.

He also characterizes naturalism thus:

> [Naturalism] sees natural science as an inquiry into reality, falli-
> ble and corrigible but not answerable to any suprascientific tribunal,
> and not in need of any justification beyond observation and the
> hypothetico-deductive method. Naturalism has two sources, both
> negative. One of them is despair of being able to define theoretical
> terms generally in terms of phenomena ... The other ... is un-
> regenerate realism, the robust state of mind of the natural scientist
> who has never felt any qualms beyond the negotiable uncertainties
> internal to science ...
> Naturalism does not repudiate epistemology, but assimilates it
> to empirical psychology. Science itself tells us that our informa-
> tion about the world is limited to irritations of our surfaces, and
> then the epistemological question is in turn a question within
> science: the question how we human animals can have managed
> to arrive at science from such limited information. Our scientific
> epistemologist pursues this inquiry and comes out with an account
> which has a good deal to do with the learning of language and the
> neurology of perception ... Evolution and natural selection will
> doubtless figure in this account, and he will feel free to apply
> physics if he sees a way.

The picture presented in the first of these quotations is of an approach which sees epistemology not as a separate, a priori discipline,
but as an integral, interlocking part of our whole web of beliefs about
the world. There is nothing to suggest any challenge to the legitimacy
of familiar epistemological questions. Quine's conception of naturalism
seems, here, aposteriorist in intent and reformist in spirit. But the
picture presented in the second quotation is of an approach which sees
epistemology as internal to the natural sciences, as assimilated, in effect, to psychology. It is, in short, strikingly scientistic. It is also strikingly
ambivalent about the legitimacy of familiar epistemological questions,
for despite Quine's explicit disavowal of any intent to repudiate epistemology it seems that it will at the very least involve some significant
restriction of traditional epistemological concerns – it rests, we are told,
on an 'unregenerate realism' which declines to take seriously any
epistemological issue not strictly internal to science. One might say that
it seems revolutionary in spirit, if reformist in letter.

But the passages quoted are not from different contexts of discussion, nor from different periods of Quine's work; in fact, not only are
they from the same paper, they are from the same page of the same

paper, with the second passage occurring between the first sentence of the first passage and the rest.[3] Quine seems to offer, in other words, a sort of composite of aposteriorist and scientistic, and of reformist and revolutionary, pictures. And this assimilation of these very different conceptions of naturalism is not an isolated or occasional slip; on the contrary, it is quite ubiquitous.

Putnam's reaction, that Quine's naturalism is 'all extremely puzzling',[4] is understandable. My goal is to dispel the puzzlement.

Here is a sketch of my diagnosis. Broad, reformist, aposteriorist naturalism is a straightforward consequence of Quine's repudiation of the a priori, of his gradualist conception of philosophy as differing only in degree of generality and abstraction, not in the metaphysical or epistemological status of the truths it seeks, from the natural sciences. But Quine uses the term 'science' ambiguously, sometimes in the usual sense, to refer to those disciplines ordinarily classified as sciences, sometimes in a broader sense, to refer to our presumed empirical knowledge, generally. His gradualism disinclines him to attach much significance to the distinction between the broader and the narrower uses. But this ambiguity masks the distinction between aposteriorist and scientistic naturalism, between the idea that epistemology is part of our whole web of empirical belief ('part of science' in the broad sense) and the idea that epistemology is internal to the sciences ('part of science' in the narrow sense). This explains how Quine shifts, apparently unselfconsciously, from aposteriorism to scientism. Because the traditional problems of epistemology do not lend themselves readily or obviously to resolution within the psychological or biological sciences of cognition, however, Quine then finds himself, in his scientistic mood, under pressure to shift and narrow the questions with which he is concerned – to such a point that continuity with the familiar questions of epistemology is broken, and Quine finds himself tempted to cast doubt on the legitimacy of the old projects. This explains how Quine shifts, apparently unselfconsciously, from a reformist to a revolutionary stance. I shall take the elements of this diagnosis in turn.

Quine repudiates the a priori (expressly, of course, he repudiates the analytic, but since he shares with the Positivists against whom he is arguing in 'Two Dogmas' the assumption that only analytic truths could be known a priori, this constitutes in effect a repudiation of the a priori too). Gradualism is the thesis that philosophy is a kind of a posteriori inquiry, continuous with empirical inquiry generally; since the natural sciences constitute a major and impressive part of such inquiry, gradualism highlights the similarities in purpose and method between philosophy and the natural sciences. It thus encourages Quine

· to use the word 'science' as a convenient way to refer to our presumed knowledge of the world, quite generally. (There is further encouragement in the fact that, as Quine reminds us, the word 'science' originates in the Latin word for knowledge.)

It will be convenient to introduce a typographical convention to mark the distinction of the two senses of 'science': '*science*' for the narrower usage, referring to the disciplines ordinarily called 'sciences', and 'SCIENCE' for the broader usage, referring to our empirical beliefs generally, and thus including commonsense, history, etc., and, according to Quine, mathematics, logic and philosophy as well as *science*. In terms of this convention, aposteriorist naturalism becomes the thesis that epistemology is part of SCIENCE, i.e., an integral part of the web of empirical belief; scientistic naturalism becomes the thesis that epistemology is part of *science*, i.e., internal to the sciences. Quine's ambiguous use of 'science' makes it all too easy to run the two together (and the equivalence of 'epistemology is part of SCIENCE' to 'epistemology is continuous with *science*' further encourages this elision).

Textual evidence of this diagnosis of what I will call 'Quine's first shift' (from the aposteriorist to the scientistic) is not hard to find. Sometimes the picture Quine presents is unambiguously gradualist, reformist, aposteriorist:

> What reality is like is the business of scientists, in the broadest sense, painstakingly to surmise; and what there is, what is real, is part of that question. The question how we know what there is is simply part of the question . . . of the evidence for truth about the world. The last arbiter is so-called scientific method, however amorphous . . . a matter of being guided by sensory stimuli, a taste for simplicity in some sense, and a taste for old things.[5]

Quine's talk of 'the business of scientists, in the broadest sense' indicates that 'science' refers to 'SCIENCE'. What is being claimed is that what there is, and how we know what there is, are questions that belong to SCIENCE, questions which do not transcend the web of empirical belief. And in this context, especially with the hint supplied by 'so-called', 'scientific method' can be taken to refer to our criteria of empirical evidence, generally, rather than to any method of inquiry supposed peculiar to *science*.

But in many passages the ambiguity of 'science' leads to a fudging of aposteriorist with scientistic naturalism. One such passage, ironically enough, is this one from Quine's reply to Putnam in the Hahn-Schilpp volume; the irony is that Quine is here supposedly replying to Putnam's charge of 'scientism':[6]

> . . . I should like to clarify what Putnam and others have called my scientism. I admit to naturalism and even glory in it. This means banishing the dream of a first philosophy and pursuing philosophy rather as a part of one's system of the world, continuous with the rest of science. And why, of all the natural sciences, do I keep stressing physics? Simply because it is the business of physics, and of no other branch of science,
>> to say . . . what minimum catalog of states would be sufficient to justify us in saying that there is no change without a change of position or states.[7]

Here 'I admit to naturalism' might at first be thought to carry the conversational implication that Quine is disavowing what Putnam calls 'scientism'. Not only does Quine not say this explicitly, however, but he describes this remark as 'clarifying' what Putnam calls his scientism. 'Banishing the dream of a first philosophy and pursuing philosophy rather as part of one's system of the world' sounds like reformist aposteriorist naturalism; and 'continuous with the rest of science' could be read compatibly with this as 'continuous with the rest of SCIENCE'. But in the next sentence Quine shifts to speaking of 'the natural sciences', i.e., of *science*, and by the sentence after that he is focusing on physics. For all that Quine presents it as clarifying his position, this paragraph is paradigmatic of its ambivalence.

Significant among the other passages where the shifts and strains in Quine's use of 'science' become conspicuous, and where it becomes apparent that those shifts and strains are both prompting and disguising a switch from aposteriorist to scientistic naturalism, are these, where Quine is discussing scepticism:

> Doubt prompts the theory of knowledge, yes; but knowledge, also, was what prompted the doubt. Scepticism is an offshoot of science . . . Illusions are illusions only relative to a prior acceptance of genuine bodies with which to contrast them . . . The positing of bodies is already rudimentary physical science.
> . . . Rudimentary physical science, that is, commonsense about bodies, is thus needed as a springboard for scepticism . . . [S]ceptical doubts are scientific doubts. Epistemology is best looked on, then, as an enterprise within natural science.[8]

'Knowledge' in the first sentence is replaced by 'science' in the second; so charity prompts one to read 'science' as 'SCIENCE'. But almost immediately this charitable impulse is frustrated by Quine's insistence on classifying 'the positing of bodies', 'commonsense about bodies' as 'rudimentary physical science'. The positing of bodies, of course, undeniably is part of SCIENCE; but as Quine strains to describe it as 'rudimentary physical science' one begins to suspect that he is proposing that it is part of *science*. So it is not surprising to find that the final sentence – 'Epistemology is . . . an enterprise within natural science' – demands to be read as scientistic rather than aposteriorist, as claiming that epistemology is part of *science*, not just of SCIENCE.

Compare:

> . . . the epistemologist is confronting a challenge to natural science that arises from within natural science . . . Ancient skepticism, in its more primitive way, likewise challenged science from within. The skeptics cited familiar illusions to show the fallibility of the senses; but this conception of illusion itself rested on natural science, since the quality of illusion consisted simply in deviation from external scientific reality . . . Our liberated epistemologist ends up as an empirical psychologist, scientifically investigating man's acquisition of science.[9]

The scientistic tone of this passage is unmistakable, but it is clear, also, that Quine is once again straining the notion of science. I shan't comment on 'external scientific reality', though it is certainly a phrase worthy of notice. Nor shall I debate at length whether it is true that ancient scepticism challenged SCIENCE from within, though I think it relevant that ancient scepticism relied, not on a contrast of illusion with reality, but rather on conflicts among appearances. The point I want to stress here is that Quine's argument again requires a shift from 'ancient scepticism . . . challenged SCIENCE from within' to 'ancient scepticism . . . challenged *science* from within'; which is doubly dubious, since one might reasonably question whether there was such a thing as *science* at the time of ancient scepticism. Only by switching from the broad to the narrow interpretation of 'science' can Quine reach his strikingly scientistic conclusion: 'our liberated epistemologist ends up as an empirical psychologist, scientifically investigating man's acquisition of science', i.e., *scientifically* investigating man's acquisition of *science*.

In the passage just discussed, Quine confines himself to ancient scepticism; Cartesian hyperbolic scepticism is not mentioned. When he does discuss Cartesian scepticism, one gets a hint of the pressures leading to Quine's second shift, from reformist to revolutionary naturalism. In this passage, Quine seems *almost* to claim that in its generalized, Cartesian form, scepticism is incoherent:

> Transcendental argument, or what purports to be first philosophy, tends generally to take on rather this status of immanent epistemology insofar as I succeed in making sense of it. What evaporates is the transcendental question of the reality of the external world.

but immediately draws back:

> Radical skepticism stems from the sort of confusion I have alluded to, but is not of itself incoherent.[10]

Noting the strain that is apparent as Quine tries to suggest that ancient scepticism is internal to *science* leads naturally to the second component of my diagnostic conjecture. It has to be conceded that there is a degree of vagueness about what would count as pursuing reformulated but recognizably continuous versions of familiar epistemological projects, and what as pursuing new projects altogether. Nevertheless, it is clear that when he is urging that epistemology is part of *science* Quine finds himself obliged to re-characterize the problems of epistemology so radically as to break continuity. This is what I will call 'Quine's second shift', from reformist to revolutionary naturalism.

This second shift is hardly surprising. On the face of it, after all, it is quite implausible to suppose that the traditional projects of epistemology could be successfully undertaken by *science*. Philosophy is continuous with *science*, I agree; but it doesn't follow that there is no difference *of degree* between philosophy and *science*. And – as the argument of the last chapter revealed – the reasonable expectation is that the kinds of assumption about human cognitive capacities and limitations on which epistemology may need to call will be of the kind of generality and abstraction characteristic of the philosophical rather than the *scientific* end of the continuum of SCIENCE. And so it is to be expected that commitment to the claim that epistemology is part of *science* would put one under pressure radically to reconceptualize the projects of epistemology – for there is no serious prospect for successful resolution of the familiar projects within *science*.

Confirmation can be found in what Quine has explicitly to say about his attitude to the old projects, which is strikingly equivocal. The comment in the second, revolutionary quotation at the beginning of this section, that 'naturalism does not repudiate epistemology, but assimilates it to empirical psychology', is characteristic. In 'Epistemology Naturalized' Quine speaks of 'epistemology, or something like it' as 'fall[ing] into place as a chapter of psychology';[11] in 'Things and Their Place in Theories', of 'epistemology, for me, or what comes nearest to it' as studying 'how we animals can have contrived . . . science';[12] in *The Roots of Reference*, after admitting that his projects are 'a far cry . . . from the old epistemology', Quine goes on to observe that this is 'no gratuitous change of subject-matter, but an enlightened persistence rather in the original epistemological problem'[13] – suggesting at once that there is no change of subject-matter, and that there is, but not a gratuitous one.

And Quine's ambivalence between a reformist and a revolutionary naturalism is paralleled, throughout his work, in what he has to say about what he takes the tasks of epistemology to be: in reformist mood, he is suggesting a novel (a posteriori) approach to familiar problems; in revolutionary mood, an abandonment of the old problems in favour of new problems which, unlike the old, look susceptible of natural-scientific solution.

In the first edition of *The Web of Belief*, for instance, Quine seems to subscribe to the traditional conception of the distinction between the characteristic problems of psychology and the typical projects of epistemology:

> The story of the origins and intensities of our beliefs, the story of what happens in our heads, is a very different story from the one sought in the quest for evidence. Where we are rational in our beliefs the stories may correspond; elsewhere they diverge. The former story is for psychology to tell. On the other hand, our present concern is with grounds, with reasons, with the evidential relations which hold among beliefs . . .[14]

This suggests a familiar picture according to which, while it may fall to psychology to tell us what a subject's evidence for a belief is, it is the task specifically of epistemology to analyse the concept of, and supply criteria for appraising the worth of, evidence. But this passage is omitted from the second edition of *The Web of Belief*;[15] and in 'Epistemology Naturalized' one finds Quine straining to insist that the investigation of the concept of evidence is the proper business of psychology:

> Epistemology . . . falls into place as a chapter of psychology . . . It studies a natural phenomenon, viz. a physical human subject.

This human subject is accorded a certain experimentally controlled input – certain patterns of irradiation in assorted frequencies for instance – and in the fullness of time the subject delivers as output a description of the three-dimensional external world and its history. The relation between the meager input and the torrential output is a relation that we are prompted to study for somewhat the same reasons that have always prompted epistemology; namely, in order to see how evidence relates to theory, and in what ways one's theory of nature transcends any available evidence.[16]

One might get the impression that Quine hopes that psychology will be capable of resolving the problems of epistemology because, in his 'enlightened' epistemology, the normative character of the notion of evidence has been given up. Another passage even more strongly suggests a 'descriptivist' position:[17]

Whatever evidence there *is* for science is sensory evidence ... But why all this [Carnap's] creative reconstruction, all this make-believe? The stimulation of his sensory receptors is all the evidence anyone has had to go on, in arriving at his picture of the world. Why not just see how this construction really proceeds? Why not settle for psychology?[18]

However, although Quine sometimes gives the impression that he is psychologizing epistemology by making it purely descriptive, Putnam reports that Quine insists that he never meant to eliminate the normative.[19] And this deserves to be taken seriously, in view of the fact that in 'Epistemology Naturalized' itself, despite the descriptivist tone of the passages just quoted, Quine is at pains to disassociate himself from the 'epistemological nihilism' he attributes to Kuhn, Polanyi and Hanson.[20] A better interpretation has Quine, not denying their normative character, but shifting and narrowing the scope of epistemological concerns. The clearest confirmation is to be found in Quine's reply to White in the Hahn-Schilpp volume:

A word, now, about the status, for me, of epistemic values. Naturalization of epistemology does not jettison the normative and settle for the indiscriminate description of ongoing processes. For me normative epistemology is a branch of engineering. It is the technology of truth-seeking, or, in more cautiously epistemic terms, prediction. Like any technology, it makes free use of whatever scientific findings may suit its purpose. It draws upon mathematics in scouting the gambler's fallacy. It draws upon experimental psychology in exposing perceptual illusions, and upon cognitive psychology in scouting wishful thinking. It draws upon neurology and physics, in a general way, in discounting testimony from occult or parapsychological sources. There is no question here of ultimate value, as in morals; it is a matter of efficacy for an ulterior end, truth or prediction. The normative here, as elsewhere in engineering, becomes descriptive when the terminal parameter has been expressed.[21]

I shan't comment on the way Quine strains to suggest that we needed cognitive psychology to tell us that wishful thinking tends not to be truth-conducive, nor pause to ask to what branch of *science* it is supposed to fall to tell us whether, and if so why, successful prediction indicates the truth of a theory. My concern is to point out, first, that Quine no longer speaks in terms of the appraisal of evidence, but of the reliability of belief-forming processes; and, second, that his focus is on what processes can be certified as truth-conducive by *science* itself. The two points are obviously connected; but I shall comment on them, in the first instance, separately.

Traditionally, epistemology has been concerned with the criteria for the appraisal of evidence; traditionally, also, it has been taken for granted that a subject's evidence for a belief must be construed as something accessible to the subject – either as consisting (in coherentist pictures) entirely of other beliefs of his, or as including (in foundationalist and foundherentist pictures) his sensory and perhaps introspective experiences as well. One can find in Quine's writings a number of important, though often quite cryptic, suggestions about the proper construal of the notion of evidence. First: Quine talks of 'sensory evidence', of 'the information conveyed by one's senses', of the 'surface irritations' which prompt a subject's assent to this or that sentence.[22] Second: Quine stresses the 'interanimation of sentences' and holds that 'there can be mutual reinforcement between an explanation and what it explains'.[23] The former indicates sympathy with the idea, characteristic of experientialist foundationalism, and of foundherentism, that a subject's evidence for a belief cannot be exclusively a matter of further beliefs, but must include experiential evidence. The latter indicates sympathy with the idea, characteristic of coherentism, and of foundherentism, that relations of evidential support are to be conceived in terms of mutual reinforcement rather than as exclusively one-directional. This hints at a theory of evidence neither foundationalist nor coherentist in character, but combining elements of both (and perhaps explains why commentators cannot agree whether Quine is to be classified as foundationalist or as coherentist).[24] I can testify, at any rate, that Quine's hints in this direction had some influence on my development of the foundherentist account. The new conception of evidence to which Quine's hints point is consonant with a reformist aposteriorist naturalism. 'Sensory evidence', in this conception, has to refer to sensory experiences conceived of as both prompting, and in virtue of prompting, supporting, a subject's beliefs. One would anticipate, therefore, that an analysis of this concept would turn out to be partly causal; and that its partly causal character would encourage the characteristic concern of aposteriorist naturalism with the nature and limitations of human beings' cognitive capacities.

In scientist mood, however, Quine seems to suggest *displacing* the concept of evidence in favour of the concept of reliability. Traditionally, as I said, the subject's evidence for a belief is conceived as something accessible to the subject – as the etymology of 'evidence' suggests. But already in 'Epistemology Naturalized' Quine is suggesting that 'what to count as observation . . . can be settled in terms of the stimulation of sensory receptors, *let consciousness fall where it may*.'[25] This presages, it seems, the shift apparent in the reply to White, where Quine no longer writes of the strength or weakness of the subject's evidence, but of the truth-conduciveness or otherwise of the process by which a belief is acquired.

The same shift, away from the cogency of evidence and towards the reliability of processes of belief-acquisition, is implicit in the characterization of naturalism offered in *The Roots of Reference*:

> . . . the epistemologist is confronting a challenge to natural science that arises from within natural science . . . [I]f our science were true, how could we know it?[26] The epistemologist . . . can fully grant the truth of natural science and still raise the question, within natural science, how it is that man works up his command of natural science from the limited impingements that are available to his sensory surfaces.[27]

This establishes, I hope, the diagnostic claim of this chapter: that Quine offers a sort of composite of three, mutually incompatible, styles of naturalism, of the aposteriorist and the scientistic, the reformist and the revolutionary.

II

My position is a development of *one* of these three different, and incompatible, themes in Quine, a reformist, aposteriorist naturalism – though my reformist aposteriorist naturalism, unlike Quine's, is narrow in scope. So it is incumbent on me to argue, not only against apriorism, but also against scientism. There are, if the classification offered at the beginning of this chapter is acceptable, four forms of scientism to be dealt with: the four permutations of revolutionary versus reformist, broad versus narrow. There is, therefore, a certain economy of effort to be achieved by presenting, first, considerations which seem persuasive against both forms of broad scientism: the revolutionary kind, according to which all traditional epistemological projects are misconceived and should be replaced by new, *scientific*, projects, and the reformist kind, according to which all traditional epistemological projects can be accomplished within *science*.

The strategy is to identify two familiar epistemological questions, at least, which cannot plausibly be argued either to be illegitimate or to be resoluble by *science*. The two issues I shall discuss are (in this section) the problem of induction and (in the next) the problem of the epistemic status of *science*.

In Quine's work the problem of induction is the chief focus of the evolutionary aspects of his epistemology. But it is worth remarking, by way of preliminary, on the ambiguities of 'evolutionary epistemology', a phrase which has proved itself no less seductive than 'epistemology naturalized'. Some of those who appeal to evolution in epistemology may only be making an analogy, while others are making a literal application of the theory. (Only the latter thereby qualify as epistemological naturalists.) Even within the latter party there are striking differences: the most notable, and the most pertinent to this book, being the contrast between Popper, who writes of the evolution of world-3 entities, problems, theories, etc., and who takes the Darwinian theory to favour his falsificationist, strictly deductivist approach, and Quine, who applies the theory of evolution at a more familiar level, to human cognitive capacities, and who claims that it offers some modest reassurance about induction. (An additional complication is that by Popper's lights, the theory of evolution does not count as a scientific theory.) The fact that Quine and Popper take such exactly opposite views of the bearing of evolution on induction is a useful warning that the issues here are not as simple as they may appear.

But the present purpose is not, luckily, to develop a comprehensive account of what, if any, role the theory of evolution should play in epistemology, but to argue that there are epistemological questions about induction which (a) are legitimate, and (b) cannot be resolved by *science* – cannot, in particular, be resolved by appeal to the theory of evolution. And to do this, as it turns out, one only needs to take a close look at Quine's arguments.

Quine's own description of the role of evolution in his epistemology is ambivalent, ambitious in one way, modest in another. The theory of evolution, he claims, can solve the only part of 'the perennial problem of induction' that makes sense – which sounds like a large and important role for evolution; but, he also says, the familiar project of justifying induction is misconceived – which sounds as if there isn't much of the perennial problem left for evolution to resolve. Thus:

> Why induction should be trusted . . . is the perennial philosophical problem of induction.
>
>   One part of the problem of induction, the part that asks why there should be regularities in nature at all, can, I think, be dismissed . . . What does make clear sense is this other part of the problem of induction: . . . Why should our innate subjective spacing of qualities have a special purchase on nature and a lien on the future? There is some encouragement in Darwin. If people's innate spacing of qualities is a gene-linked trait, then the spacing that has made for the most successful inductions will have tended to predominate through natural selection. Creatures inveterately wrong in their inductions have a pathetic but praiseworthy tendency to die before reproducing their kind.[28]

But:

> These thoughts are not meant to *justify* induction . . . What natural selection contributes . . . is a reason why induction works, granted that it does.[29]

Quine's description of his evolutionary epistemology, then, though manifesting the now-familiar ambiguity between a reformist and a revolutionary approach, is thoroughly scientistic. But when one looks at the details of the arguments of 'Natural Kinds', it turns out that Quine's description of the role evolution plays in his epistemology is seriously misleading.

What is actually offered in 'Natural Kinds' is a two-stage argument. In the first stage, Quine argues that only inductions involving natural kind predicates or logically equivalent predicates are correct or reliable. In the second, he argues that the theory of evolution, by supporting the expectation that our innate quality spacings correspond at least approximately to the real natural kinds, explains why we have a tendency to make correct inductions. It is the second stage of the argument that makes the appeal to *science*; the first makes no such appeal, but rests on intuitions about the correctness or incorrectness of certain inferences from observed to unobserved instances. The relevance of the second, specifically evolutionary, stage of the argument presupposes the success of the first, philosophical, stage. And the first stage, if not exactly an attempt at the 'perennial problem of induction', *is* directed to Goodman's 'new riddle of induction'; for its purpose is to argue *which* inductions are correct. Quine tells us that the purpose of the second, evolutionary stage is 'to explain the success of induction'; but this does not mean what one was led to expect: it means, not 'explain why certain inductions are [or, are mostly, or are probably] truth-conducive', but, 'explain why human beings are innately disposed to make, by and large, those inductions which are correct'.

In case they are not obvious, let me spell out the morals here. Quine's suggestion that the old problem of 'justifying induction' is misconceived turns out to be best interpreted as an oblique way of saying that it is a mistake to try to show that inductive arguments are mostly or probably truth-preserving, because only some – those involving projectible predicates – *are*; as urging us to focus on the new riddle rather than the old problem of induction, on the question: which predicates are projectible? And so he not only *acknowledges the legitimacy* of the new riddle of induction, but *proposes a solution* – that only natural kind predicates or predicates logically equivalent to natural kind predicates are projectible – *which involves no appeal to evolution* (or to any *scientific* work), but is *entirely philosophical* in character.

And on these two points Quine is surely correct. The question: what is peculiar about 'grue', and what, if anything, justifies our confidence that the fact that all so far observed emeralds have been grue gives no support to the conclusion that all emeralds are grue? is manifestly a genuine question; and pretty clearly a question which no amount of information about the evolution of human beings' innate quality spaces (or any other information supplied by *science*) could answer.

This is not to say that Quine's answer to the question about 'grue' is correct. In fact, I think, it is not. '[A] projectible predicate is one that is true of all and only the things of a kind',[30] Quine claims. But the idea that green things constitute a natural kind, while grue things do not, is most implausible; *neither* do. Quine himself seems partly aware of this, for he writes that 'green things, *or at least green emeralds*, are a kind' (my italics),[31] thus running together the plausible claim that emeralds constitute a kind with the implausible claim that green things do.

Lying behind the failure of Quine's response to the grue paradox is his assimilation of the notions of natural kind and similarity. These are different notions: two horses, say, are things of the same natural kind (and one would scarcely describe them as similar in virtue of their both being horses); but two squarish things, though they are, in respect of their shape, similar, do not thereby count as of the same natural kind. A natural kind is better construed as a knot of similarities, a cluster of similarities holding together in a lawful way.

There *is* a connection between induction and natural kinds. My argument derives from Peirce, who held that the reality of 'generals' (meaning, roughly, 'kinds/laws') is a necessary condition for the possibility of the scientific method – for explanation, prediction, and induction. If there are natural kinds, the thought is, there are clusters of similarities holding together in a lawful manner; so the fact that observed things of a kind have had a certain feature is some reason to expect that other, unobserved things of the same kind will also have that feature - for this may be one of the properties in the knot tied by the laws of nature.[32]

If this line of thought is correct, the reality of kinds and laws is a necessary condition of successful inductions. It is not, of course, sufficient. We know that not all inferences from observed to unobserved instances of things of the same natural kind will lead to true conclusions. We do not suppose that things of a kind will be alike in *all* respects; we know, for instance, that while (male) cardinals are red, and blue-jays blue, swans may be white or black, and horses, dogs, human beings, etc., come in various colours.

What, then, about the grue paradox? It may be a mistake to set up the question (as Quine, following Goodman, does) as: what makes 'green' a projectible predicate and 'grue' a non-projectible one? For we don't suppose that *all* inductions involving familiar colour predicates are reliable (even when the predicate in the antecedent of premiss and conclusion is, as required, a natural kind predicate). A better way to set up the question would be: what makes us so sure that inductions involving 'grue' are *not* correct? Here is a suggestion. A thing is grue iff either it is examined before the year 2001, and is green, or is not examined before the year 2001, and is blue.[33] Why are we so confident that the truth of 'all so far observed emeralds have been grue' offers no support for 'all emeralds are grue'? Well, for the conclusion to be true it would have to be the case that all emeralds not examined before 2001 are blue. The 'grue' induction doesn't predict any change in the colour of any emerald at the beginning of 2001. But it does require that the colour of emeralds varies systematically depending on when they are examined. Now, we have reason to think that in some cases colour is one of the properties in a cluster that constitutes a natural kind; we have reason to suppose that in some cases the colour of things changes systematically depending on whether they are examined (the flesh of apples, for example); we have reason to suppose that in some cases the colour of things of a kind changes systematically depending on the time of year at which they are examined (the leaves of deciduous trees, for example); we have reason to suppose that in some cases the colour of things of a kind varies systematically depending on location (bears in the Arctic or Antarctic versus elsewhere, for example); but we have *no* reason to suppose that in any case the colour of things varies systematically depending on the year in which they are examined. In fact we have indirect reasons against this; while we have theories about what is apt to cause the colours of things to change or to vary, none of them hint at any mechanism that would make colour variation depend on date of examination.

This approach to the 'grue' paradox has a characteristically foundherentist cast in the way it conceives of the notion of 'inductive inference' as focusing on part of a phenomenon better construed more holistically and in terms of supportiveness and explanatory integration: on the relation between a belief about all observed things of some kind, and a belief about all such things, which beliefs are ordinarily embedded in a whole nexus of further beliefs about, e.g., what sorts of features tend to be universal among things of a kind, what sorts of factor potentially cause variations in what features, and so on. The hope is that as this reorients one's attitude to 'grue', it also illustrates the differences between my conception of supportiveness of evidence and the more usual notion of inductive validity.

This has been something of a detour from the main line of argument; but the fact that, like Quine's proposed solution to the 'grue' paradox, the diagnosis I have suggested makes no appeal to evolution or any *scientific* work, echoes the main theme of this section: that there are legitimate epistemological questions which cannot plausibly be claimed to be soluble by *science*.

III

Another such question is: whether *science* has a special epistemic status, and if so, why. Broad revolutionary scientistic naturalism has to deny that this is a legitimate question – while at the same time urging that epistemological projects be superseded by *scientific* ones; broad reformist scientistic naturalism, acknowledging its legitimacy, has to insist that it is a question that can be resolved by *science* itself. Neither attitude is at all plausible.

Recall that Quine is anxious to disassociate himself from the cynical sociologism of some recent philosophy of *science*, the 'epistemological nihilism', as he calls it, of Kuhn, Polanyi and Hanson.[34] There are two distinct themes in the work to which Quine alludes: the sociological claim that which *scientific* theory or paradigm gets accepted and which rejected is a matter of politics and propaganda as well as, or perhaps instead of, the weight of evidence; and the epistemological claim that the whole notion of theory- or paradigm-independent evidence on the basis of which it could be decided that this or that theory or paradigm is epistemically better, is illegitimate. (If the epistemological thesis were true, the strong version of the sociological claim would follow more or less tautologically; but the sociological claim has no tendency to imply the epistemological.) Though he doesn't explicitly distinguish them, Quine apparently rejects both: he thinks that there *is* something epistemically special about *science*, and that this is something to do with its reliance on observation. The pertinence of all this for present concerns, of course, is that thereby Quine first acknowledges the legitimacy of the question about the epistemic status of *science* (which, *qua* broad revolutionary scientistic naturalist, he could not), and, second, suggests an answer to this question which is philosophical rather than *scientific* in character (which, *qua* broad reformist scientistic naturalist, he could not). In other words, Quine is found acknowledging implicitly what I said explicitly in the previous paragraph.

The question of the epistemic status of *science* seems patently legitimate, and the broad revolutionary scientistic attitude, that it is somehow misconceived, patently implausible. Even those Quine calls 'epistemological nihilists' accept its legitimacy; their radicalism consists not in their repudiating the question, but in their answering it negatively.

The broad reformist scientistic attitude, that the question may be answered by *science* itself, is no less implausible. The point is not that there is no room for the investigation, within *science*, of the reliability or otherwise of this or that statistical or experimental, etc., technique; it is rather that it is implausible to suppose that that predictive success is an indication of truth, or that beliefs sustained mainly by the subject's desires or fears tend not to be true, or that perception is of things and events around one rather than of sensa from which one infers or constructs things and events . . . are to be settled exclusively by or exclusively within *science*.

From the perspective of my reformist aposteriorist naturalism, however, it is possible to devise the beginnings of a quite plausible answer to our question. Does *science* have a special epistemic status? Thinking about this question at a commonsense level, unalloyed by any sophisticated epistemological theory, I should be inclined to answer 'yes and no'. 'Yes', because *science* has had spectacular successes, has come up with deep, broad and detailed explanatory hypotheses which are anchored by observation and which interlock surprisingly with each other; 'no', because although, in virtue of these successes, *science* as a whole has acquired a certain epistemic authority in the eyes of the lay public, there is no reason to think that it is in possession of a special method of inquiry unavailable to historians or detectives or the rest of us, nor that it is immune from the susceptibility to fad and fashion, politics and propaganda, partiality and power-seeking to which all human cognitive activity is prone.[35] (This concedes something to the Kuhnians' sociological point, while resisting their epistemological cynicism.)

Can this commonsense answer be given any plausible theoretical underpinning? I think it can. *Science*, as I see it, has done rather well, by and large, at satisfying the criteria by which we judge the justification of empirical beliefs, central to which are explanatory integration and experiential anchoring. These criteria are not internal to, nor restricted to, *science*; they are the criteria we use in appraising the evidence for everyday empirical beliefs as well as for *scientific* theorizing. Nor are they restricted to *scientific* cultures: primitive people attributing lightning and thunder to the anger of the gods, like *scientists* attributing it to electrical discharges in the atmosphere and the sudden expansion of air in their path, are seeking explanatory stories to accommodate their experience. But *science* has had notable success by these standards.

What I mean may be made vivid by returning to the analogy of the crossword puzzle. The theoretical successes of *science* are like the great strides one makes in completing some long central entries in a crossword, after which filling in other entries is apt to become significantly easier. Or, to use the more official literal vocabulary of foundherentism: one of the things that is epistemically special about *science* is its very substantial contribution to the explanatory integration of our web of empirical belief.

At the same time, it has also scored well with respect to experiential anchoring. Two features of *scientific* inquiry have contributed to its success on this score: experimental contrivance and co-operative inquiry, both of which have enabled *science* greatly to extend the range and variety of experience available to anchor its explanatory theorizing.

One might put it like this: *science* has a distinguished epistemic standing, but not a privileged one. By our standards of empirical evidence it has been, on the whole, a pretty successful cognitive endeavour. But it is fallible, revisable, incomplete, imperfect; and in judging where it has succeeded and where failed, in what areas and at what times it is epistemically better and in what worse, we appeal to standards which are not internal to, not simply set by, *science*.

I hope that this not only establishes that broad scientism, whether revolutionary or reformist, is indefensible, but also constitutes a significant point in favour of aposteriorist naturalism.

The major themes of this chapter have been: that 'naturalistic epistemology' is multiply ambiguous; that Quine is ambivalent between aposteriorist and scientistic, and between reformist and revolutionary varieties of naturalism; and that broad forms of scientism, whether revolutionary or reformist, are untenable.

This does not yet amount to a comprehensive critique either of reformist or of revolutionary scientism, however, since, in and of itself, it does no damage to narrow scientism. The next order of business, therefore, is a critique of narrow reformist scientism. As I observed in section I, as Quine makes his first shift (from aposteriorist naturalism to scientistic naturalism) he moves from suggesting a novel – a proto-foundherentist – account of evidence, to focusing on the truth-conduciveness of belief-forming processes; i.e., in the direction of reliabilism. He does not, however, anywhere claim that an account of the truth-conduciveness of belief-forming processes would *constitute an account of* justification or evidence. Alvin Goldman, however, does; he looks to be, therefore, a better exemplar of the reformist scientism that must be disposed of next. So, conveniently, the necessity of explaining why I regard reformist scientistic naturalism as indefensible coincides with the desirability of answering a question which may well, by this point, be bothering the attentive reader: why, given the availability of an apparently simpler alternative approach which, as desired, accommodates both the causal and the evaluative aspects of the notion of justification, do I employ all the elaborate apparatus of S- versus C-evidence, etc., etc.? Why not, in short, settle for reliabilism? These two intersecting issues are the concern of the next chapter.

7

The Evidence Against Reliabilism

We should all agree that a person can only believe reasonably when he has evidence for the propositions believed.

Price *Belief*[1]

The theory offered in this book is evidentialist in character, in the sense that the account of justification proposed is couched in terms of the subject's evidence for a belief. But while the initial formula – 'how justified A is in believing that p depends on how good his evidence is' – is both simple and intuitively plausible, the eventual explication is undeniably complex, and, if it is still plausible, hardly, any longer, 'intuitively'. It would be understandable, therefore, if some readers suspected that it would be simpler, and better, to opt for a reliabilist theory of some kind. Reliabilism, after all, it might be urged, allows that the concept of justification is partly causal in character, can acknowledge that justification comes in degrees, need be neither foundationalist nor coherentist in structure, recognizes the relevance of psychology to epistemology – and it seems a lot more straightforward and a lot less complicated than the theory I am proposing. So the first section of this chapter is my response to the question: why not settle for reliabilism?

My response could be summed up, briefly and bluntly, as follows. First, a reliabilist account of justification is just incorrect. Justification is a matter of the *experiential anchoring* and *explanatory integration* of the subject's *evidence* with respect to a belief; an explication in terms of the *truth-conduciveness* of *belief-forming processes* simply uses the wrong concepts, and consequently yields counter-intuitive consequences. Second, the appearance that a reliabilist theory is simpler is an illusion, soon dispelled when one considers what is required to articulate it in any detail; the distinction of the state and the content senses of 'belief', for example, is implicit in the idea of the truth-conduciveness of a belief-forming process. Third, the apparent affinity of reliabilism with a gradational conception of justification turns out to disappear as soon as the theory is articulated in sufficient detail to accommodate the role of undermining evidence. Fourth, though a reliabilist explication, *qua* reliabilist, need not be either foundationalist or coherentist in structure, this does not mean that reliabilism constitutes, nor even that it offers any clue to the construction of, an account of the structure of justification which falls into neither category. The supposed advantages of reliabilism are more apparent than real.

To establish this, however, certain difficulties must be overcome. An initial problem is that the term 'reliabilism' refers to any number of different theories, not all of which are in any straightforward sense rivals of the theory offered here. The inspiration, it seems, is a remark of Ramsey's, that 'roughly: reasonable degree of belief = the proportion of cases in which habit leads to truth':[2] a remark which has to be understood against the background of Ramsey's sympathy with Peirce's account of belief as a habit of action, and his proposal to characterize degrees of belief in terms of dispositions to bet, and which perhaps is only intended to apply to beliefs of a general character; and which Ramsey himself says it is not possible to make precise. Armstrong, acknowledging Ramsey and some others, uses the term 'reliability theory' for the account offered in *Belief, Truth and Knowledge*, where reliability comes in to characterize the basic or non-inferential component of a foundationalist theory of knowledge. 'Reliabilism' first refers to a theory of justification in Alvin Goldman's 'What is Justified Belief?', where it characterizes a style of foundationalism in which the justification both of basic and of derived beliefs is explained in terms of the reliability of belief-forming processes. By the time of Goldman's *Epistemology and Cognition*, however, though 'reliabilism' still refers to a theory of justification, it no longer refers to a style of foundationalism specifically, but is said to be neutral between foundationalism and coherentism; and 'reliable' turns out to mean, not 'gives true upshots more often than not' but 'gives true upshots more often than not *in normal worlds*' – a qualification which, however, in a later paper, Goldman withdraws.

A reviewer who holds that reliabilism is (or was in 1986) 'the past decade's reigning epistemology' also describes Goldman as its leading exponent, 'known for his subtle and eloquent defense' of the reliabilist approach.[3] Choosing Goldman as my target has, I hope, the virtue of forestalling any accusation that I am criticizing a caricature of a theory, or a straw man instead of a real opponent. And there are two other reasons for this choice: first, that Goldman conceives of reliabilism specifically as an explication of justification, and even, by the time of *Epistemology and Cognition*, as a theory of justification that rises above the dichotomy of foundationalism and coherentism; and second, that Goldman's reliabilism is closely associated with his championship of a strong conception of the relevance of cognitive psychology to epistemological questions. So Goldman's approach seems to be both pretty straightforwardly (a) a rival of double-aspect foundherentism as a theory of justification and (b) a rival of aposteriorist reformist naturalism as an account of the relation of the *science* of cognition to epistemology; specifically, to represent a narrow form of the scientistic reformist naturalism with which, in chapter 6, I contrasted my position.

So section I will be a critique of Goldman's reliabilism, and section II a critique of his scientistic reformist naturalism.

I

So: why *not* just settle for reliabilism? Because, as an explication of justification, reliabilism goes wrong in two main ways. First: by explicating justification in terms of truth-ratios, reliabilism misrepresents the connection between justification and truth. Our criteria of justification are, indeed, what *we take to be* indications of the truth, or likely truth, of a belief. Reliabilism, however, identifies the criteria of justification with whatever *is in fact* truth-indicative, whether or not we take it to be. Adapting some terminology of Donnellan's, one could say that reliabilism makes the connection of justification and truth attributive, when really it is referential.[4] The effect is to trivialize the question, whether our criteria of justification really are truth-indicative: the solution of the problem of ratification is already trivially contained in the reliabilist response to the problem of explication.[5] Second: by explicating justification in terms of the processes by which a subject arrived at a belief, reliabilism by-passes the subject's perspective. Our criteria of justification are, indeed, focused on the causes of a belief – on the subject's [S-]evidence. Reliabilism, however, explicates justification in terms of belief-forming processes. But while a subject's S-evidence consists – as the etymology of 'evidence' suggests it ought to – of states of which the subject is aware, the process by which the belief was formed is something of which the subject may be quite unaware. Avoiding the terminology of 'internalism' versus 'externalism', I shall say that reliabilism makes justification an extrinsic notion, when really it is evidential. In sum: 'a belief is justified iff it was arrived at by a reliable process' is wrong both in focusing on belief-forming processes (in its extrinsic character), and in appeal to truth-ratios (in its referentialist character).

It would be convenient if it were possible to organize this chapter straightforwardly along the lines laid down in the previous paragraph; but this is precluded by the fact that Goldman has offered not one, but three significantly different (ostensibly) reliabilist theories. So I shall have to show that none of these three theories constitutes an acceptable account of justification. The price in terms of complexity is not negligible, but there are benefits to compensate. For it will soon become apparent that Goldman has felt the need to shift from one to another to a third form of reliabilism in an attempt to avoid just the difficulties sketched above; so a systematic critique of each of his three theories in turn will make the conclusion pretty inescapable that those objections are insuperable.

There is one more complication, fortunately also potentially fruitful. The argument of this section will not be, simply, that none of Goldman's three theories works; it will be, rather, that on his first two attempts to articulate a reliabilist account of justification Goldman makes modifications in a attempt to avoid anticipated objections which effectively, though covertly, sacrifice the reliabilist character of the explication; while on the third attempt he offers an account which has more claim to be genuinely reliabilist, but which is still, I shall argue, susceptible to the objections he previously tried to avoid. If it works, my argumentative strategy will have the advantage of illustrating the strength of the pull towards evidentialism and referentialism, as well as revealing the weakness of reliabilism; but it has the disadvantage that it requires some characterization of what is to count as a genuinely reliabilist theory. I hope I can allay any suspicion that the characterization on which I rely is prejudicial to reliabilism by using Goldman's own: a reliabilist theory must be *couched in terms of the truth-ratios of belief-forming processes.*[6]

The explication of justification offered in 'What is Justified Belief?' relies on a distinction between belief-independent processes (i.e., processes, such as perception, which do not require beliefs as input) and belief-dependent processes (i.e., processes, such as inference, which do require beliefs as input). An unconditionally reliable process is a belief-independent process which usually yields true beliefs as output; a conditionally reliable process is a belief-dependent process which usually yields true beliefs as output given true beliefs as input. Goldman offers the following recursive definition:

A If S's belief in p at t results ('immediately') from a belief-independent process that is (unconditionally) reliable, then S's belief in p at t is justified.

B If S's belief in p at t results ('immediately') from a belief-
   dependent process that is (at least) conditionally reliable, and if
   the beliefs (if any) on which this process operates in producing
   S's belief in p at t are themselves justified, then S's belief in p
   at t is justified.
   (Otherwise, S's belief in p at t is not justified.)[7]

The theory has a foundationalist structure, with beliefs arrived at by
unconditionally reliable processes as basic, and beliefs arrived at from
basic beliefs by conditionally reliable processes as derived.

So far, so straightforward. Almost immediately, however, Goldman
makes two qualifications. He is troubled by the fact that it is logically
possible that there should be a benevolent demon who so arranges
things that beliefs formed by wishful thinking are usually true. He
expresses some uncertainty about whether the appropriate reaction is
to allow that, in such a possible world, beliefs formed by wishful thinking would be justified, or to modify the account so as to require that
the belief-forming processes be reliable in *our* world, or in a 'non-
manipulated environment'. He eventually concludes, however, that,
given the goal of explicating our pre-analytic conception of justification,
the real moral of these reflections is that '[w]hat matters, then, is what
we *believe* about wishful thinking, not what is *true* . . . about wishful
thinking'. Oddly enough, he says that he is 'not sure how to express this
point in the standard format of conceptual analysis';[8] oddly, because the
way to do so is, surely, to replace the reference to processes which *are*
reliable by reference to processes which *we believe to be* reliable.

Goldman then considers another possible objection to his account,
according to which, as he now puts it, 'a belief is justified in case it is
caused by *a process that is in fact reliable, or by one we generally believe to
be reliable*'[9] (my italics): the objection is that even if a belief of S's was
caused by such a process, S is not justified in the belief if he has no
reason to believe that it was, or, worse, has reason to believe that it was
caused by an *un*reliable process. This time Goldman proposes to add
another necessary condition on justification, that:

there is no reliable or conditionally reliable process available to S
which, had it been used by S in addition to the process actually
used, would have resulted in S's not believing that p at t.[10]

As it stands, this additional requirement is still couched in reliabilist
terms; but Goldman concedes that it is 'somewhat . . . vague', and
continues by observing that 'it seems implausible to say that all 'available'

processes should be used, at least if we include such processes as gathering new evidence', and that 'we should have in mind here such additional processes as calling previously acquired evidence to mind, assessing the implications of that evidence, etc.'.[11]

It hardly requires elaborate argument to show that Goldman's two concessions effectively cancel the ostensibly reliabilist character of the explication on offer. Their upshot is something like this: S is justified in the belief that p if he arrived at that belief by a process we believe to be reliable (whether it *is* reliable or not) unless his evidence indicates otherwise. What was originally presented as an account of justification solely in terms of the *truth-conduciveness* of belief-forming *processes* is transmuted into an account which depends on what processes of belief-formation *we believe to be* truth-conducive, and on whether the subject has *evidence* available to him indicating that his belief was not so arrived at.

The problem is not only that Goldman's modifications effectively cancel the reliabilist character of his theory; it is also that to articulate the second modification would require an explication of the notion of evidence and of criteria for the appraisal of its worth. But if we had *that*, surely, it could stand by itself as a theory of justification, and would not need to serve as appendage to a reliabilist account.

Though he presents his account categorically ('S is justified iff . . .'), Goldman remarks early in the paper that justification really comes in degrees, and that it would be easy to modify his account so as to accommodate this gradational character, along the lines of 'S is justified to such-and-such a degree iff his belief was arrived at by a process reliable to that degree'.[12] It is worth noting that Goldman's second modification to his first account effectively rules out this manoeuvre, and leaves the ability of his theory to recognize degrees of justification dubious at best.

In due course, apparently, Goldman himself came to the conclusion that the theory offered in 'What is Justified Belief?' won't do; for in *Epistemology and Cognition* he offers a new version which he claims can avoid the difficulties faced by earlier reliabilist accounts.

The main task of the philosophical theory of justification, according to *Epistemology and Cognition*, is to give 'criteria of rightness for a system of J-rules', where J-rules are 'permissive rules for justified belief-formation'. Among possible such criteria Goldman distinguishes the deontological, which are categorical, and the consequentialist, which are conditional, characterizing the rightness of a system of rules via its conduciveness to some end or value. Among consequentialist criteria he distinguishes 'explanationism' (where the end or goal is explanatoriness), 'pragmatism' (where the goal is action-related) – and reliabilism, where the end is a truth-ratio. He also distinguishes, within the reliabilist category, resource-dependent reliabilism (where the required truth-ratio is relative to the available resources) and resource-independent reliabilism, where it is not.[13]

Goldman indicates that his sympathies are in accordance with the following resource-independent 'criterion schema' (so-called because it specifies no definite truth-ratio):

A J-rule system R is right if and only if:
R permits certain (basic) psychological processes, and the instantiation of these processes would result in a truth ratio of beliefs that meets some specified high threshold (greater than 50%).[14]

The reference to 'basic processes' in this formula is an indication that by the time of *Epistemology and Cognition* Goldman is aspiring only to what he calls 'primary epistemology', which is individual rather than social and which focuses on innate cognitive processes rather than learned cognitive methods.[15]

As it stands, of course, this – though it has even less detailed structure than the foundationalist reliabilism of 'What is Justified Belief?' – looks vulnerable to the same kinds of objection anticipated in that earlier paper. Once again, in fact, Goldman proposes modifications to avoid these objections, now no longer anticipated but articulated by his critics.

One of those objections, that there is a whole class of cases in which the intuitive judgement is that the subject's belief is not justified, despite the fact that his belief was arrived at by a reliable process, because he has reason to believe the process was not reliable, or no reason to believe it is, is pressed by BonJour, who, as one would expect, insists that reliabilism is wrong because it fails to look at justification from the subject's perspective. Among the counter-examples BonJour proposes is the case of Maud, who arrives at a belief by means of her perfectly reliable clairvoyant powers, and who persists in believing that she has such powers even though she has strong evidence that no such powers are possible; and Norman, who arrives at a belief by means of his completely reliable clairvoyant powers, but has no evidence either for or against the possibility of there being such powers, or of his possessing them.[16] Reliabilism implies that Maud and Norman are justified in their beliefs, but the correct verdict is that they are not.

Goldman does not dispute the bona fides of BonJour's

counter-examples; indeed, he introduces a case of the same kind himself, the case of Millicent, who arrives at a belief by means of her perfectly reliable visual powers, but also believes, with excellent reason, that her visual apparatus is malfunctioning.[17] Millicent, Goldman admits, is not justified in her belief. So he suggests that being permitted by a right system of J-rules, though necessary, is not sufficient for justification. Another necessary condition is also required:

> S's believing that p at t is justified if and only if:
> (a) S's believing at t that p is permitted by a right system of J-rules, and
> (b) this permission is not undermined by S's cognitive state at t.[18]

Initially, Goldman suggests that S's justification for believing that p is undermined if S believes, justifiedly or not, that believing that p is not permitted by a right system of J-rules. To accommodate Millicent, who needn't have any concept of a right system of J-rules, he modifies this to: S's justification for believing that p is undermined if S believes, justifiedly or not, some q such that if q were true the belief that p would not be permitted by a right system of J-rules. And to accommodate Maud and Norman, who don't believe any such q, he modifies it again, to: S's justification for believing that p is undermined if *either* S believes, justifiedly or not, some q such that if q were true the belief that p would not be permitted by a right system of J-rules, *or* there is some q such that if it were true the belief that p would not be permitted by a right system of J-rules, and S would be justified in believing that q.[19]

The no-undermining clause now depends on the interpretation of 'S would be justified in believing that q', or, as Goldman puts it, of *ex ante* justification. All he offers by way of an account of this notion is the following:

> A theory of *ex ante* justifiedness can be constructed, I think, along lines very similar to my account of *ex post* justifiedness, though I will not pursue all the details. One difference is that we may have to require right rule systems to feature obligation rules as well as permission rules. Thus, we might suppose that a right rule system would *require* Maud to utilize certain reasoning processes, processes that would lead her from the scientific evidence she possesses to belief in the proposition that she does not have any reliable clairvoyant power.

And as for Norman, he:

> ... *ought* to reason along the following lines: 'If I had clairvoyant power, I would surely find *some* evidence for this ... Since I lack any such signs, I apparently do not possess reliable clairvoyant processes'. Since Norman ought to reason this way, he is *ex ante* justified in believing that he does not possess reliable clairvoyant processes. This undermines his belief...[20]

Goldman is confident that 'the no-undermining clause ... handles BonJour's cases'. But, even supposing that it did, this does not put Goldman in the clear unless the no-undermining clause, and in particular the account of *ex ante* justification, can be spelled out in reliabilist terms. Goldman's 'I will not pursue all the details' is hardly reassuring. It is *not* possible straightforwardly to adapt the account of *ex post* justification; for one thing, that account refers to the process by which the subject arrived at the belief in question, whereas an account of *ex ante* justification can't refer to the process by which the subject arrived at the belief in question, since it applies precisely where the subject *didn't* arrive at the belief, but would be justified if he had. Presumably the route Goldman would propose to take would be to refer to reliable processes which are *available to*, though not used by, S; but this (as he had said candidly in 'What is Justified Belief?') is quite a problematic notion. Another problem is that the reasons for appending the no-undermining clause to the account of *ex post* justification apply equally to the account of *ex ante* justification, but that the account of *ex ante* justification cannot accommodate such a clause without vicious circularity.

It should not escape attention that Goldman's description of the BonJour cases, and his informal discussion of *ex ante* justification, are couched in terms of *the subject's reasons* for doubting the reliability of the process of belief-acquisition, and the subject's failure to take *this evidence* into account. But no explication of reasons or evidence is offered. As before, it is hard to quell the suspicion that Goldman's response to the evidentialist objection leaves him with an account which is no longer reliabilist, and indeed no longer really a theory at all.

Two lines of defence suggest themselves. One possibility would be for Goldman to argue that, even if the no-undermining clause turned out not to be expressible in reliabilist terms, at least a necessary condition of justification would be that the subject have arrived at his belief by a reliable process. This response relies on the fact that BonJour's counter-examples (and Goldman's in the same vein) are of cases where the intuition is that the subject is *not* justified though his belief *was* arrived at by a reliable process; a fact reflected in Goldman's description of the objection as to the effect that the requirement that the subject have arrived at the belief by a reliable process is *too weak*. But it takes only a moment's reflection to realize that the evidentialist intuition that underlies BonJour's examples *also* supports a converse class of counter-examples, where the subject *is* justified even though his belief was *not* arrived at by a reliable process. Suppose that Nigel arrives at a belief by the use of his eyes, which are in fact malfunctioning, so that the process is not reliable; but that he has just been informed by his eye doctor of the results of the numerous tests to which he has been submitted, and has every reason to believe that his eyes are working normally. The intuition that Nigel *is* justified seems as robust as the intuition that Maud or Millicent is *not*. If this is right, the requirement that S have arrived at the belief by a reliable process is too strong as well as too weak; and the analogous modifying move would have to be to a disjunctive formula: *either* S arrived at his belief by a reliable process and the no-undermining clause is satisfied, *or* S did not arrive at the belief by a reliable process but an overriding clause is satisfied. And now reliability of the belief-forming process wouldn't be even a necessary condition of justification.

Thus far it has been assumed that Goldman is, indeed, as he concedes, obliged to modify his account to meet BonJour's objections. Actually, however, it is not so clear that this is correct. For Goldman presents himself as offering criteria of rightness, not for J-rules, but for *systems* of J-rules. And if one takes the concern for systems of rules seriously, it might seem that it is unnecessary, after all, to modify the theory to take account of Maud, Norman and co.; for it could be said that, though their beliefs might be permitted by a right J-rule, they would *not* be permitted by a right *system* of J-rules. So the second line of defence that suggests itself is this: the BonJour objection requires *no* modification of the proposed criterion schema, which already avoids the supposed counter-examples by its appeal to systems of J-rules. The trouble with this defense, of course, is that it takes Goldman out of the frying pan into the fire. For he has nothing whatever to say about the relation of the rightness of a system of J-rules and the rightness of the rules that make up the system, beyond the simple observation that 'rules are *interdependent* with respect to their epistemically relevant properties', except to remark that the reference to systems of rules will enable him somehow – he doesn't say how – to avoid the lottery paradox.[21] Justification has, indeed, as I have argued at length, a quasi-holistic character; my point is not that Goldman is wrong about this, but that unless and until he offers some detailed articulation of the relation of global to local reliability his acknowledgement of this point is purely *pro forma*. This 'second line of defence' shows, at best, not that Goldman's theory of justification is correct, but that it avoids the BonJour objections only because it is really no substantive theory at all.

In 'What is Justified Belief?' Goldman had anticipated the objection that, by tying justification directly to truth-ratios, reliabilism would yield counter-intuitive consequences under the hypothesis of a benevolent demon who makes beliefs arrived at by wishful thinking, for example, come out true.[22] In *Epistemology and Cognition* he faces the objection articulated by Cohen,[23] that reliabilism yields counter-intuitive consequences under the hypothesis of an evil demon who brings it about that our beliefs are comprehensively false. If there is such an evil demon, reliabilism implies that we have no justified beliefs. But the intuitive verdict is that if there were an evil demon we would nevertheless have justified beliefs, but that our criteria of justification would have turned out not to be – as we hope and believe they are – indicative of truth.

Once again, as with BonJour, Goldman admits the force of the objection; once again, he modifies the theory to avoid it. The trick is to read 'would result in a truth-ratio that meets some specified high threshold', not as 'would result *in the actual world* in a truth-ratio that meets some . . . high threshold', but as 'would result *in normal worlds* in a truth-ratio that meets some . . . high threshold'. A normal world, Goldman tells us, is a world 'consistent with our *general* beliefs about the actual world'[24] ('general' because he wants to count worlds with different individuals and events than the actual world as normal); he also tells us that the beliefs which define normal worlds are *not* to include any that concern regularities about our cognitive processes.[25]

Does this modification meet the objection? The argument Goldman has in mind is, presumably, that on the revised theory, if there were an evil demon the actual world would not be a normal world, but those of our beliefs that were arrived at by processes that would be reliable in a normal world world nevertheless be justified. (And, with respect to the problem of the benevolent demon, that if there were such a demon the actual world world not be a normal world, but those of our beliefs that were arrived at by processes that would not be reliable in a normal world would not be justified.) This has a superficial plausibility; but the fact of the matter is that 'if there were an evil demon, we should nevertheless be justified in those beliefs that were arrived at by processes that would be reliable in normal worlds' *is nothing but an empty form of words*. Those beliefs of ours with respect to which 'normal' is characterized are, Goldman specifically says, *not* to include any beliefs about what our cognitive processes are, nor about which are reliable. So the qualification 'in normal worlds' implies *no* restriction on what processes are reliable – the reliable processes might include radar, clairvoyance, dreams or omens, or they might be restricted to unimpeded sensory perception, introspection, undistorted memory, valid inference – in fact they might be anything whatsoever. To say that we would be justified in those beliefs that were arrived at by processes which would be reliable in normal worlds makes no discrimination at all among beliefs.

Unlike the manoeuvre hinted at in 'What is Justified Belief?', the shift to 'processes *we believe to be* reliable', Goldman thinks the normal world qualification answers the objection while remaining 'objectivist', i.e., it still makes justification a matter of fact rather than a matter of opinion.[26] This is doubly wrong. Like the earlier modification, the normal worlds clause *does* require reference to our beliefs (a normal world is one 'consistent with our general beliefs about the actual world'); and, unlike the earlier modification, which *did* supply an answer, albeit not a reliabilist answer, to the objection, the normal worlds qualification gives no answer at all.

It doesn't come as much of a surprise to find that, a couple of years after the publication of *Epistemology and Cognition*, Goldman had come to the conclusion that the normal worlds manoeuvre should be abandoned. I agree; it was, as I have argued, an unqualified failure.

Abandoning it, however, leaves Goldman with the same old problem he had faced ever since 'What is Justified Belief?', of how to handle what may as well be called for short 'the referentialist objection'. By the time of his third relevant piece, 'Strong and Weak Justification', however, what seemed in *Epistemology and Cognition* to be not much more than an infelicity in his classification of the objections he thought reliabilism must answer has become a significant obstruction. The two main lines of objection are: that it is wrong to explicate justification in terms of truth-ratios (the referentialist objection); and that it is wrong to explicate justification by reference to belief-forming processes (the evidentialist objection). *Both* objections indicate that a simple reliabilist account is *both too strong and too weak*; both are, after all, to the effect that reliabilism uses the wrong concepts in the explication. In *Epistemology and Cognition*, however, Goldman classified the evidentialist objection as saying that reliabilism is too weak (because BonJour's examples happen to be of cases where the process is reliable but the subject's evidence indicates otherwise, not vice versa) and the referentialist objection as saying that reliabilism is too strong (because his critics had happened to stress that reliabilism has counter-intuitive consequences on the hypothesis of an evil demon, not a benevolent demon).

In 'Strong and Weak Justification', then, one finds Goldman abandoning the normal worlds manoeuvre, which he has (mis)construed as a way of avoiding the objection that reliabilism is too strong, by arguing that there are really two concepts of justification, a weaker and a stronger, and that reliabilism – actual-world reliabilism, that is – is a correct analysis of the latter.

This can't be right: the referentialist objection surfaces (as Goldman was well aware in 1978) in the form of the problem about the benevolent demon as well as in the form of the problem about the evil demon. It is *not* simply that the reliabilist account is too strong; so Goldman's latest manoeuvre cannot succeed.

But it may be as well to augment this rather schematic argument with another, which would work even if I were mistaken in my critique of Goldman's classification of the objections to reliabilism. Goldman now holds that there is both a strong concept of justification, which requires that the belief have been arrived at by a reliable process, and a weak, which requires only that the subject not be culpable or blameworthy in holding the belief. A 'benighted cognizer' who has the misfortune to live in a pre-scientific community in which omens and oracles are taken seriously and the experimental method has never been heard of, according to Goldman, may well be justified in the weaker sense, not blameworthy, in his beliefs, even though his beliefs are not justified in the strong sense. The suggestion is that if there were an evil demon we would be in a position analogous to this benighted cognizer; and so we would be justified in the weak, but not in the strong, sense. This time, then, Goldman's strategy is not to introduce a new modification to avoid the unwanted consequences of simple reliabilism, but to try to explain away the intuition that the consequences are unwanted: the intuition that we *would* be justified in our beliefs even if, because of the machinations of an evil demon, the processes by which they were arrived at were not reliable, is correct with respect to the weaker concept of justification; but this does not affect the correctness of reliabilism as an account of the stronger concept.

I don't think there are two concepts of justification; but I grant that we may feel pulled, as Goldman says, between the verdict that the benighted cognizer *is*, and the verdict that he *isn't*, justified in his beliefs. But this is quite insufficient to establish what Goldman needs to establish, *viz.*, that the verdict that the benighted cognizer *isn't* justified is based on the fact that his beliefs were not arrived at by reliable methods, and that this can be extrapolated to apply to *us* under the

hypothesis of an evil demon. Instead, in my view, the intuitive appeal
of the verdict that the benighted cognizer isn't justified is based on the
fact that (one assumes) his beliefs don't satisfy our criteria of evidence,
don't meet what we take to be indications of truth; and if this is so, it
would support the *contrary* verdict in the evil demon case. In other
words, the argument Goldman gives as to why the attributive character
of reliabilism only seems counter-intuitive – that we have forgotten the
distinction of strong and weak justification – is quite inadequate to
establish the conclusion that reliabilism is a correct account of the
stronger concept.

To repeat, my thesis is not only that none of Goldman's reliabilist
accounts of justification is defensible; it is also that the shifts and changes
in Goldman's position are such as very strongly to support the conclusion
that *no* reliabilist explication is defensible. One last line of defence
needs to be explored, however. Goldman makes it clear that he offers
his reliabilist analyses *as explications of our pre-theoretical concept of justification*;[27] and my argument has been that, *so construed*, reliabilism is
wrong. But it might be suggested that a reliabilist account should not
be so construed, but should be frankly acknowledged to be, not an
explication of our pre-theoretical conception, but a proposed alternative to, a revision of, that conception. But this suggestion is unmotivated.
Only if we had reason to believe that the pre-analytic conception was
somehow incoherent, or that it was not appropriately related to the goal
of inquiry, would there be a persuasive rationale for such a revisionary
proposal. I don't believe we have such grounds; rather, I think that
(though there was no guarantee in advance that this would turn out to
be so) our ordinary standards of evidence, reasons, warrant etc., stand
up rather well to meta-epistemological scrutiny, and do not need
replacement.

II

Already at the time of 'What is Justified Belief?' Goldman was urging
the merits of a close *rapprochement* of epistemology with psychology.
The interdisciplinary project Goldman calls 'epistemics' was then described, however, in quite modest terms. Goldman observes, for example, that psychologists have made distinctions (e.g., between occurrent
and dispositional belief) which epistemologists might with profit employ, and that psychologists have been interested in such characteristics
of belief-forming processes as power and speed, to which epistemologists might profitably turn their attention; this sounds like a harmless
but unexciting form of expansionist naturalism. His most ambitious

suggestion, at this time, is that by telling us what cognitive processes are possible for human cognizers psychology might contribute, by way of the principle that 'ought' implies 'can', some constraints on the epistemological project of giving rules for the conduct of inquiry; which amounts to a limited kind of aposteriorist reformist naturalism.[28]

By the time of *Epistemology and Cognition*, however, Goldman is making much more startling claims. The division of labour now envisaged between philosophical analysis and empirical psychology assigns to the former only the task of supplying a schematic account such as Goldman's 'criterion schema' for the rightness of J-rules; according to Goldman, it is for psychology to supply a substantive theory of justification, to adjudicate between foundationalism and coherentism, to determine whether there is such a thing as a priori knowledge . . . etc. This is a bold affirmation of scientistic reformist naturalism.[29]

One notices, however, that much of what Goldman says about the specific, detailed psychological work he discusses in the second half of *Epistemology and Cognition* is very modest relative to the bold scientism he affirms in the first half: psychologists have refined the concepts of belief and memory in ways that might be useful to the epistemologist; psychology has discovered interesting things about the circumstances in which people are apt to make certain kinds of logical or statistical errors; cognitive science may discover new problems for epistemo-logy . . . and so on.[30]

Furthermore, though both Goldman's analysis of justification and his style of naturalism change over time, they do not change in parallel; there seems to be no logical connection between the shift from the early, rather weak claims about the relevance of psychology and the later, much stronger claims, and the changes in Goldman's account of justification in the same period; and, significantly, no shift in his natur-alism is indicated when he decides to drop the qualification 'in normal worlds'. There are grounds, in other words, for suspecting that Goldman is not aware, or not fully aware, of his shift from a very modest to a very ambitious conception of the epistemological role of psychology – and hence grounds, also, for wondering about the cogency of the motiva-tion for his later scientism.

My quarrel is not with Goldman's earlier expansionist and aposteriorist naturalism, but with his later aspirations to a naturalism which, like mine, is reformist, but also, unlike mine, scientistic. Goldman's own rationale for his reformist scientism depends on his reliabilism; so one strategy available to me would be, simply, to rely on the arguments already advanced that reliabilism is indefensible. But there is some illumination, as well as extra security, to be had by taking the trouble to argue, in addition, that *even if a reliabilist account of justification were correct*, Goldman's hope of turning substantive epistemological questions over to psychology to adjudicate would not be realistic. So I shall take this steeper, but more rewarding, path.

The first step is to investigate whether, supposing the schematic account of justification offered in the first, philosophical half of *Epistemology and Cognition* were acceptable, Goldman's claim that cognitive psychology can supply the substantive theory would be defensible. It might seem that Goldman's reliance on psychology to supply the substance of a theory of justification answers the objection made in the first section of this chapter, that the philosophical analysis he proposes in *Epistemology and Cognition* doesn't really amount to a theory at all. But this is not so. Goldman says that his account of the rightness of a system of J-rules is only schematic, because it doesn't specify a minimal truth-ratio that must be achieved by a permitted process; he nowhere claims, however, that cognitive psychology can or should be expected to specify an appropriate ratio. I have complained that Goldman's theory lacks substance for other, more significant, reasons: that the no-undermining clause amounts to no more than 'unless the subject's evidence indicates otherwise'; that no account is offered of the interdependence of J-rules, nor, therefore, of what it might be for a *system* of rules to be reliable; and that the requirement that belief-forming processes be reliable in normal worlds makes the account vacuous. Goldman nowhere claims, however, that psychology can or should be expected to plug any of these gaps either – in fact the no-undermining clause, the reference to systems of rules, and the normal worlds qualification are all conspicuous by their absence from the second half of *Epistemology and Cognition*.

So what *is* the epistemological substance Goldman thinks we should look to psychology to supply? The argument he has in mind must be, I take it, something like this: philosophical analysis tells us that a belief is justified iff it was arrived at by a reliable process; psychological investigation can tell us what processes are reliable. More particularly, it can tell us whether the reliable processes for the formation of empirical beliefs all involve only other beliefs as input, or whether some include non-belief input, and hence whether foundationalism or coherentism is correct.[31] (Goldman is operating with a definition according to which any theory which requires experiential input for the justification of empirical belief counts as foundationalist; as is clear from chapter 1, this conception is defective, but this is not an issue that need detain us now.) And psychological investigation can tell us whether there are any unconditionally reliable belief-forming processes which require no experiential input, and hence whether there is a priori knowledge.[32] I shall call these, jointly, 'the scientistic argument'.

If this is the argument Goldman has in mind, it is frustrated by other themes of *Epistemology and Cognition*. The first problem is this. According to *Epistemology and Cognition* correct J-rules should permit only processes which are reliable in normal worlds, and normal worlds are characterized as those conforming to certain general beliefs of ours, which, however, *are not to include any beliefs about what cognitive processes are reliable*. No amount of psychological investigation of the reliability of cognitive processes in the actual world could tell us what processes would be reliable in normal worlds. (It is no accident that the qualification 'in normal worlds' is last mentioned on p. 113 and does not occur in the second, psychological part of *Epistemology and Cognition*.)

Of course, Goldman has repudiated the 'normal worlds' requirement, and the objection just made would not apply to the actual-world reliabilist theory of the strong concept of justification offered in 'Strong and Weak Justification'. This doesn't entirely solve the problem, however, since that theory is, if the argument of section I was right, vulnerable to the referentialist objection with which Goldman has been struggling, unsuccessfully, since 'What is Justified Belief?'.

There is, in any case, a second problem arising from another theme of *Epistemology and Cognition*, a theme which Goldman has *not* repudiated. Goldman distinguishes primary epistemology (which focuses on the individual subject and concerns itself with innate cognitive processes) and secondary epistemology (which concerns itself with learned cognitive methods and takes account of social aspects of knowledge).[33] But by Goldman's lights the justifiability of accepting this or that cognitive-scientific finding about the reliability of these or those cognitive processes depends on the reliability of the methods used in this or that *scientific* research. This is a matter of considerable importance, given that one must choose between rival findings, or 'findings', offered by proponents of rival methodologies. And questions of the reliability of methods can only be settled by secondary epistemology. The scientistic argument, in other words, violates Goldman's own epistemological ordering.

All this, though, shows at most that Goldman's use of the scientistic argument is problematic given other aspects of his theory; it does not show that the scientistic argument fails in and of itself. There is, however, another objection which does not rely on the incompatibility of the scientistic argument with other details of Goldman's theory. The conclusion in dispute, remember, is that investigation by psychologists or cognitive scientists could be sufficient by itself to resolve, for instance, the question of coherentism versus experientialism, by showing whether there are any reliable processes for the formation of empirical beliefs which involve only other beliefs as input. It is true that psychological investigation may tell us, for instance, whether and in what circumstances a subject's background beliefs are likely to lead him to misperceive. But any such investigation of course presupposes the *reliability* of perception in some circumstances (otherwise the psychologist would have no way to be sure what were *mis*perceptions). It is also true that psychologists sometimes point to this or that kind of experimental result as supporting, say, a conception of perception as always inferential (Gregory, for instance, interprets data about misperceptions of puzzle-pictures in this way). But the arguments about what conception of perception is correct, and what experimental data are most significant in deciding what conception of perception is correct, are themselves of a characteristically philosophical cast. 'Psychological', here, has a broad and a narrow sense parallel to the broad and narrow senses of 'science' in Quine's work: 'PSYCHOLOGICAL questions' are questions about human cognitive processes, capacities and limitations, '*psychological* questions' are questions within the purview of the *science* of psychology. The point the scientistic argument misses is that some PSYCHOLOGICAL questions are also philosophical. This is not a merely verbal point; for it depends on the thesis of the continuity of *science* and philosophy.

No doubt this response to the scientistic argument would fail to impress Goldman, who, I think, rejects the continuity thesis. As I read him, Goldman distinguishes philosophical from *psychological* questions by taking the former to be conceptual and evaluative and the latter empirical and descriptive in character, and this would not permit any possibility of questions being both philosophical and PSYCHOLOGICAL.[34] I shall have some more to say in defense of the continuity thesis in chapter 10. For now, though, I shall conclude that, on this assumption, even if reliabilism were correct, scientistic reformist naturalism would fail.

The argument of this chapter has been, first, that a reliabilist explication of the concept of epistemic justification is not defensible; second, that even a narrow scientistic reformist account of the relation of epistemology to the *sciences* of cognition is not defensible either – and would not be defensible even if reliabilism were correct.

As the reader may perhaps already have conjectured from the tone of my critique of Goldman's scientism, I suspect that his aspirations to found a new interdisciplinary enterprise in which psychology supplies the straw and philosophy makes the bricks, since it has no very cogent motivation, may be explained in part by the hope that epistemology might come to share something of the prestige and intellectual excitement that the booming fields of AI and cognitive psychology enjoy. There is some evidence confirming this suspicion in Goldman's remarkably candid observation, near the end of 'Epistemics: the Regulative Theory of Cognition', that 'a return to [psychologistic conceptions of epistemology] is especially timely now, when cognitive psychology has renewed prestige and promises to enhance our understanding of fundamental cognitive processes'.[35] (I shall resist the temptation to introduce the term 'opportunistic naturalism', though it comes *nearly* irresistibly to mind as I read this remark!)

There is an irony, then, in the fact that other recent writers, no less enchanted than Goldman by the prestige and the promises of cognitive science, have argued, not that it can resolve outstanding epistemological issues for us, but that it has undermined the very legitimacy of epistemological questions. The next task, then, is to show that this revolutionary scientistic line is no more defensible than Goldman's reformist scientism.

8
Revolutionary Scientism Subverted

[W]e ... have in favor of the literal ascription of belief ... both the available science and the evidence of our day-to-day experience ... [N]obody *seriously* (as opposed to philosophically) doubts it ...

Fodor *Representations*[1]

The goal of this chapter is to defend the legitimacy of the epistemological projects in which I am engaged against the arguments – and the rhetoric – of revolutionary scientistic naturalists, Stich and the Churchlands, who claim that developments in the *sciences* of cognition show these projects to be misconceived.

Epistemology, these revolutionaries point out, has been centrally concerned with questions about the appraisal of evidence for, justification of, processes for the formation of, beliefs. But developments in the *sciences* of cognition now indicate, they claim, that there may be no such things as beliefs. And if so, as Stich puts it, the question: what beliefs ought we to hold? is as misconceived, as superstitious, as the question: what deities ought we to propitiate?[2]

The concern here will be with the consequences of the 'no-belief thesis' for epistemology specifically. But, of course, the no-belief thesis, if true, would threaten the legitimacy of other disciplines and practices too: if there are no beliefs, then historical, economic and sociological explanations, much if not all literary narrative, and most of the machinery of the law would have to be deemed, like epistemology, merely superstitious.

Some epistemologists, especially those of a Popperian persuasion, might be inclined to contest the assumption that the legitimacy of epistemology depends on the bona fides of beliefs. But this course is not open to me; I must tackle the revolutionaries' arguments directly.

I note by way of preliminary, however, that both Stich and Paul Churchland exhibit a certain ambivalence about what exactly it is that they are arguing *for*. Sometimes one gets the impression that they are committed to the full-blown no-belief thesis, that there *are no* beliefs; more usually, they go only so far as the tentative thesis that *probably there are no* beliefs; and sometimes they stop short at the thesis that *it is possible that there are no* beliefs. At one point Stich writes that the concept of belief '*ought not* to play any significant role in a science aimed at explaining human cognition and behavior' and that 'despite appearances . . . [it] *does not* play a role in the best . . . theories put forward by contemporary cognitive sciences' – but, only a few pages later, that it is 'too early to tell' whether there are beliefs, and then, a few lines later, that it is 'more than a mere logical possibility' that there are not.[3] That people believe things is an empirical claim. The serious issue is whether any good reasons have been given for thinking that this admittedly contingent thesis *is in fact false*.

A second preliminary is to note that the serious issue is whether *any good reasons* have been offered for at least the tentative no-belief thesis; for Stich and the Churchlands rely sometimes less on argument than on rhetoric – in effect, on the seductive effect of the prestige and intellectual excitement of the *sciences* of cognition. The first section of this chapter, therefore, will have to be devoted to disentangling the revolutionaries' rhetoric from their reasons.

Rhetoric aside, what is on offer is, on the one hand, evidence which, it is claimed, shows that the *sciences* of cognition can provide explanations of action without positing beliefs, desires, etc.; and, on the other, in-principle arguments allegedly showing that this is no accident, since the ontological bona fides of intentional states are at best doubtful.

The concern of the second section of this chapter will be to show that the *scientific* work which allegedly provides explanations of action without positing beliefs, etc., either (a) provides explanations of action but, contrary to what is claimed, does posit beliefs, or, (b) does not posit beliefs but, contrary to what is claimed, does not provide explanations of action. Stich's appeals to work in cognitive psychology and computational AI tend to fall into the first category, Churchland's appeals to work in neurophysiology and connectionist AI into the second.

The concern of section III will be to tackle the 'in-principle' arguments against beliefs. Part of this task can be achieved by playing Churchland and Stich off against each other. Churchland holds that beliefs are mythical because not 'smoothly reducible' to neurophysiological states; Stich, that beliefs are mythical because their content, their reference to things and events in the world, violates the 'autonomy principle' to which psychological explanations supposedly conform. But Stich realizes that Churchland's demand for smooth reduction is excessive, and Churchland acknowledges, at least implicitly, that organism/environment relations can play a legitimate role in *science*. To go deeper, though, requires an argument to the effect that both in-principle arguments rest on a misunderstanding of what is required for human beings' capacity for intentional action and inquiry to be acknowledged as part of the natural – of the physical – world; and prompts the further thought that Churchland's and Stich's thesis that there are no beliefs rests, at bottom, on misconceptions about what beliefs are.

All this can establish at most that the revolutionaries' arguments fail, and that even the tentative no-belief thesis is unproven. In the fourth section, however, I shall point out that the no-belief thesis leaves the revolutionaries without an intelligible account of assertion; in the absence of which their arguments are not just inconclusive, but self-defeating.

I

Patricia Churchland's revolutionary paper, 'Epistemology in the Age of Neuroscience', contains, so far as I can tell, no arguments whatever that the familiar epistemological projects are illegitimate or misconceived; but its rhetoric is remarkable. Epistemology, the message is, is out of date; it is being superseded by developments in neuroscience. She phrases her announcement thus: 'We are in the midst of a paradigm shift'. The significance of the Kuhnian vocabulary soon becomes apparent: Churchland concedes that the old epistemological paradigm 'has not been decisively refuted', a concession well-designed to convey, without argument, the impression that the old paradigm, if not *decisively* refuted, at least faces anomalies which seriously threaten its legitimacy; at the same time, the fact that in the Kuhnian picture paradigm shifts are supposed to be more a matter of conversion than of rational argument or weight of evidence operates in a subterranean way to make her failure to offer any arguments at all why the old paradigm is misconceived seem legitimate. It is impossible to avoid the suspicion that Churchland is urging conversion to the new, neuroscientific paradigm *simply on the grounds that it is the coming thing*. (Opportunistic naturalism, indeed!) But the dizzying prospect she holds out of an epistemology revolutionized by cheap computing should not be allowed to disguise the fact that she has given no reasons for supposing revolution necessary.[4]

Stich's title, *From Folk Psychology to Cognitive Science*, is a small masterpiece of suggestion. 'Folk psychology' sounds as if it is bound to be crude, primitive, out of date; 'cognitive science', benefiting from the favourable connotations of both 'cognitive' and 'science', sounds as if it is bound to be sophisticated, rigorous and up to date.

This rhetoric manages to insinuate itself into the first of Stich's arguments against 'folk psychology'. 'However wonderful and imaginative folk theorizing and speculation has been', Stich urges, 'it has turned out to be screamingly false in every domain where we now have a reasonably sophisticated science'.[5] This is not merely (as he 'concedes') a rather weak induction, i.e., a good argument which, however, only weakly probabilifies its conclusion; it is a bad argument which gives no support whatever to its conclusion. The fatal flaw is the shiftiness of Stich's use of the term 'folk'. Stich talks casually, though hardly idiomatically, of 'folk astronomy', 'folk physics', etc., giving the impression that any old but now discredited body of ideas is to be counted as a folk theory. If the adjective 'folk' is applied to a theory or body of ideas in virtue of the fact that it used to be widely accepted by the lay public *but is now discredited*, however, no reasons have been given for supposing that the idea that a person's actions can be explained by reference to his beliefs and desires *is* a folk theory, and the induction doesn't get off the ground. If, on the other hand, the adjective 'folk' is being used in a neutral way, simply to refer to ideas or theories which have been accepted by the lay public for a long time, no reasons have been given for supposing that folk theories have invariably turned out to be false, and once again the argument doesn't get off the ground. What Stich is *suggesting*, of course, is that folk psychology stands to cognitive science as, say, ancient Babylonian to modern astronomy; but his argument has no tendency to establish this.

Paul Churchland observes that the folk-psychological belief-desire model of the explanation of action is empirical; then that, because of the fallibility of introspection, it must be regarded as theoretical in character; hence, that it is a competitor of other, *scientific* theories in the same domain; and then that, compared to these *scientific* theories, it is seen to be a degenerating research programme which ought to be abandoned.[6]

But it does not follow from the fallibility of introspection that mental states such as beliefs and desires are theoretical entities, any more than it follows from the fallibility of perception that physical objects such as rocks and furniture are theoretical entities. And it does not follow from the synthetic, empirical character of the proposition that people have beliefs and desires that it is a *scientific* rather than a philosophical proposition – a point which Churchland, despite his ostensible commitment to the thesis of the continuity of philosophy and *science*,[7] systematically misses. The real work in reaching the conclusion is effected by neat rhetoric, by manoeuvring with the word 'theory'. Churchland is taking advantage of the fact that in casual discourse 'theory' often carries the connotation 'merely hypothetical, not a known fact'. And sleight of words *almost* deceives the mind's eye as he shifts from 'not known infallibly to introspection' to 'theory' to 'research programme' and then, as soon as he has elevated the belief-desire model to the status of 'research programme', immediately demotes it by the accusation, 'degenerating'. This seems to me like calling the postulation of rocks, furniture, etc., a 'degenerating research programme' on the grounds, first, that it has been sustained for many centuries without major modification and, second, that it is simple, coarse-grained and gerrymandered relative to the ontology of modern physics. True, Churchland also offers the observation that folk-psychological explanations are 'isolated', but this claim depends on stressing the isolation of such explanations from physics, neuroscience, etc., while ignoring their deep embedding in economics, sociology, history, criminology, and so on. Stripped of its rhetorical boosters, Churchland's argument gets no further off the ground than Stich's.

So I shall put aside these more or less transparent rhetorical manoeuvres to discredit 'folk psychology', and turn to the specific evidence offered.

II

On the face of it, it is surprising to be told that cognitive science poses a threat to the bona fides of belief. A striking feature of cognitive psychology, by contrast with the behaviourist approach which it has now largely displaced, after all, is that it does not scruple to posit internal mental mechanisms, states and processes. In fact, Stich does not claim, and neither is it true, that all or most or even much work in cognitive science is inhospitable to beliefs. But some work, he claims, indicates that it is a serious possibility that there just are no beliefs. Though the evidence he offers is presumably selected as the best he can find for his thesis, it is utterly unconvincing.

Stich first appeals to work by Nisbett and Wilson on the phenomenon called 'attribution'.[8] The central idea of attribution theory, as Stich reports it, is that people sometimes explain their own behaviour by appeal to rather crude theories, and that this attribution of causes itself has behavioural effects; typical experiments in this field lead a subject to make a mistaken inference about the cause of some behaviour of his, and then to behave as if this mistaken inference were correct. Stich discusses an experiment in which two groups of insomniac patients were given placebo pills; one group was told that the pills would produce rapid heart rate, irregular breathing, etc., i.e., the symptoms of insomnia, the other that they would produce regular breathing, lowered heart rate, etc. Attribution theory predicts that the first group would take less time to get to sleep, since they would attribute any arousal symptoms to their having taken the pills, while the second group would take more time to get to sleep, since they would infer that, since their arousal symptoms persist despite their having taken pills that should relax them, their thoughts must be especially disturbing. Both predictions, reportedly, were borne out. Questioning subjects about what they thought caused them to take more/less time to go to sleep, however, Nisbett and Wilson found that none offered what attribution theory conjectures to be the correct explanation; arousal subjects typically replied that they found it easier to get to sleep later in the week! To explain the discrepancy between subjects' verbal accounts of their mental processes and the hypothesized true explanations of their responses, Wilson proposes a model which he describes as postulating two relatively independent cognitive systems, one, largely unconscious, to mediate non-verbal behaviour, and the other, largely conscious, to explain and verbalize what happens in the unconscious system.

Stich claims that, since beliefs are supposed to play a role in the explanation of both verbal and non-verbal behaviour, neither of Wilson's two systems can be thought of as a system of beliefs. But this interpretation is a gratuitous piece of axe-grinding. If the true explanation of the time taken by subjects to get to sleep is as attribution theory says, there is a discrepancy between the true explanation and the explanation given by the subjects themselves. But the obvious explanation of this discrepancy is that people's awareness of their own mental states is imperfect and apt to be influenced, as, notoriously, their perceptual judgements are influenced, by their expectations and preconceptions – an explanation which poses no threat to beliefs.

And this is the explanation which Nisbett and Wilson themselves propose: 'Evidence is reviewed which suggests *there may be little or no direct introspective access to higher-order cognitive processes*'. Wilson's subsequent paper suggesting a 'two-systems' model is also clearly concerned with the limits of introspection. Wilson's 'second system', the system which 'mediates verbal reports and explanations', turns out to be, specifically, those mechanisms by which people arrive at reports of their own mental states and processes, and not, as Stich suggests, a system responsible for all verbal behaviour whatsoever. Any doubts about the status of Stich's suggestion that Wilson is hypothesizing that there are no such things as beliefs are surely finally dispelled by Wilson's own description of the two-systems model: '. . . a model will be offered to explain the origin *of beliefs about mental states*';[9] or, indeed, by the subtitle of his paper: 'the origins and accuracy of *beliefs about one's own mental states*'.

This is just as well. For on Stich's interpretation Wilson's position would be self-defeating. The discrepancy of which an account is required is between the subjects' own explanations of the time they took to get to sleep, and the hypothesized true explanation. And the hypothesized true explanation *itself refers to the subjects' beliefs*: arousal subjects take less time to get to sleep *because they believe* that their arousal symptoms are caused by the pills, while relaxation subjects take longer to get to sleep *because they believe* that their thoughts must be especially disturbing.

Paul Churchland also refers to this work of Nisbett and Wilson, but interprets it, correctly, as indicating the fallibility of introspection.[10] But he then argues from the fallibility of introspection to the theoretical status of the belief-desire account; and then that folk psychology is a false theory and its ontology merely mythical. So he too misuses Nisbett and Wilson's work in support of a conclusion flatly at odds with what that work presupposes.

The other work to which Stich appeals is in AI, where some who had formerly tried to model various human cognitive processes by operations on sentential or sub-sentential units had recently (at the time of Stich's book) begun to move away from this kind of approach. Stich describes this shift as suggesting the falsity of the assumption that cognitive processing is 'modular', a system being modular, as Stich defines it, 'to the extent that *there is some more or less isolatable part of the system which plays (or would play) the central role in a typical causal history leading to the utterance of a sentence*'.[11] Although this characterization makes modularity a matter of degree, while presumably it is either true or false that people have beliefs, and although it defines modularity in terms only of verbal behaviour, while beliefs are supposed to play a role in the explanation of non-verbal behaviour too, Stich assumes that the failure of modularity would show that there are no such things as beliefs. But there is little point in labouring over the deficiencies of the argument at this abstract level, since a close look at the work on which Stich depends – two papers of Minsky's and some brief remarks of Winograd's – makes it abundantly clear that it has no tendency to show that beliefs are mythical.

Stich refers to Minsky's 'Frames' paper, which he describes as urging a shift from models which represent knowledge as collections of sentential components, and to his 'K-Lines' paper, which violates modularity in a dramatic way. I shall discuss only the 'Frames' paper; because, although it is true that the 'K-Lines' piece replaces a sentential model by 'great webs of structure', it is offered as a model *for infantile memory only*, with an explicit warning that adult memory can be expected to be significantly different.[12]

Minsky offers only a very imprecise sketch of what frames are supposed to be (am I the only reader whose heart sinks to be told that they are like Kuhnian paradigms?). Frames are described as 'data structures for representing a stereotyped situation, like being in a certain kind of living room, or going to a child's birthday party' and as having 'attached' to them several kinds of information, e.g., 'about how to use the frame' or 'about what one can expect to happen next'. However, it is clear that Minsky intends his frame models to be *un*like what he calls 'logistic' models, i.e., models based on formal, deductive logic, and that his main objection to logistic models is that they lack a *procedural* element; they specify strings of sentences and permissive rules of inference, but give no guidance as to when which rules are to be used or how the separate bits of information are interconnected.[13] Frames are supposed to be better because they connect bits of information. So the components are not *isolated*, since they are to be connected. But the components are *isolatable*, since there are identifiable parts of a frame which could plausibly be construed as beliefs; the 'child's birthday party' frame, for example, is plausibly construed as composed of, among other things, the beliefs that party clothes should be worn, that guests should bring presents, etc., etc. This hardly threatens the legitimacy of beliefs.

Initially, it seems, Winograd favoured 'declarative' over 'procedural' models, but subsequently he came to appreciate the advantages of the latter. 'Declarative' here is approximately equivalent to Minsky's 'logistic', and it is already clear that dissatisfaction with this kind of approach need pose no threat to the bona fides of belief. However, Winograd also offers a couple of examples introduced by a favourable allusion to a comment of Maturana's, that 'many phenomena which for an observer can be described in terms of a representation' can actually be understood as 'the activity of a structure-determined system with no mechanism corresponding to a representation'.[14] These examples of Winograd's fail to engage with Stich's definition of modularity, for they do not concern 'the causal history leading to the utterance of a sentence'. But they do have a bearing on Stich's thesis; for they are cases where what looks like goal-directed behaviour allegedly turns out to be explicable without the postulation of anything like a goal or desire.

Stich seems to be inviting one to draw the conclusion that *everything* that looks like goal-directed behaviour might be so explicable.

Winograd's first example is a pretty straightforward case in which what might initially seem like goal-directed behaviour is plausibly described as really reflexive. There might be some temptation to think of a suckling baby as having a 'representation' of the relevant anatomy, but, he suggests, a better explanation is that it has a reflex to turn its head in response to a touch on the cheek, and a reflex to suck when something touches its mouth – an explanation which calls for no ascription of beliefs or desires to the baby.[15] There is no reason to contest Winograd's description of this case; but neither is there any reason to suppose that, of itself, it goes any way towards showing that adults' activities – my going to the fridge to get a glass of milk, for example – are not sometimes goal-directed. The baby's response is simple and inflexible in the way characteristic of reflexes, not responsive to circumstances in the way characteristic of what we take to be goal-directed behaviour; the suckling baby would react in the same way whatever touched its cheek and whatever touched its mouth.[16]

But it seems that Stich's point must be precisely that adults' actions, or rather, 'actions', may turn out to be more like babies' responses than we realize. (No doubt this is why he appeals to Minsky's K-Lines paper even though it is concerned with infantile memory only. But the appeal is obviously question-begging.) Paul Churchland makes explicitly the claim that is implicit in Stich's argumentative strategy: babies' activities, he says, are recognizably continuous with children's and adults'; so folk psychology, which ascribes beliefs and desires to children and adults but not to infants, makes a distinction where there is no real difference.[17]

This makes it apparent that Stich is using Winograd's other example to suggest that the flexibility and responsiveness to circumstance characteristic of what we take to be genuinely intentional action may after all be explicable without reference to beliefs or desires. One might be tempted to say of a computer programme, Winograd writes, that it has the goal of minimizing the number of jobs in the waiting queue; but it is unlikely that it has a goal structure in memory, more likely that 'there may be dozens or even hundreds of places throughout the code where specific actions are taken, the net effect of which is being described'.[18] Presumably the implication is meant to be that, as in the first case it is false that the baby has a representation of the relevant anatomy, so here it is false that the computer has the goal of minimizing the job queue. And Stich wants us to draw the further conclusion that adult human behaviour, or 'behaviour', like the infant's responses and the computer's queue-minimizing pattern, may be explicable without reference to the agent's beliefs or desires.

Consider what would be required of a human agent to whom we would unhesitatingly apply the characterization: he wants to minimize the job queue. He tends, by and large, to act in ways that reduce the job queue; he responds with irritation to events which impede his efforts to minimize the job queue; he expresses regret when he misses an opportunity to minimize the job queue; when asked what he is trying to do, he replies that he wants to minimize the job queue. Now, imagine a computer which simulates all this behaviour (the screen reads 'DAMN!' and a robot-arm punches the operator in the nose if he types in a new job just as the computer has processed the last one in the queue; in response to the command 'LIST PROGRAMME PRIORITIES' the screen reads '1 MINIMIZE JOB QUEUE, 2 . . .', etc., etc.). I feel inclined to say that the computer does 'have the goal of minimizing the job queue'; I feel a need for scare quotes, but I feel this when applying *any* mental predicate to a computer. Now imagine instead a computer as sketched in Winograd's remarks: its programme priorities do not include 'MINIMIZE JOB QUEUE', but rather a string of more specific characterizations, e.g., 'MINIMIZE JOB THROUGHPUT TIME', 'DELETE IMPROPERLY WORDED JOB SPECIFICATIONS', 'CANCEL 27TH AND SUBSEQUENT JOB ORDERS', or whatever. What would we say about a human agent whose behaviour was like this? – probably, that he did not have the goal of minimizing the job queue, but that minimizing the queue was the unintended or unforeseen consequence of things he did intend to do. So Winograd's second case has no tendency at all to show that human agents don't have beliefs or desires, and the first has no tendency to show this either unless one assumes that adult human behaviour is just like infants' reflex responses.

But the assumption that all adult human behaviour is, like those responses, 'structure-determined' is extraordinarily far-fetched. In one significant respect, after all, infants are *un*like children and adults: they can't talk. Since children learn to talk gradually, in a sense there is continuity; but our willingness to ascribe beliefs to a small child runs in parallel with the child's gradual acquisition of language.

Does this make me a *Cartesian* naturalist? Yes and No. Yes: in that I regard human beings' capacity for language as constituting an enormously significant enhancement of our cognitive abilities – without which there would indeed be no place for the familiar projects of epistemology. (Though I would add, with Hobbes, that the capacity for language which enables men, unlike brutes, to engage in ratiocination, also enables

men, unlike brutes, to 'multiply one untruth by another').[19] No: in that
I am not thereby denying that there are continuities between humans
and other animals, or that these continuities are of epistemological
interest.

Certainly, though, I am a more Cartesian naturalist than Paul
Churchland, who holds that 'when we consider the great variety of
cognitively active creatures on this planet – sea slugs and octopuses,
bats, dolphins and humans', and take into account 'the ceaseless
reconfiguration in which their brains or central ganglia engage', we
must first acknowledge that truth is not the primary aim of this cognitive activity, and then draw the conclusion that maybe truth should
cease to be a primary aim of science, and that talk of truth may make
no sense.[20]

Churchland writes that 'neuroscience is unlikely to find "sentences in
the head," or anything else that answers to the structure of individual
beliefs and desires', and 'on the strength of this', he says, he is 'willing
to infer that folk psychology is false, and that its ontology is chimerical.
Beliefs and desires are of a piece with phlogiston, caloric and the al-
chemical essences', and '[w]e therefore need an entirely new kinematics
and dynamics with which to comprehend human cognitive activity'. A
decade earlier, Churchland continues, though he was already willing to
draw this conclusion, he could not clearly imagine what a systematic
alternative to folk psychology might look like; but now an alternative is
available:

> The microstructure of the brain and the recent successes of
> connectionist AI both suggest that our principal form of represen-
> tation is the high-dimensional activation vector, and that our
> principal form of computation is the vector-to-vector transfor-
> mation, effected by a matrix of differently weighted synapses. In
> place of propositional attitudes and inferences from one to another,
> therefore, we can conceive of persons as the seat of vectorial
> attitudes and various non-linear transformations from one vector
> to another.[21]

But what kind of phenomenon is it that the successes of connectionist
AI to which Churchland points explain? Not cases of what is ordinarily
taken to be goal-directed action (as: my cooking a dish by consulting
a recipe, calling the grocery stores in the Yellow Pages, and consulting
a map to find the store that sells curry leaves . . .) but, on the one hand,
pre-propositional cognitive capacities like recognizing the vowel sound
'ā', and, on the other, motor and co-ordinative skills like catching a

ball.[22] There is no reason to deny that there are important cognitive capacities which are pre-propositional, in the sense both that they are necessary conditions of a creature's having propositional knowledge, and that they may be shared by adult humans and human infants, the higher animals, and perhaps, in primitive forms, by sea slugs and earthworms. Nor is there any reason to deny that there are many things people can do which they cannot articulate how to do – ride a bicycle or recognize a face, for instance. The work to which Churchland refers has significantly improved our understanding of pre-propositional cognitive processing and of control of motor skills. But it clearly doesn't follow from its success in simulating, say, a speaker's ability to recognize the vowel sound 'ā', or in training up a computer to discriminate between a rock and a mine on the ocean floor, that connectionist neuroscience has any tendency to encourage the idea that there are no beliefs, or that appraisals of evidence are nothing but superstition, or that truth is not a goal of inquiry.

Tempting as it is to overreact to Churchland's unseemly rush from the non-propositional workings of the ganglia of the sea slug to his vulgar pragmatism about the goal of inquiry, I acknowledge that it might be desirable for epistemologists to pay more attention than they mostly have to the pre-propositional, to knowing how, and to tacit knowledge. (I say 'than they *mostly* have' in recognition of the very significant contributions made to these issues by Michael Polanyi[23] – to whose work, however, Churchland nowhere refers.) But it is not an overreaction to conclude that the work to which Churchland appeals offers no support for even the tentative no-belief thesis.

I have been unable to find evidence that *any* recent work in connectionist neuroscience offers any support for this thesis. In *Wet Mind: The New Cognitive Neuroscience*, published in 1992, Kosslyn and Koenig report developments in the understanding of brain structures underlying perception, memory, speech production, writing, the control of movements, etc. Since there are several entries under 'Action programming subsystem' in the index, but none under 'belief' or 'desire', one might get the impression that Churchland may be right after all – until one notices that under 'Action, guidance of' the index briskly tells the reader, '*see* Movement'. Chapter 7, entitled 'Movement', reports what is known about the brain structures that control muscles and coordinate their movements relative to perceived objects. Though they sometimes use 'action' and 'movement' interchangeably, Kosslyn and Koenig grasp the distinction philosophers make between the two; in the final chapter, entitled 'Gray Matters', and devoted to those issues about the workings of the mind with respect to which cognitive neuroscience has *not*, so far, much to offer, the first issue mentioned is 'the ultimate source of decision making in the brain'. '[T]here must be a "decision subsystem"', Kosslyn and Koenig observe, but so far neuroscience can't tell us much about it. Neither, they observe in the same chapter, can connectionist neuroscience yet tell us much about reasoning. And they pose the problem of understanding the brain's 'decision subsystem' in terms of *selecting a goal* and *devising a way to achieve it.*[24] I am at a loss to see how this could be interpreted as hostile to the bona fides of beliefs.

III

I have laboured over the details of the *scientific* work alleged to support the no-belief thesis to make it unmistakably clear that it is not *science*, but preconceptions in the philosophy of mind, on which the thesis really depends. It is important to be under no illusion that these preconceptions carry the authority of *science*.

I think people have beliefs, goals, hopes, fears, etc., and that agents' propositional attitudes contribute to explanations of their actions. I don't think there is soul stuff, immaterial substance; and neither do I see how supposing that there is would make it easier to understand how a person's beliefs and desires explain his actions. People are physical organisms in a physical environment, physical organisms capable of thought, of intentional action, of inquiry. I do not assume, however, as Churchland does, that it can be true that people are physical organisms capable of thought, of intentional action, of inquiry, only if intentional states could be 'smoothly reduced' to neurophysiological states, nor, as Stich does, only if they could be identified with 'autonomously describable' states of the brain.

Though Churchland and Stich both think there are good in-principle arguments against an ontology of intentional states, the arguments they have in mind are quite different. Rather than call them 'anti-realists' about intentional states, as Fodor does,[25] I shall call them 'atheists', because that will enable me, by analogy with 'Catholic atheist' versus 'Protestant atheist', to classify Churchland as a smooth-reductionist atheist and Stich as a functionalist atheist – and those who believe in beliefs as 'believers'. (It would be possible to accommodate the differences noted in the previous section by expanding this to 'smooth-reductionist connectionist atheist' versus 'functionalist computationalist atheist', but that would be too burdensome even for me.)

As the title of one of his papers, 'Eliminative Materialism and the Propositional Attitudes', indicates, Churchland is a philosophical materialist of the most aggressive stripe: from the premiss that neuro-science is unlikely to find 'sentences in the head' via a 'smooth reduction' of intentional states and laws to neurophysiological states and laws, he is willing to infer that there are no intentional states. The appropriate reaction is to grant that no such smooth reduction is likely to be forth-coming, but to refuse to draw the atheist conclusion; Churchland's requirements for the ontological bona fides of intentional states are just too high.

This is also the reaction of functionalists, according to whom, though each belief that p, desire that q, etc., has some physical realization, different beliefs that p, desires that q, etc., may have different physical realizations, since intentional states are to be individuated and classified functionally, so that many different physical stories may correspond to the same functional explanation.

Stich agrees, up to a point. 'Those of us who take the special sciences seriously', he writes, 'have come to expect that the classificatory schemes invoked in those sciences will cut across the classificatory grain imposed by physics'.[26] But whereas functionalist believers, such as Fodor, see this as a way of reconciling intentional psychology and physicalism, Stich maintains that the functionally individuated states posited by psychology cannot be intentional; he is, therefore, a functionalist atheist.

Stich's in-principle argument can be summed up, not quite so suc-cinctly as Churchland's eliminative materialism, in one of his chapter titles: 'The Syntactic Theory of the Mind'. The syntactic theory is so-called by contrast with Fodor's 'representational' theory; and the point of entry of Stich's argument is a tension he observes in Fodor's view, according to which, on the one hand, intentional states are essentially contentful but, on the other, only their formal, computational properties can be relevant to the causation of action. Stich urges that the proper conclusion (though Fodor, of course, does not draw it) is that inten-tional states, *qua* intentional, contentful, do not play any causal role.

Why does Stich take the content of intentional states to be causally irrelevant? He relies chiefly on what he calls 'the autonomy principle': 'the states and processes that ought to be of concern to the psychologist are those that supervene on the current, internal, physical state of the organism'.[27] Hence, according to Stich, psychology ought not to con-cern itself with the content of a person's mental states, since this would require it to get involved with relations to the things and events the subject's beliefs, etc., are *about*. In favour of the autonomy principle Stich offers the 'replacement argument': two subjects who are physical-ly identical ('molecular duplicates') would behave in exactly the same ways, and so, since psychology is the science which aspires to explain behaviour, any states or properties not shared by molecular duplicates must be irrelevant to psychology.

Immediately, however, Stich admits that this argument 'plainly will not do'. For if we allow in all the usual kinds of descriptions of behaviour, it is just *false* that molecular duplicates will behave in exactly the same ways. For example, Stich can, but his duplicate cannot, sell his (Stich's) old car. Stich proposes, therefore, to modify the argument by granting that molecular duplicates will not satisfy *all* the same behavioral descriptions, and retreating to the premiss that molecular duplicates will satisfy all the same *autonomous* behavioural descriptions.[28]

But with this modification, even if Stich has succeeded in making his premisses true, he has certainly made his argument invalid. From 'psychology explains behaviour' and 'molecular duplicates would behave in the same autonomously describable ways', it obviously doesn't follow that only states shared by molecular duplicates are relevant to psychology. If Stich thinks it does, it must be because he is taking for granted that it is appropriate to require of psychology only that it explain autonomously describable behaviour; but that, of course, is just the point at issue.

So Stich's autonomy principle is unproven. To see that it is also untrue, it is only necessary to look a little more closely at Stich's example. Suppose, Stich writes, that he has been kidnapped and his duplicate 'sent out into the world in my place'. You offer the duplicate $1,000 for the old car, and he 'agrees to the sale with the same sincere delight that I would exhibit . . . signs all the appropriate documents just as I would . . . the signatures would convince a handwriting expert'. Nevertheless, 'my replica does not sell you the old clunker'.[29] But, for the same reason Stich's molecular duplicate couldn't sell the car, he couldn't agree to the sale or sign the documents either. He could say to the potential purchaser, 'It's a deal!', and write 'Stephen P. Stich' on the documents, but what he would be doing is *pretending to agree to the sale* and *forging Stich's signature*. There are two senses of 'non-autonomous description' in play: (a) description which applies to a subject in virtue of his being that particular person, and (b) description which applies to a subject in virtue of his relations to things and events in his environment. What Stich needs to establish, in support of his 'syntactic theory of the mind', is that psychology ought not to be expected to explain behaviour under any non-autonomous descriptions in the broader sense, (b); the most his examples show is that psychology should not be expected to explain behaviour under non-autonomous descriptions in the narrower sense, (a). (And this may be no more than an instance of the presumption that *scientific* explanations should be general in character rather than restricted to specific individual things or persons.) When one notices that even 'says to the prospective purchaser, "It's a deal!"' and 'writes "Stephen P. Stich" on the documents' are non-autonomous descriptions in the broader sense, one realizes that Stich's principle is completely implausible.

Our actions are *inter*actions with things, persons, etc., in our environment; and the reference of beliefs to such things, persons, etc., so far from unfitting them for a role in the explanation of action, is precisely *required* if they are to play such a role. How could my belief that the ice is thick enough to bear my weight possibly contribute to the explanation of my setting off to walk across the lake, *unless* it was about the ice on the lake?

The last paragraph indicates that, though I repudiate Stich's functionalist atheism, I don't throw in my lot (sorry, I couldn't resist!) with Fodor's functionalism, either – for my insistence on the explanatory relevance of what a belief is about is as much at odds with Fodor's 'methodological solipsism' as with Stich's autonomy principle. In fact, though I agree with Fodor that psychological explanation requires intentional states, and that this is compatible with a conception of persons as physical organisms even though no simple reduction of intentional to physical states and laws is likely to be forthcoming, beyond those points I disagree with him in just about every respect.

How do we determine, for instance, that I believe that the ice is thick enough to bear my weight? We attend to my behaviour, verbal and non-verbal: my readiness to assent to, or assert, 'the ice is thick enough to bear my weight', or words to that effect; my setting off to walk across the lake; my encouraging others to cut across it rather than take the long way round; my shock or surprise if, as I walk across, the ice cracks beneath me; and so on. We judge the sincerity of my verbal behaviour by my non-verbal behaviour; however firmly I avow that the ice is thick enough, if I encourage my enemy to walk across but will not set foot on the ice myself, you will rightly doubt that I believe what I say. Though we ascribe beliefs on behavioural criteria, however, we acknowledge that people may have beliefs which are not manifested in what they do or say, whether because there is no occasion, or because there is reason for inhibition – the boss or the Inquisitor is listening.

An account that accommodates these observations rather comfortably is Price's characterization of beliefs as 'multi-form dispositions', complexes of dispositions to verbal and non-verbal behaviour: to assent to or to assert certain sentences in, as Price neatly puts it, 'unstudied speech', to behave in these or those ways, to feel shock or surprise if such-and-such happens . . . etc.[30]

This suggests a resolution of the ambivalence one feels about whether to ascribe beliefs to animals, on the one hand, and computers, on the other; since in each case some but not all strands of the full multi-form disposition are present, the answer that suggests itself is: they have something belief-like, but not beliefs in the full sense. It also suggests a plausible way to accommodate degrees of belief via degrees of strength of the relevant dispositions.

It might be thought that construing a belief as a complex of dispositions including dispositions to act in certain ways is at odds with the fact that we explain people's actions by reference to their beliefs.[31] (Think of the standard detective story ploy, where the police trap a suspect by leading him to believe that incriminating evidence is to be found in such-and-such a place, and then follow as he goes off to hide or destroy it.) Surely, the objection goes, 'he Φ'd because he believed that p' is more informative than 'he Φ'd because he had a disposition to Φ'. It is not clear, however, that the objection survives further reflection about dispositional explanations. True, we are likely to say, not 'the glass broke because it was brittle', but 'the glass broke because he dropped it'; but the reason may be that we think of the brittleness of glass as a permanent, background condition, and pick out as explanatory the changed feature of the situation. We might well say, 'she broke her hip because her bones had become brittle', when brittleness is the new factor; as the suspect's belief is in the example above.

This approach is somewhat in the spirit of Bain and Peirce,[32] but much less in the spirit of Watson or Skinner. A person's disposition to such-and-such patterns of verbal and other behaviour is something to do with the state of his brain (as brittleness is with the microstructural configuration of the glass) – something, in other words, to do with the contents of the black box into which Watson or Skinner would forbid us to look.

Something, however, not autonomously describable, but inherently triadic. What I have said so far has presupposed an essential point about a connection between the dispositions to verbal behaviour and the dispositions to non-verbal behaviour characteristic of belief: that, in normal cases, the subject is disposed to assent to sentences which represent as such and such some thing or place or event, etc., with respect *to which* he is disposed to act thus and so. My belief that the ice is thick enough to bear my weight involves a disposition to assent to sentences which *represent the ice on the lake* as thick enough to bear my weight, and a disposition to *walk across the ice* if I want to get to the other side of the lake.[33] Figure 8.1 is an attempt to make this clearer.

Intentional action is action guided by the agent's representations of

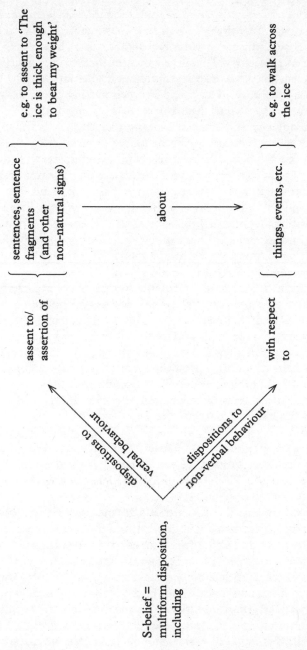

Figure 8.1

things and events in the world. I have focused on sentences in the agent's language. But drawing a sketch map, as well as giving verbal directions, is an indication of the belief that this is how you get there; so 'representations' should include not only bits of language, but any non-natural signs. Not, however, sentences in the 'language of thought' hypothesized by Fodor. The point is precisely that S-beliefs are complex dispositions including dispositions to respond to/to use sentences in a public language, or other non-natural signs; it is the dispositions, not the sentences, that are in the head.

Until just now 'belief' has been used, in this chapter, with deliberate ambiguity; for the writers I have been discussing do not respect the distinction of S- versus C-beliefs (which partly explains the fruitless search for 'sentences in the head'). But the account of beliefs as multi-form dispositions is intended, of course, as an account of belief states, S-beliefs. Questions about how the relevant C-belief is to be identified will be postponed until after a brief exploration of some consequences of the suggested approach to S-beliefs.

A disposition to assent to a sentence depends on capacities for recognition and response: on recognizing words, on understanding sentences composed of familiar words. This is consonant with language users' capacity to recognize and to utter sentences they have never heard before. It even suggests, though only vaguely, how propositional capacities might depend on pre-propositional capacities; thus combining the thesis that intentional action is the privilege of sign-using creatures with hints at continuities through human adults, human infants . . . all the way to Churchland's friend the sea slug. (This thought has also occurred to some writers much more knowledgeable than I about the relevant *scientific* literature; thus, Goschke and Koppelberg: 'the specific features of human cognition may well result from the intimate interaction of context-sensitive connectionist operations and the capacity to use external symbol systems'.)[34]

Now I can explain why my attitude to the familiar dichotomies of computationalism versus connectionism, reductionism versus functionalism, is rather like that of the Irishman asked for directions: 'I wouldn't start from here'. I agree with functionalists that we can expect there to be different physical explanations corresponding to the same intentional explanation (though my reasons are based less on the logical possibility of silicon-based Martian intentional agents than on the empirical fact of different human languages). I agree with reductionists, however, that, of itself, this neither answers nor illegitimates the question, what the neurophysiological realizations of intentional states are. I should feel as uneasy as Churchland about the apparent evasiveness of functionalism if I believed, as Churchland does,[35] that the problem is not that there are *too many* candidates for neurophysiological realization of the belief that p, but that there are *none*. But I think Churchland believes there are no candidates because he is looking for the wrong kind of thing – for 'sentences in the head' rather than (*inter alia*) for dispositions to respond thus and so to words, phrases and sentences in the subject's language. And if one grants this, and – as one then would be obliged to – acknowledges the implausibility of the autonomy principle or of methodological solipsism, then connectionism versus computationalism, like reductionism versus functionalism, no longer looks like an exclusive dichotomy.

This leaves me with a problem about what to call my approach ('modest neo-behaviourism'? 'baroque reductionism'?[36] . . .). I have settled on 'sign-mediation' or 'SM' account.

The SM account has the merit of making an internal connection between the concepts of belief and of truth: to believe that p is, *inter alia*, to be disposed to assent to, i.e., acknowledge the truth of, sentences to the effect that p. This comports with the truism that to believe that p is to accept p as true; as in the *OED*'s definition of 'belief' as 'acceptance as true . . . of statement, etc.'. Accepting p as true requires more than a disposition to verbal assent; but there is no need to fear that sincerity can be explained only as requiring that the subject actually *believe* p. Assent is sincere if accompanied by a disposition to act on the proposition concerned.

The SM account suggests a new spin to the familiar suggestion that ascriptions of intentional action imply minimal rationality on the agent's part. 'Rational' has at least two relevant senses: capable of reasoning ('RATIONAL', contrasting with 'a-rational' or 'non-rational') and: using this capacity properly or well ('*rational*', contrasting with 'irrational'). '*Rational*', in turn, has a stronger and a weaker interpretation: in conformity with the agent's goals and beliefs ('*weak rationality*') and: in conformity with the agent's reasonable goals and justified beliefs ('*strong rationality*'). The SM account implies that beliefs are the privilege of creatures capable of employing non-natural signs, and thus requires RATIONALITY. Not all of a RATIONAL creature's activities are intentional, of course, but the SM account implies that any action that is explicable by reference to the agent's beliefs and desires is *weakly rational*. It does not imply, however, that intentional action must be *strongly rational* – for the beliefs which ground it may be quite unjustified, and the goals which guide it quite at odds with the agent's real interests.

The SM account comports with the plausible thought that the capacity for reasoning, deliberation, intentional action, inquiry, grows as language mastery grows; and that it is enhanced by richness, inhibited by poverty of one's linguistic resources. (Newspeak is a language deliberately impoverished so as to make politically incorrect thoughts not merely in*expres*sible, but un*think*able; and thereby to inhibit politically incorrect action.)[37]

In the form in which I have presented it, the SM account has the consequence not only that thinking is in signs, but that it is appropriate to speak of thinking in *a* language. This will be controversial, but I welcome it. Introspection speaks in its favour; so do such commonplace remarks as 'I was just *thinking aloud*', 'I can speak French, but I still *think in English*'; so do novelists who write, quite unselfconsciously, such lines as: 'Five perpetrators. Though an educated man, Douglas *thought in police jargon*';[38] and even, in unguarded moments, Fodor, who, describing an agent reflecting on a chess game, writes, '[w]hen, however, he had considered for a while which pawn to push, it all began to look boring and hopeless, and *he thought: "Oh, bother it"* and decided to resign'.[39]

There remains a tangle of issues concerning the ascription of belief-*content* – a tangle thus far evaded by vague talk about a person's being disposed to assent to sentences 'to the effect that' p. In the very simplest cases, some sentence a subject's disposition to assent to which is a component of the S-belief in question will adequately identify the C-belief. But in ascribing to you the belief that p, I am representing *your* belief in *my* language; and so, since even within a language-at-a-time, probably, no two speakers use words in exactly the same way, belief-ascriptions have to be adjusted for linguistic variation. So, often enough, ascription of a C-belief will require attention to a substantial sample of a subject's use of language, and to his non-verbal behaviour. And sometimes the adjustment will call for elaborate periphrasis: 'He believes he has arthritis in his thigh – well, he calls it 'arthritis', that's why he asked the doctor to prescribe ARTHRIGHT, but obviously he doesn't realize that the word really refers only to inflammation of the joints'.[40] (In some cases, as with Stich's Mrs T., who reportedly would assent to 'McKinley was assassinated' but not to 'McKinley is dead', or even to 'I am not dead', there will be no saying what, if anything, the subject believes. In such peculiar cases one hesitates to ascribe *any* belief; but it would be unreasonable to take this to constitute grounds for hesitating to ascribe beliefs to normal subjects.)[41]

These problems will arise for any believer, but another is particularly acute for me. Since I have maintained that the fact that beliefs are *about* things and events in the world is vital to an understanding of how they contribute to the explanation of action, I stand in need of an account of C-beliefs as *de re* ('relational' in the sense in which Quine uses the term, not in the exactly opposite sense in which Fodor uses it). This leaves the problem of how to reconcile the apparently non-extensional character of belief-ascriptions with a *de re* conception. It may be possible to achieve this by using Burdick's attractive construal of beliefs as of ordered pairs of which the first member is an ordinary, extensional object and the second a predicate representing the relevant 'mode of presentation'. My belief that the ice is thick enough to bear my weight, for example, might be construed as my holding-true 'thick enough to bear my weight' of <the ice on Lake So-and-So, 'the ice on the lake beside which I am standing'> – the SM story, of course, is my explanation of 'holding-true'.[42]

This has been, obviously, the merest gesture towards a sketch; but, fortunately, a full account is not necessary to the thesis of this section, which is that it is unproven that acknowledging that people are physical organisms in a physical environment obliges one to deny that they have beliefs, or that their beliefs contribute to the explanation of their intentional actions; a thesis established, I hope, by the more pedestrian parts of this section without the help of its very speculative second half. Perhaps, indeed, none of this elaborate argument was strictly necessary; for the attitude would not be unreasonable that the fact that some theoretical stance in the philosophy of mind has the consequence that people don't have beliefs is always better grounds for rejecting that stance in the philosophy of mind than for accepting the consequence that people don't have beliefs.

It is pertinent to this last thought that neither Stich nor Churchland can really sustain their commitment to this consequence, even as they argue for it.

IV

Stich's and Churchland's practice is strikingly (perhaps Stich would prefer 'screamingly') at odds with their official doctrine. Here, with my italics, are some sentences taken from pp. 166–7 of Stich's *From Folk Psychology to Cognitive Science*:

> *I think* there is an *important kernel of truth* in the replacement argument.
>
> *I think* the right move to make in response to this objection is to grant the point.

> *[W]e should not expect* a psychological theory to . . . explain behavior under any [sic!] and every description.

> [L]et us ask *whether there is any reason to think* that autonomous behavioral descriptions include all those that a psychologist will find useful. *In thinking about this question* it is helpful to *reflect on the analogy* between organisms and industrial robots.

Not to labour the point too much, let me just observe that Stich and Churchland: utter a great many sentences, while maintaining that language use is peripheral or epiphenomenal; express, and in many instances overtly avow, their beliefs, while insisting that there are or may be no such things as beliefs; appraise this or that development in cognitive psychology or neuroscience as progressive or well supported by the evidence, and deplore folk psychology as a 'degenerating research program', a false theory the ontology of which is mythical, while maintaining that epistemic appraisals are merely superstitious and that truth is not a goal of inquiry. On the last point, I am unable to resist just a couple more quotations (again, the italics are mine):

> Stich: [T]here is a strong presumption, on my part at least, that scientists generally *have good reasons* for building their theories as they do.[43]

> Churchland: [T]he empirical sciences . . . have provided a steady flow of *evidence relevant to the making of* . . . *a rational choice* [among alternative theories of the mind].[44]

> [T]he constellation of moves, claims and defenses characteristic of functionalism constitute[s] *an outrage against reason and truth* . . . [T]he functionalist stratagem is a smoke screen for the *preservation of error and confusion.*[45]

Churchland, who seems somewhat more aware of the tension than Stich, indulges in the fantasy that in the future '[l]ibraries become filled not with books, but with long recordings of exemplary neural activity . . . not . . . sentences or arguments'.[46] But *he* offers us books, books consisting of sentences and (at least occasionally) arguments.

The problem is not simply that Stich and Churchland fall short, in practice, of high standards that they preach (or that they fall long of low standards that they preach). It is that, if there really are no such things as beliefs, it is a mystery what is going on when – as from time to time they undeniably do – people utter sentences. If there are no beliefs, it seems that there is no difference between a person's asserting that p and a parrot's uttering ⌈p⌉. (And, in particular, that there is no difference between Churchland's or Stich's asserting that there are no such things as beliefs, and a parrot's uttering 'there are no such things as beliefs').

Churchland anticipates this kind of objection, and replies that it is question-begging.[47] He is right thus far: the problem is stated in terms that presuppose connections between the concepts of assertion and belief which he must repudiate. But his reply doesn't solve the problem, which is that no *alternative* account of assertion is on offer; which is what creates the mystery of which I am complaining. The question to be pressed is, 'what *is* assertion, if not a manifestation of belief?'. 'Something else' just isn't an adequate answer.[48]

After observing that the no-belief thesis, 'if true, could neither be taken seriously nor accepted' and 'must be simultaneously unbelievable and indubitable', Heil suggests that we allow the possibility that the abolitionists, as he calls them, might, for all the conceptual instability of their thesis, be *showing* something that cannot be *said*.[49] In Heil's case this may be a rhetorical device to make an opening for the useful critique of abolitionism he then presents. For myself, after reiterating that the no-belief thesis is, if true, literally incredible, I shall only say that Stich and the Churchlands seem to me to be kicking away the ladder while they are climbing it.

One could be forgiven for getting the impression that, in urging the merits of their bizarre thesis, Stich and the Churchlands betray an enthusiasm for revolution for its own sake. This impression is conveyed not only by the weakness of the evidence they offer, and the conflict between their doctrine and their practice, but also by their note of ambitious wistfulness for greener pastures than the old, overgrazed epistemological fields. That this impression is not entirely off the mark is confirmed by the fact that more recently, in *The Fragmentation of Reason*, though he no longer maintains the no-belief thesis, Stich continues to do battle with epistemology – only now in a spirit which one might describe as rather relativistic than scientistic. Churchland, as we saw, slides from the sea slug to vulgar pragmatism; Stich now takes us there directly.

Stich is by no means the original vulgar pragmatist, of course; in our time, that dubious honour goes to Richard Rorty. So as I turn to this other revolutionary tendency – which would be, if it succeeded, no less damaging than revolutionary scientism to the enterprise in which I am engaged – I shall take on Rorty first.

9
Vulgar Pragmatism: an Unedifying Prospect

SHE: For the last time, do you love me or don't you?
HE: I DON'T!
SHE: Quit stalling, I want a *direct* answer.

Jane Russell and Fred Astaire, 'carrying on the conversation'[1]

So: the main target of the present chapter is Richard Rorty, since the publication of *Philosophy and the Mirror of Nature*[2] probably the most influential critic of the epistemological enterprise in contemporary English-speaking philosophy. The secondary target is Stich, who has of late shifted his allegiance from the scientistic to the 'pragmatist' camp.

There are significant differences between Rorty's and Stich's arguments, and in the conclusions they reach. But they have in common at least this: both repudiate the idea that criteria of justification should be judged by their truth-indicativeness. Rorty thinks the idea makes no sense; Stich, that it is narrow-minded and parochial.

Referring to Rorty and Stich as 'vulgar pragmatists' is intended as an implicit challenge to their claim to be the philosophical descendants of the classical pragmatists, a challenge that will be made explicit in the closing paragraphs of this chapter. But the main goals here are epistemological rather than historical. The major theme is that neither Rorty nor Stich has any good arguments that the familiar epistemological projects are misconceived. A secondary theme will be that both Rorty and Stich fail to grasp that to believe that p is to accept p as true; with the result that the 'edifying' philosophy into which Rorty wants the exepistemologist to put his energies masks a cynicism which would undermine not only epistemology, not only 'systematic' philosophy, but inquiry generally; and that the liberated post-analytic epistemology which Stich envisages turns out to consist in a search for more efficient techniques of self-deception. As my title says: not an edifying prospect.

Still, the hope is, by revealing the poverty of the revolutionaries' post-epistemological utopias I can begin to articulate why, in my view, epistemology is indispensable – and to sketch some of the contours of the problem of ratification, of the relation of justification and truth.

I

Rorty wants, he says, to replace *confrontation* with *conversation*. This sounds like a plea to stop the bombing and get around the conference table. But it means something more like: we should abandon the conception of philosophy as centred in epistemology, as seeking 'foundations' for knowledge in 'privileged representations', and accept that there is nothing more to the justification of beliefs than local and parochial convention, our practices of objection, response, concession. This bears on its face the characteristic stamp of Rorty's This-or-Nothingism: *either* we accept this particular composite, a certain conception of the role of philosophy within culture, of the role of epistemology within philosophy, of the role of 'foundations' within the structure of knowledge, this 'neo-Kantian consensus', *or* we jettison the whole lot and take 'carrying on the conversation' as our highest aspiration.

According to Rorty, the idea that there is such a discipline as epistemology, as a distinctively philosophical theory of knowledge which is to inquire into the foundations of science, and *a fortiori* the idea of philosophy as centred in epistemology, is quite a recent one. It could arise only in the context of a perceived distinction between science and philosophy, an idea implicit in the work of Descartes and Hobbes, which came to seem obvious only since Kant. Locke, learning from Descartes to look inward, conceived of the theory of knowledge as the science of the mind; then Kant's Copernican revolution made this 'science of the mind' distinctively philosophical by raising it to the a priori level (pp. 131–64).

The philosophical theory of knowledge has developed, furthermore, under the influence of a variety of perceptual or ocular metaphors, an analogy of knowing with seeing, which encourages a confusion of knowledge that p with knowledge of x, of justification with causation, and of which the idea of 'foundations' of knowledge is a product. This conception of epistemology and its role in philosophy, and this set of metaphors, are 'optional' (pp. 146, 159, 162–3).

That this 'foundationalism' is fundamentally misconceived has been revealed, Rorty argues, as the epistemological tradition has worked itself out in analytic philosophy, by the combination of Quine's and Sellars' critical arguments. Between them, Sellars' critique of the notion of the given, and Quine's of the notion of the analytic (and hence, by implication, of the a priori) combine to undermine the whole conception of epistemology as foundational. Sellars' critique unmasks the confusion of justification with causation; Quine's reveals the hopelessness of seeking foundations of an a priori character (pp. 169ff.).

Neither Quine nor Sellars, Rorty thinks, fully appreciates the revolutionary impact of their combined work, but he is convinced that it makes the conclusion inescapable that justification is nothing more than a matter of social practice. To say that A knows that p is to say 'something about the way human beings interact' (p. 175). For a belief to be justified is for it to be defensible against 'conversational objections'. '[W]e understand knowledge when we understand the social justification of belief', Rorty writes, 'and thus have no need to view it as accuracy of representation' (p. 170).

The last clause is an indication of just how radical Rorty's position is. The differing criteria of different times or cultures or communities, he holds, are 'incommensurable'; no agreement can be expected about which standards of defending beliefs are correct. And neither does it make sense to seek to ratify these or those criteria of justification by arguing that beliefs which satisfy them are likely to be true; for this requires the idea of truth as correspondence, as faithful picturing – another legacy of the ocular metaphor, and covertly unintelligible. Justification is not only a social, but also an entirely conventional, matter: it makes no sense to suppose that our practices of criticizing and defending beliefs could be grounded in anything external to those practices (p. 178).

Rorty urges (not, like the scientistic revolutionaries discussed in chapter 8, the replacement of epistemology by some natural-scientific successor-subject, but) the repudiation of the idea that the abandonment of epistemology leaves any gap that needs to be filled. Still, he thinks there remains a role for the ex-epistemologist; but it is to be 'hermeneutic' rather than epistemological, 'edifying' rather than systematic, rather poetic than philosophical in the traditional sense, a matter of 'carrying on the conversation', of seeking new vocabularies instead of persisting in a hopeless attempt to commensurate incommensurable discourses (pp. 315ff.).

Well, no, certainly one wouldn't want to waste one's time doing *that*! But while pondering the futility of trying to commensurate incommensurable discourses may have convinced some to abandon epistemology, it leads me to suspect that the tautological is being transmuted into the tendentious: e.g., that we judge by the standards by which we judge, into, it makes no sense to ask what the basis of our standards might be; or: that we can't describe anything except in language, into, there is nothing outside language for our descriptions to represent accurately or inaccurately.

But I digress. The question at issue is: does Rorty have any arguments that establish that it makes no sense to suppose that criteria of justification need, or could have, objective grounding?

Fortunately, it is not necessary to engage in detailed discussion of Rorty's claims about the history of epistemology. (This *is* fortunate, because there are significant difficulties in determining just what Rorty's historical story is. Is the enterprise he repudiates supposed to have begun with Descartes? with Locke? with Kant? Does he gloss over the relevance to Descartes' project of the then recently-discovered writings of the ancient sceptics because to acknowledge its importance might lead us to perceive the disputed conception as much older, much less 'recent', than he would have us suppose? And so on.) The point on which I want to insist is simple: it is of course true that what we now perceive to be the problems and projects of epistemology have evolved during a long and complicated historical process, a process involving multi-layered and overlapping shifts and refinements in the ways problems were conceptualized and tackled; but this has not the slightest tendency to show that 'epistemology' is just a term for a bunch of pseudo-problems. It is, surely, a fact familiar from the history of the sciences as well as from the history of philosophy that reformulating, refining and refocusing problems is one way of making progress. I would go so far as to say that a discipline in which problems had ceased to evolve *would* be dead.

Nor is it necessary to engage in detailed consideration of Rorty's claims about the influence of ocular metaphors. (This is doubly fortunate, because there are significant difficulties here, both in reconciling Rorty's stress on the importance of a style of metaphor which was at least as predominant in Plato as in Descartes or Locke or Kant with his claim that the disputed conception of the philosophical theory of knowledge is recent, and in reconciling it with the resolutely non-cognitivist theory of metaphor he elsewhere defends.) For, once again, the point on which I want to insist is simple. I don't deny the epistemological importance of metaphors – how could I, given my concern to replace the model of the mathematical proof by an analogy with a crossword puzzle as better representing the structure of justification? But it has yet to be shown that ocular metaphors have led to a preoccupation with problems which, cleared of their metaphorical accretions, would be seen to be misconceived.[3]

The arguments considered thus far amount to little more than an inference from 'optional' to 'misconceived', obviously a non sequitur.

The focus must be on Rorty's arguments that 'foundationalism' is not just optional, but misconceived. It is impossible to assess these arguments, however, without disambiguating 'foundationalism' and 'epistemology as foundational'. Sometimes Rorty uses these expressions to refer to experientialist versions of the style of theory of justification characterized as 'foundationalist' in chapter 1; sometimes to refer to the idea that epistemology is an a priori enterprise the goal of which is to legitimize the claim of science (i.e., *science*) to give us knowledge; sometimes to what might less confusingly be called 'epistemic objectivism', the thesis that criteria of justification require objective grounding. The required distinctions may be marked as follows:

> (experientialist) foundationalism: theory of justification distinguishing basic beliefs, held to be justified, independently of the support of any other beliefs, by experience, and derived beliefs, held to be justified by the support of basic beliefs [i.e., which postulates basic beliefs justified by experience as the foundations of knowledge];
>
> *foundationalism*: conception of epistemology as an a priori discipline – of the explication of criteria of justification as an analytic enterprise, of their ratification as requiring a priori proof of their truth-indicativeness [i.e., which regards a priori epistemology as founding *science*];
>
> FOUNDATIONALISM: thesis that criteria of justification are not purely conventional but stand in need of objective grounding, being satisfactory only if truth-indicative [i.e., which takes criteria of justification to be founded by their relation to truth].

FOUNDATIONALISM does not imply *foundationalism*, nor *foundationalism* foundationalism. It could be that though criteria of justification stand in need of ratification (as FOUNDATIONALISM holds), ratification is not to be achieved a priori (as *foundationalism* holds) but within, or with the help of, empirical knowledge. Or it could be that the way to ratify criteria of justification is (as *foundationalism* holds) a priori, but that the correct criteria are not foundationalist, but coherentist or foundherentist.

The allegation of a confusion of justification with causation, like the appeal to Sellars' critique of the given, is relevant to foundationalism;

the appeal to Quine's critique of analyticity, to *foundationalism*; and only Rorty's remarks about the unintelligibility of truth-as-mirroring to FOUNDATIONALISM. So I shall comment only briefly on the first two lines of argument, since clearly it is on FOUNDATIONALISM, not *foundationalism* or foundationalism, that the legitimacy of epistemology depends.

Sellars' critique of the idea of the given does damage the experientialist foundationalist style of theory of justification – though strong more than weak versions.[4] And Rorty is right, experientialist foundationalism is not defensible, even in its weaker forms. The allegation of a confusion of justification with causation, however, can be answered – indeed, has been answered in my account (chapter 4) of the interaction of the causal and the evaluative aspects of justification. This is important because, like experientialist foundationalism, foundherentism insists on the relevance of the subject's experience to the justification of his empirical beliefs, and thus acknowledges a causal element.

This last observation throws another point into sharp relief: that experientialist foundationalism fails is quite insufficient to oblige one to accept anything like Rorty's conversationalist alternative. One might, like Davidson (who agrees with Rorty that experientialist foundationalism rests on a confusion of justification with causation) opt for some form of coherentism; or, like myself (disagreeing with Rorty and Davidson on this issue) for foundherentism.

Rorty is right, also, in thinking that *foundationalism* is not defensible. But the appeal to Quine's critique of analyticity is neither necessary nor sufficient to establish this.[5] Not sufficient: because even if there are no analytic truths it follows that there is no a priori knowledge only on the assumption that only analytic truths can be known a priori; more importantly, not necessary: because, given that the ratification of criteria of empirical justification will require synthetic assumptions (assumptions about human cognitive capacities), that *foundationalism* is false would follow from the repudiation of the synthetic a priori alone.

Rorty is also rightly critical of Quine's attempt to turn epistemology into psychology. Given the significance he attaches to the fact that the distinction between science and philosophy is relatively recent, it seems likely that he has in mind some such further argument as this: once the idea is abandoned that philosophy deals with the sphere of the a priori, science with the a posteriori, the idea of a distinctively philosophical theory of knowledge is seen to be untenable. But if this is what he is thinking, it misses a significant subtlety, one on which I have been insisting since chapter 6, and have marked by the *science*/SCIENCE distinction: giving up the idea that philosophy is distinguished by its a priori character encourages a picture of philosophy as continuous with *science*, as part of SCIENCE; but this does not oblige one to deny that there is a difference of degree between *science* and philosophy. So it by no means follows that all legitimate questions about knowledge must be answerable by *science*; nor, therefore, that (as Rorty may be thinking) any question about knowledge not answerable by *science* is not legitimate.

So the whole weight of Rorty's case against epistemology, to repeat, rests on the repudiation of FOUNDATIONALISM, which depends on considerations about truth. And here one finds less argument than assertion. (Also a rather neat piece of strategy: though section 5 of chapter VI of *Philosophy and the Mirror of Nature* is entitled 'Truth Without Mirrors', and section 6 'Truth, Goodness and Relativism', *there is no entry under 'truth' in the index*! Rorty is, I take it, letting us know the importance he attaches to the concept.)

A key passage is this one, from one of the sections with unlisted telephone numbers:

> [T]here are . . . two senses apiece of 'true' and 'real' and 'correct representation of reality,' and . . . most of the perplexities in epistemology come from vacillation between them . . . [C]onsider the homely use of 'true' to mean 'what you can defend against all comers' . . . It is [this] homely and shopworn sense of 'true' which Tarski and Davidson are attending to . . . The skeptic and Putnam . . . switch to the specifically 'philosophical' sense of . . . 'true' which, like the Ideas of Pure Reason, [is] designed precisely to stand for the Unconditioned . . . (p. 308)

This is (especially coming from a philosopher who likes to align himself with Dewey) a stunningly untenable dualism. We seem to be offered a choice between identifying truth with what is defensible against conversational objections, and taking it to be – well, something else, something not specified but hinted at in the allusion to Kant and to Putnam's distinction of metaphysical *versus* internal realism; something, anyway, rather pretentious, something aspired to despite, or even because of, its inaccessibility.

To deal with this false dichotomy, I need, first, a more discriminating and less confusing classification of concepts of truth. At the strongly irrealist end, there is (i) Rorty's proposed identification of 'true' with 'what you can defend against all comers'. Between this irrealist conception and anything that would appropriately be called 'realist' is (ii) Peirce's conception of truth as the hypothetical ideal theory, the 'ultimate opinion' that would survive all experiential evidence and full logical scrutiny. If realism with respect to truth is taken, as seems appropriate here, as requiring a conception which is non-epistemic, i.e., which allows that even a hypothetical ideal theory might be false or incomplete, then the realist category would include (iii) Ramsey's redundancy theory, according to which 'it is true that p' is just an elaborate way of saying that p; (iv) Tarski's semantic theory, which makes truth a relation between closed formulae and infinite sequences of objects; (v) Wittgenstein's and Russell's Logical Atomist correspondence theories, which make truth a structural isomorphism of proposition to fact, and Austin's correspondence theory, which makes truth a relation of conventions linking statements to states of affairs; and (vi) a conception of truth as copying or mirroring Things-in-Themselves. I will sometimes refer to (i) as 'irrealist'; (ii) as 'pragmatist'; (iii) and (iv) as 'minimally realist'; (v) as 'strongly realist'; and (vi) as 'grandly transcendental'.

Simple as it is, this classification enables us to struggle free of the wool Rorty is trying to pull over our eyes. Rorty hopes we will choose his first option as obviously more palatable than his second. But, to repeat, the dichotomy is false – grossly false, in fact. It is not just that we are being manoeuvred into a choice between extremes (the irrealist versus the grandly transcendental), but also that the manoeuvring consists in part of tendentious reclassification of the intermediate positions. We can, and most certainly should, decline to choose either of the options Rorty offers us. It cannot be said too plainly that there is *no* sense of 'true', homely or otherwise, in which it means 'what you can defend against all comers'; neither does Tarski, or Davidson,[6] think there is. Declining the irrealist option does not oblige us to go grandly transcendental. We may opt, instead, for a Peircean pragmatism, for a minimal or for a stronger realism.

Nor should we allow Rorty's grossly false dichotomy to disguise the fact that he is relying on our being repelled by the grandly transcendental instead of supplying arguments against pragmatist (for reasons to be explained below, I am strongly disinclined to give Rorty the word), or minimally realist, or strongly realist conceptions of truth. Indeed, he hasn't really any *arguments* even against the grandly transcendental.

The present goal, remember, is to show that Rorty has no good arguments against the legitimacy of epistemology. Since only his repudiation of FOUNDATIONALISM is relevant to the legitimacy of epistemology, the issue is whether he has any good arguments against FOUNDATIONALISM. And since his repudiation of FOUNDATIONALISM depends on his views about truth, I conclude that, since he has no arguments against pragmatist, minimally realist, strongly realist, or even grandly transcendental views of truth, he has, *a fortiori*, no good arguments against them, nor, therefore, against FOUNDATIONALISM, nor, therefore, against epistemology.

This is not, of itself, sufficient to establish the legitimacy of epistemology. But I think that a closer look at the post-epistemological future Rorty envisages, and the conception of justification that motivates it, will begin to make it apparent that abandoning epistemology is not an appealing prospect.

Rorty's conversationalist conception of justification takes justifying a belief to be a matter of social practice or convention, variable both within and between cultures, and nothing more. A natural interpretation, and one which comports with Rorty's frequent admiring references to the later Wittgenstein, would take conversationalism as a conjunction of two theses: contextualism at the level of explication, conventionalism at the level of ratification.

Contextualism is a style of theory of justification; it contrasts with foundationalism, coherentism, foundherentism. Its characteristic thesis is that 'A is justified in believing that p' is to be analysed along the lines of 'with respect to the belief that p, A satisfies the epistemic standards of the epistemic community to which A belongs'.

Conventionalism is a meta-epistemological thesis, a thesis about criteria of justification; it contrasts with epistemic objectivism, i.e., FOUNDATIONALISM. Its characteristic thesis is that epistemic standards are entirely conventional, that it makes no sense to ask which criteria of justification (those of this or that epistemic community) are correct, which are really indicative of the likely truth of a belief.

Though contextualists sometimes make observations about the structure of justification which have a vaguely foundationalist air ('contextually basic beliefs are those which stand in no need of justification within the epistemic community; all other justified beliefs are justified by reference to these contextually basic beliefs') contextualism is distinct from foundationalism, for (i) it insists on the addendum 'in the epistemic community to which A belongs', and (ii) it does not posit beliefs justified otherwise than by the support of further beliefs. And though contextualists maintain, as coherentists do, that justification is a matter of relations among beliefs, contextualism is distinct from coherentism too, for (i) it insists on the addendum 'in the epistemic community to which A belongs', and (ii) it does not make relations of coherence sufficient for justification.

So contextualism has sometimes been welcomed as a third alternative to the traditionally rival theories – and some readers may have been wondering why I didn't consider it more carefully before proposing *my* 'third alternative'. The reason can now be made clear. Contextualism may appear a harmless, even attractive, option with respect to the problem of explication, but it leads to a radical, indeed revolutionary, attitude to the project of ratification – to conventionalism, the second element in Rorty's conversationalism.

Contextualism is pointless unless (a) different epistemic communities have different epistemic standards and (b) there is no distinguished epistemic community, C*, such that the standards of C* are, while those of other communities are not, truth-indicative. For if (a) were false the characteristic contextualist thesis would be vacuous; and if (b) were false the status of the epistemic standards of C* would be so distinguished relative to the standards of other communities as to oblige one to concede that for A to be *really and truly* justified, he should meet the standards of C*. Rorty is a little coy about what exactly the 'incommensurability' to which he appeals amounts to (though he is quite concerned to distinguish it from the meaning-variance thesis with which, in Kuhn's work, it is associated); but the likeliest interpretation seems to be: that there is no higher court of appeal in which agreement could be reached among the different epistemic standards of different communities – i.e., that it is an amalgam of theses (a) and (b).

Since contextualism contrasts with foundationalism (as well as coherentism and foundherentism) and conventionalism with FOUNDATIONALISM, this makes it even less surprising that Rorty, *qua* conversationalist, should fail to distinguish foundationalism and FOUNDATIONALISM. But doesn't it suggest that Rorty has a reply to one of the arguments used earlier, that a refutation of foundationalism is irrelevant to the standing of FOUNDATIONALISM? No: because, although contextualism indeed provides strong motivation for conventionalism, the falsity of foundationalism does not provide strong motivation for contextualism; the options of coherentism and foundherentism remain.

Rorty perhaps fails to appreciate this because (naturally enough, he does not consider the foundherentist option, and) he shows the occasional tendency to describe his position as 'coherentist' (p. 178). But he does that for no better reason than that his position is opposed to 'foundationalism' – thus compounding his indiscriminate use of 'foundationalism' with a correspondingly undiscriminating use of 'coherentism'.

Conversationalism, on the present interpretation (= contextualism + conventionalism), is quite a tightly-knit conception, since contextualism, as we saw, provides strong motivation for conventionalism. It is, however, both relativist and cynical.

It is relativist, because contextualism makes justification depend on the epistemic community to which the subject belongs, and, since conventionalism precludes the possibility of any higher-minded conception of really-truth-indicative justification* (justification by the standards of C*), it must treat the epistemic standards of any and every epistemic community as on a par.

And it is cynical, because if one really believed that criteria of justification are purely conventional, wholly without objective grounding, then, though one might conform to the justificatory practices of one's own epistemic community, one would be obliged to adopt an attitude of cynicism towards them, to think of justification always in covert scare quotes. The problem is not that, in general, one cannot engage in a practice one regards as wholly conventional. It is that, in particular, one cannot coherently engage fully – non-cynically – in a practice *of justifying beliefs* that one regards as wholly conventional. For *to believe that p is to accept p as true*. (This, to repeat a point from the argument of chapter 8, is not a sophisticated remark about truth but a truism about belief.) And, since to believe that p is to accept p as true, for one who denies that it even makes sense to suppose that there is any connection between a belief's being justified according to our practices, and its being true, it is impossible to see why a belief's being justified, conforming to those practices, should be thought to have any bearing on whether one should hold it.

From time to time, however, Rorty protests against the accusations – which, you will gather, I am not the first to make – that he is 'relativist' or 'cynical'. His defensive remarks have more than a little of the flavour of Berkeley's protests that he is not denying the reality of physical objects. ('I'm not a relativist, I believe in objectivity – you just have to realize that objectivity is a matter of social agreement, not correspondence to some supposed "reality"'). But the real reason he thinks the accusation of relativism can be brushed off is to be found elsewhere. Even in the *Mirror*, there is evidence against, as well as evidence for, the interpretation of Rorty's conversationalism as combining conventionalism with contextualism. Sometimes, at least, Rorty sounds less contextualist than, as I shall say, tribalist; for example, 'The Quine-Sellars approach [i.e., the Rorty approach] to epistemology . . . say[s] that truth and knowledge can only be judged by the standards of inquirers of our own day' (p. 178). This suggests not contextualism but tribalism: 'A is justified in believing that p iff A satisfies the criteria of *our* epistemic community'. And by the time of *Objectivity, Relativism and Truth* (1991) Rorty's commitment to tribalism ('solidarity'), rather than relativism, seems clear.

This enables Rorty to answer the criticism that he is relativist, but it does not get him off the hook; on the contrary, it reveals just how deep his difficulties are. Tribalism is entirely arbitrary and unmotivated unless one thinks that the criteria of one's own epistemic community are better than those of other communities; that is, it pulls *against* conventionalism, to which, however, Rorty is unambiguously committed. Hence conversationalism is either (first interpretation, = contextualism + conventionalism) both relativist and cynical, or (second interpretation, = tribalism + conventionalism), no longer relativist, but still cynical, and incoherent to boot.

This begins to explain why Rorty's own *modus operandi* seems so odd, and why his accounts of the post-epistemological philosophy he envisages are so puzzling.

We have ('as a matter of social practice', Rorty would say) criteria for what counts as good reasons, as flimsy evidence, as jumping to conclusions, and so forth. And Rorty apparently aspires to conform to those criteria when he tries to persuade us that those criteria are wholly without objective grounding, entirely conventional. If he really believes that those criteria are entirely conventional, however, he can't be fully engaged in this enterprise; he must, rather, be abiding by those standards only as a ploy to persuade others less enlightened than himself by playing the game by their rules. He must be a cynic.

In the introduction to *Philosophy and the Mirror of Nature*, no doubt as a pre-emptive strike against the charge of cynicism, Rorty tells the reader that he will be not so much arguing against more traditional conceptions as suggesting an alternative vision of what philosophy might better be. But in fact much of the body of the book is taken up with arguments against 'foundationalism' (though, as I have said, it is hard to find arguments, as opposed to rhetoric, against FOUNDATIONALISM). By the time of *Contingency, Irony and Solidarity*, Rorty has a different defensive strategy: he describes those who, like himself, have grasped the 'contingency' of language, the conventionality of justification, as 'ironists'. Ironists, he tells us, use the 'final vocabulary' they find themselves with, but, realizing there are no objective grounds for choice between vocabularies, are 'never quite able to take themselves seriously'.[7] I shall not pause to protest the skilful insinuation that we non-ironists are humourless prigs;[8] nor to press the point that acknowledgment of the possibility and the importance of linguistic innovation is most certainly not the exclusive privilege of Rorty's ironists. The important point for now is to see that this re-description does not mitigate, though it does quite cleverly disguise, the cynicism on which I have been dwelling. The cleverness lies in suggesting that the ironist is simply more aware than the rest of us of the possibility that our criteria of justification may turn out to be in need of revision, and hence is less dogmatically committed to them. But this suggestion is thoroughly misleading; Rorty's ironist is no fallibilist, he is a cynic hiding behind a euphemism. He engages in 'our' practices of justifying beliefs only at arms' length not because he thinks they might need revising, but because he thinks it makes no sense to ask whether they are or aren't really indicative of truth.

This reinforces the diagnosis suggested earlier, that construed – as Rorty's earlier work allows, and his later work encourages us to construe it – as combining conventionalism and tribalism, Rorty's conversationalism is incoherent. Tribalism requires 'solidarity' with 'our epistemic practices'; 'irony' reveals that Rorty's supposed solidarity is no more than *pro forma*, cynical conformity with those practices.

It also reinforces the impression one gets from the *Mirror*, that Rorty's conception of the tasks to which the newly enlightened ex-epistemologist is to turn his energies is less edifying than baffling. (One is entitled to wonder, in any case, why, if the problems of epistemology really are misconceived, one should expect there to *be* any work conveniently awaiting the ex-epistemologist.) The edifying philosopher, one is told, will compare and contrast the incommensurable discourses which, as epistemologist, he confusedly hoped to commensurate (p. 343); what does this mean, one asks oneself, if not that he is to turn sociologist of knowledge? One is told that he will study 'abnormal' discourse (p. 320); what could an abnormal discourse be, one asks oneself? If an attempted conversation between participants from incommensurable discourses, what more illuminating conclusion could the ex-epistemologist hope to reach than that there is irresoluble disagreement? And one is told that he will 'carry on the conversation' of Western culture (pp. 377–8); but what, one asks oneself, if the various discourses which constitute Western culture really are incommensurable, could this be but participation in what he already knows must inevitably be mutual incomprehension?

There could be no honest intellectual work in Rorty's post-epistemological utopia. Unless there is such a thing as better and worse evidence for accepting this or that proposition as true – objectively better or worse evidence, that is – there can be no real inquiry of any kind: epistemological . . . or scientific, forensic, historical, mathematical. Since not even Rorty himself accepts this conclusion, and since his argument for abandoning epistemology rests, at bottom, on nothing more than a manifestly false dichotomy of extreme realism versus extreme irrealism about truth, the legitimacy of epistemology seems pretty secure.

II

Or *seemed* pretty secure; but now, with *The Fragmentation of Reason*,[9] we have Stich's new critique to deal with.

Stich doesn't deny that it makes sense to ask whether these or those epistemic standards are truth-indicative, he only insists that it is parochial and narrow-minded, a kind of 'epistemic chauvinism', to *care* whether one's beliefs are true; and he doesn't want to abandon epistemology altogether, but to revolutionize it, to shift its focus away from these narrow-minded concerns and onto the really important questions: how to improve cognitive processing so as better to achieve the things people really value – such as survival, fame, fortune, power, etc., etc. Stich is also unlike Rorty in welcoming, rather than resisting, the description 'relativist'. (But in the shifting kaleidoscope of Rorty's contribution to the conversation one finds this description of 'the tradition in Western culture' from which he would have us turn away: '[t]he idea of Truth as something to be pursued for its own sake, not because it will be good for oneself, or for one's real or imaginary community . . .'.[10] The sentiment, though not the prose, could be Stich's.)

To avoid any confusion, it should be said that now Stich admits that people do, after all, have beliefs. It should also be said that he now conceives of beliefs along the lines of 'sentences in the head' (pp. 109ff.). This may be partly responsible for some of the difficulties I shall diagnose. At any rate, someone who thinks it illuminating to imagine the subject's head equipped with two boxes of sentences, one labelled 'beliefs' and the other 'desires',[11] runs the risk of failing to notice that *assent, acknowledgement of truth*, is part of the concept of belief.

It should also be noted that Stich's critique is informed by certain preconceptions about what epistemology does, specifically, by Goldman's conception of theories of justification as giving criteria of rightness for systems of rules of belief-formation, and his framework of deontological versus consequentialist theories, and, within the consequentialist category, of reliabilist versus explanationist versus pragmatist accounts. This too may be partly responsible for some of the difficulties I shall diagnose. At any rate, someone focused exclusively on processes of belief-formation runs some risk of losing sight of the connection of justification and evidence, and someone assuming that justification must be tied to truth either as directly as reliabilism ties it or not at all runs the risk of choosing the latter option for no better reason than the implausibility of the former.

Stich presents himself as arguing against 'analytic epistemology', by which he means 'any epistemological project that takes the choice between competing justificational rules or competing criteria of right-ness [note the use of Goldman's terminology] to turn on conceptual or linguistic analysis' (p. 91). This Stich describes as parochial, chauvinis-tic: epistemic standards, he argues, are culturally acquired and vary from culture to culture, and so do the evaluative epistemic concepts embedded in everyday thought and language. And '[u]nless one is inclined towards chauvinism or xenophobia in matters epistemic, it is hard to see why one would care much that a cognitive process . . . accords with the set of evaluative notions that prevail in the society into which one happened to be born' (p. 94). Unlike Rorty, Stich is rather repelled than attracted by tribalism.

But what if it could be shown that satisfaction of these or those epistemic criteria is an indication that one's belief is true? This, according to Stich, is still parochial; it assumes that having true beliefs is some-thing to be valued. And this, he maintains, is 'for most people . . . very dubious indeed' (p. 98). In fact, according to Stich truth is neither an intrinsically nor an instrumentally valuable property for a belief to have.

A belief, according to the 1990 time-slice of Stich, is a brain state mapped by an interpretation function onto a proposition which has a truth-value, and which is true just in case the proposition onto which it is mapped is true. Stich proposes a 'causal/functional account of our commonsense interpretation function', i.e., of the function mapping brain states on to propositions. He then points out that there are many possible alternatives to this function. The 'standard' function, Stich continues, maps the belief he would express by 'There is no water on the sun' onto the proposition that there is no H_2O on the sun, but an alternative function might map it onto the proposition that there is no H_2O or XYZ on the sun. He describes the standard function and the possible alternatives as generating different notions of reference (ref-erence, REFERENCE*, REFERENCE** . . . etc., and truth (truth, TRUTH*, TRUTH** . . . etc.). Truth, he concludes, is just one among many possible truth-like values a belief might have (pp. 110ff.).

Once one grasps this, Stich thinks, one will come to doubt that truth is intrinsically valuable, realizing that valuing truth for its own sake is 'a profoundly conservative thing to do' (p. 118).

And, he continues, one will also realize that it is no less questionable whether truth is instrumentally valuable. Consider, for example, poor Harry: he believed that his flight left at 7.45 a.m., and this belief was true; unfortunately, the plane crashed, and Harry died. An alternative interpretation function would map the belief Harry would express by 'my flight leaves at 7.45 a.m.' onto the proposition that Harry's flight leaves at 8.45 a.m., and so make Harry's belief TRUE**** (though not, of course, true). Harry would have been better off with this TRUE**** belief than the true one he had. And this kind of argument, Stich continues, generalizes to lots of other goals that people take to be valuable. So '[t]rue beliefs are not always optimal in the pursuit of happiness or pleasure or desire satisfaction . . . [or] peace or power or love'. Hence, 'the instrumental value of true beliefs is far from obvious' (pp. 123, 124).

Urging, therefore, that we break out of the old, parochial, conservative, truth-oriented mould, Stich offers a 'pragmatic' account of cognitive evaluation. Cognitive processes are to be evaluated as tools for achieving whatever it is that the subject actually values. The formula would presumably be something like: P is a good cognitive process, for A, iff P produces beliefs which conduce to whatever A values. This account is, as Stich notes, both relativistic and pluralistic: 'in general it will not make sense to ask whether one system is better than another (full stop) . . . [I]t may well turn out that one system is best for one person or group, while another system is better for another person or group' (pp. 135–6).

It is open to question whether, in the relevant sense, epistemic standards really are local, parochial, culturally variable. Yes, there are scientific and pre-scientific cultures, there are cultures where the authority of a sacred text is respected and cultures where it is not; and yes, there may be, even within one culture, a great variety of *theories* of evidence or justification professed. But I am not sure that there is, or has been, a culture in which the fit of a proposition into an explanatory net of propositions anchored in sense and introspection (that is, explanatory integration and experiential anchoring) is not grounds for thinking it true. And I notice that the evidence Stich offers of cultural diversity is astonishingly thin: he refers to *one* piece of work, which he reports as claiming – contrary to the usual English–Yoruba translations – that Yoruba does not distinguish knowledge and true belief as we do, but the first- from the second-hand.[12] Interesting as it is, if true, that Yoruba speakers are equipped with something like Russell's 1912 distinction of knowledge versus probable opinion,[13] this is inconclusive, to put it mildly, with respect to the claim that our epistemic standards are simply idiosyncratic and parochial.

It would be unwise, however, to put much weight on this point here, because the relevance of cultural diversity to Stich's main thesis is marginal. For one thing, he is careful to hedge his bets, as: 'other languages and other cultures *certainly could and probably do* evoke conceptions of cognitive evaluation that are significantly different from our own' (p. 94, my italics). But, more important, that our epistemic standards are, or could be, culturally local, features as premiss only in a relatively minor, softening-up phase of Stich's argument. The main phase acknowledges the possibility that our standards (local or not) might be demonstrably truth-indicative, and maintains that, *even so*, a preference for those standards would be 'chauvinistic', depending on a 'profoundly conservative' preference for truth over TRUTH*, TRUTH**, TRUTH*** . . . etc.

One can see why Stich thought the reader might need to be softened up before the main phase of the argument, though, because what he offers next is remarkably feeble. What he would need to do is to show that truth is valuable only if either intrinsically or instrumentally valuable, and that it is neither; what he offers is little more than mere assertion that it is 'not obvious' that truth is either. Stich admits that his arguments are 'not knockdown' (p. 120). His strategy is dismayingly familiar from his earlier work: he hints that he has arguments for a startling thesis, offers considerations which go nowhere near establishing it, disarms the reader by conceding that his arguments are inconclusive, and then, urging that it is *possible* that his startling thesis is true, thrusts the burden of proof on the opposition.

Just to keep the record straight: all Stich offers to persuade us that truth is not intrinsically valuable is the observation that truth is just one of a whole range of semantic properties a belief might have (truth, TRUTH*, TRUTH** . . . etc.), the one which happens to be picked out in our culture. Frankly, I have no idea even what it might mean to say that another culture picked out, say, TRUTH* instead of truth; and I would protest the suggestion that TRUTH*, TRUTH**, etc., are *truth*-values.[14] But in any case, that truth is one of a range of semantic properties of beliefs simply has no bearing on whether it is or isn't intrinsically valuable. And all that Stich offers to persuade us that truth is not instrumentally valuable is the observation that in some circumstances, Harry's for example, a true belief may lead to one's death while a TRUE**** belief would have saved one's life. This shows – what I don't deny – that an isolated true belief may not be *optimally* instrumentally valuable. But it simply has no bearing on whether truth is or isn't instrumentally valuable, period.

This establishes, I hope, that Stich has no good arguments why, because of their orientation to truth, the familiar epistemological projects are misconceived. It is tempting to leave it at that – by way of parting shot, perhaps, noting that what Stich purports to do is not to show that accepting his startling thesis would conduce to whatever the reader values, not to show that it is TRUE*, TRUE** . . . or whatever, but to give reasons for thinking it true. But, as so often, there is a better view from the steeper path; or maybe I should say, benefit to be gained from the exercise of shouldering, for a while, the burden of proof Stich thrusts at those of us who value truth.

The first part of my argument will be that truth is *epistemically* valuable, in this sense: that each of the concepts of inquiry, justification and belief is internally connected with the concept of truth.

I speak of inquiry, in the way characteristic of philosophers, in the most general sense: inquiry-into-how-things-are, so to speak. What is the goal of inquiry, thus broadly construed? Something like: to get as much interesting and important truth about the world as possible. But the suggestion of uniqueness is misleading, since 'the' goal decomposes into two elements: truth, on the one hand, and interest or importance on the other. Obviously there is potential for tension between the two components, since it is a lot easier to get truths if one doesn't mind the truths one gets being trivial. There are plenty of unimportant or uninteresting truths.

But truth is, though not *the* goal, *an aspect of the goal* of inquiry. If you aren't trying to find out how things are, to get truth, you aren't really inquiring. (There is, however, a lot of pseudo-inquiry about; that is why, when the government institutes an Official Inquiry into this or that, some of us reach for our scare quotes.)

Because inquiry has this double goal, appraisal of a person's success in inquiry has two dimensions, which might be roughly characterized as depth and security, the former being interest- and the latter truth-oriented. (Correspondingly, appraisal of a person *qua* inquirer has two dimensions, roughly characterizable as creativity and carefulness.)

When one focuses on questions of justification, however, one is *ipso facto* restricting oneself to the second of the two dimensions. Truth-indicativeness is *the* characteristic virtue of criteria of justification. (Goldman is quite right to insist on a connection of justification and truth – the very point on which Stich parts company with him; where he goes wrong is in making the connection too direct, attributive instead of referential.)

And to believe that p is to accept p as true.

That truth is epistemically valuable is entirely compatible with the fact that in some circumstances one may be better off not inquiring, or better off having an unjustified belief, or better off having a false belief; and with the fact that some truths are trivial, boring, or unimportant.

Stich would no doubt regard all this as no more than a quaint elaboration of my 'profound conservatism'. 'So', he might say, 'the concepts on which epistemology has traditionally focused are internally connected to the concept of truth – but why, except for a culturally-inherited bias towards truth-orientation, should we be interested in *them*?'

Part of the answer is that truth *is* instrumentally valuable. Knowledge of how things are enables us to bring about desired ends and to avoid undesired ones. Not always, of course; but when (as in Harry's case) a true belief serves us worse than a false belief would have done, more complete true beliefs could have served us better (if Harry had believed, truly, that his plane was due to leave at 7.45, and that it would crash, he could have saved not only his own life, but others' too).

The other part is harder to articulate. The best way I can put it is this: beliefs are what we have – so, since the concepts of belief and truth are internally connected, it is no cultural bias to value truth. Compared with other animals, human beings are not especially fast or strong; what we do have is a capacity to figure things out. This capacity is very imperfect, and it isn't an unmixed blessing, but who could seriously doubt that it is of instrumental value to us? The present point, though, is that it is the fact that we are animals who have beliefs and act intentionally that makes the epistemic value of truth something much deeper than a cultural quirk.

That this is right is confirmed by reflection on what Stich's post-revolutionary epistemology would do. Its task, we are told, is improvement of our cognitive processing; the goal, beliefs, whether true or false, such that his accepting them as true would conduce to what the subject values. That it must be *beliefs* which are produced is clear from the case of Harry; what would leave him better off is his *accepting as true*, i.e., believing, a proposition which is not true but TRUE****. 'TRUE****' is of course a magnificently misleading piece of typographical sleight of hand, as is apparent when one translates the last clause into English: Harry would be better off believing a different proposition which is not true but his believing which conduces to something he values.

There would not be much honest intellectual work in Stich's post-revolutionary epistemology, either. The explicative task is trivial: 'good cognitive processing is processing which produces beliefs such that the subject's holding them conduces to what he values' is all there is to it. This lack of substance, by the way, is only to be expected; it is the mirror-image of the insubstantial character of Goldman's reliabilist explication. What of the regulative task, the 'improvement of our cognitive processing' that Stich aspires to undertake? The 'improvement', as we know, is to consist in our accepting as true, propositions, whether true or false, such that our believing them is advantageous. How is this to be achieved? If not by magic (though Stich's references to a helpful

Genie suggest he may be hoping for magical assistance),[15] how else than by *better techniques of self-deception*?

Since Stich might reply that this is just profoundly conservative moralizing, I had better say that, though self-deception is, by my lights, always an epistemic failing, it is not always or necessarily a moral failing. The moral qualms one rightly feels about the project of helping the fence to believe that the surprisingly cheap goods he buys are not, after all, stolen, his believing which conduces to something he values, namely, being on the right side of the law, do not extend to the project of helping the cancer victim to believe that he will recover, his believing which conduces to something he values, namely, surviving.

Stich might reply that this answers the charge of moralizing, but not the charge of profound conservatism. ('Why should I care that self-deception is an *epistemic* failing? – that's just a cultural quirk'.) Tempting as it is to reply that this reveals that Stich's post-revolutionary 'epistemology' would no longer be recognizably epistemology, it is more important to stress that it prompts, also, the realization that Stich's post-revolutionary epistemology, or 'epistemology', could not displace the more traditional projects.

Why not? Because any non-trivial specification of what would constitute 'cognitive improvement' (in Stich's peculiar sense) would require detailed knowledge of the circumstances in which true beliefs will conduce to what the subject values, and the circumstances in which false beliefs will do so. This 'detailed knowledge' would have to be just that, detailed *knowledge*; false beliefs that conduced to something Stich values wouldn't do. And so the familiar, truth-oriented epistemological questions would still arise.

It is a fine irony that this last point was made, nearly a century ago, by C. S. Peirce, the founder of pragmatism. The context is a review of Pearson's book, *The Grammar of Science*; Peirce is objecting to Pearson's thesis that the goal of science is to forward the interests of society:

> I must confess that I belong to that class of scallawags who purpose, with God's help, to look the truth in the face, whether doing so be conducive to the interests of society or not. Moreover, if I should ever tackle that excessively difficult problem, 'What is for the true interest of society?' I should feel that I stood in need of a great deal of help from the science of legitimate inference . . .[16]

So, having carried the epistemological burden thus far, I hope I may be permitted to put it down long enough to make some brief historical comments.

The passage just quoted is absolutely characteristic of Peirce, who insists on the importance of what he calls 'the scientific attitude', of 'a craving to know how things really [are]', 'a great desire to learn the truth'; and that the truth 'is SO . . . whether you, or I, or anybody thinks it is so or not'.[17] This could hardly be further removed from what Rorty or Stich calls 'pragmatism'.

Still, the philosophical tendencies known as 'pragmatism' are formidably diverse; and it would be foolish to deny that there are some elements in some pragmatist writers that might seem to suggest what I have called the 'vulgar pragmatisms' of Rorty and Stich. For example, in James's urging that philosophers pay more attention to concrete truths and curb their obsession with abstract Truth,[18] one might hear something akin to Rorty's impatience with anything supposedly grounding what is presently defensible. But this would be to forget that James maintains that the notion of concrete truth depends on the notion of abstract Truth, and could not stand alone. Again, in James's defence of the 'will to believe', of the propriety of believing without evidence if belief will enable one to live one's life better, one might hear something akin to Stich's identification of 'justified belief' with 'belief that conduces to what one values'. But this would be to forget that James also says, not only that this doctrine applies only to propositions, e.g., of a religious character, in principle incapable of settlement by evidence, but also that it is distinct from, and independent of, pragmatism.[19] It would also be to forget that, when he says that 'the true is only the good in the way of belief', James is stressing – exaggerating – the instrumental value of true beliefs. James used to complain about critics who put 'the silliest possible interpretation' on his words;[20] now, it seems, the 'friends' of pragmatism are doing the same.[21]

Which is why I have chosen some shrewd words of James's to open the next chapter and introduce my attempt at the problem of ratification.

10
Foundherentism Ratified

[W]hen . . . we give up the doctrine of objective certitude, we do not thereby give up the quest or hope of truth itself.

James *The Will to Believe*[1]

The goal of inquiry is substantial, significant, illuminating truth; the concept of justification is specifically focused on security, on the likelihood of beliefs being true. Hence my claim that truth-indicative is what criteria of justification need to be to be good.

The characteristic question of the project of ratification is: are these criteria of justification truth-indicative? The goal of this chapter is to offer what reassurance I can that the foundherentist criteria *are* truth-indicative.

The question: are our criteria of justification truth-indicative? is not the same question as: are our beliefs true or mostly true or largely true? Even if our criteria of justification *are* truth-indicative, to reach the conclusion that our beliefs are mostly true would require the further assumption that our beliefs are mostly justified. But people have many beliefs in which they are not justified, or are justified only to a very modest degree. Superstition, wishful thinking, self-deception, jumping to conclusions, and so forth, are not, after all, so rare.

The question: are our criteria of justification truth-indicative? is not the same question, either, as: are these processes of belief-formation truth-conducive? Criteria of evidence differ from rules for the conduct of inquiry rather as criteria for judging whether a meal is nutritious differ from directions for cooking or menu-planning. The difference is in part a matter of current-state-versus process-appraisal (a point familiar from chapter 7); but it is in part a matter, also, of the fact that concerns about justification are focused on one dimension, specifically, of the goal of inquiry (a point not articulated until chapter 9). This is not to suggest that the two kinds of epistemological project here distinguished are unrelated; after all, the role of the concept of explanatory integration in the explication of supportiveness is an indication that its explanatory power may contribute to the security of a belief. It is only to insist that, though related, they are distinct. But it is the distinctness of the two projects that needs emphasis here, because they have frequently been run together.

In part because of the potential tension between the two aspects of the goal of inquiry, it is doubtful whether it is possible to give *rules* – as opposed to *guidelines*, the application of which requires judgement or discretion – for conducting inquiry. This may explain why attempts to give such rules show a marked tendency to shift between the manifestly unacceptable and the obviously discretionary; e.g., between: make a conjecture, test it as severely as possible, and give it up as soon as any counter-instance is found, and: do not hang on to a theory too long, or make excessively baroque modifications to evade contrary evidence, but don't abandon a theory too easily in the face of difficulties (roughly, between a 'naive' and a 'sophisticated' falsificationist methodology). The 'conduct of inquiry' project is likely to be more resistant to precision than the 'criteria of justification' project, if, as I have suggested, the element of discretion may be ineliminable. It is likely, on the other hand, to be more hospitable to considerations concerning interactions among inquirers, both within and across generations.[2] And such concepts as epistemic character or epistemic virtue seem to have their natural home in the 'conduct of inquiry' project, since they focus on what it is to have the good judgement required by guidelines for going about inquiry; this in turn confirms, what I have thus far taken for granted, that hopes of explicating justification in terms of such concepts, or replacing it by such concepts, are unrealistic.[3] Most important for present purposes, perhaps, is that the 'conduct of inquiry' project is likely to be more hospitable to pluralism, for there may well be different, equally good, ways of proceeding in inquiry – indeed, it may well be that the best thing is for different inquirers to proceed differently; whereas pluralism with respect to criteria of justification, as I shall argue below, is not plausible. (The reflections of this paragraph are summarized in figure 10.1.)

The present task, the ratification of foundherentism, falls (as does this book as a whole) squarely within the 'criteria of justification' project.

Descartes's attempt to prove that what he clearly and distinctly perceives is true is a classic ratificatory effort. But my approach to the question of ratification will be far from Cartesian. It will not, for one

Goal of inquiry: substantial, significant truths

project of devising guidelines for the conduct of inquiry:	projects of explicating/ratifying criteria of justification:
– focused on both aspects of the goal and, because of potential for tension between its two aspects,	– truth-oriented, i.e. focused on security, likelihood, truth-indication; so *'truth-indicative is what criteria of justification have to be to be good'*

– focused on both aspects of the goal
and, because of potential for
tension between its two aspects,

    * more hospitable to pluralism
    * more recalcitrant to precision
    * guidelines, not rules
    * require discretion, good
      epistemic character
    * social dimension important

SH's focus

Figure 10.1

thing, aim at proof, or at any guarantee of truth, but only to give reasons for thinking that, if any truth-indication is possible for us, the foundherentist criteria are truth-indicative; reasons, furthermore, which are not conclusive, nor comprehensive, nor, since they depend on our theories about the world and ourselves, fully secure. And it will be naturalistic, in the sense articulated in chapters 5 and 6; it will depend in part on the defensibility of the presuppositions about human cognitive capacities built into our standards of evidence.

As the last sentence indicates, my view is that the truth-indicativeness of the foundherentist criteria rests in part on facts about human capacities. This comports with – though it does not absolutely require – the doubts expressed in chapter 9 about a fashionable style of cognitive pluralism, the thesis that different cultures or epistemic communities have widely divergent standards of evidence. So I begin with an articulation of what I mean by speaking of 'our' appraisals of evidence, 'our' standards of justification, and of my reasons for suspecting that the supposed divergence of such standards is at least exaggerated, perhaps illusory. One reason why pluralism with respect to standards of evidence has acquired an (as I believe) undeserved popularity may be confusion with pluralism with respect to procedures of inquiry. Another, I shall suggest, is confusion with a different, and more defensible, proposition about criteria of evidence, which I shall call 'perspectivalism'. My critique of pluralism with respect to criteria of justification will not only shed a little light, retrospectively, on the tribulations of contextualism and tribalism, but also, more to the point of the present chapter, will reinforce the ratificatory arguments proper, which begin in section II.

For if this kind of pluralism is, as I suspect, false, the ideas about human nature on which my ratificatory arguments will call are that much more secure.

I

In articulating the foundherentist theory of justification, I described myself as trying to make explicit what is implicit in our commonsense appraisals of evidence as good or bad, strong or flimsy. I was deliberately unforthcoming about who the 'we' of 'our commonsense appraisals' referred to, and I deliberately avoided that phrase so favoured by contextualists and tribalists, 'our epistemic practices'. Now I can be a bit more forthcoming.

It seems to have come to be taken pretty much for granted that the evidential standards of different times, cultures or communities are significantly different; and this makes it seem as if, by referring to 'our commonsense appraisals', I must be referring to the criteria of some specific group to which I belong. This is the background against which Stich can assume that 'analytic epistemologists' must be favouring the standards of their epistemic community because it is the community into which they happen to have been born. Stich tempts me to say something like: I don't accept these standards of justification because they are the standards of the community to which I happen to belong, I call them 'our' rather than 'their' standards because I accept them. But even that would grant too much; because, as I said in chapter 9, I am not convinced about this supposed diversity. It is at least an exaggeration, and perhaps altogether an illusion.

Suppose you and I are cramming for the Florida drivers' test. You think the penalty for driving under the influence is six months' loss of license, I think it is a year's. We look in the drivers' handbook and check. Or perhaps you look in yours and I look in mine, and they give different answers, so then we check whose is the later edition. Here we disagree about whether p, but agree about what would count as evidence for or against p. Now suppose you and I are both on an appointments committee. You believe that a certain candidate should be ruled out on the grounds that his handwriting indicates that he is not to be trusted; I think graphology is bunk and scoff at your 'evidence'. Perhaps you refer me to *Character as Indicated by Handwriting*;[4] I point out its reliance on a tiny number of cases, the lack of theoretical background, etc., etc. Here we disagree not only about whether p, but also, as we might say, about 'what counts as a reason' for doubting the candidate's honesty. But I don't think anyone would be much inclined to think that this kind of commonplace disagreement suggests that you and I have 'different standards of evidence' in any deep or interesting sense. We simply disagree about what evidence is relevant because we disagree in some background beliefs.

Suppose you and I are doing the same crossword puzzle, and that we have decided on different solutions to some entry. Henceforth we will disagree about what evidence is relevant to other, intersecting entries; I think, given my solution to 7 across, that 4 down must end with an 'E', you, given yours, that it must end with an 'S', say. The more entries we have filled in differently, and the longer and more central they are, the more deep-seated our differences will be, and the harder to resolve. Nevertheless, we are both trying to fit the entries to the clues, and to other entries.

My conjecture is that the very deep-seated disagreements which have encouraged the idea that standards of evidence are culture-relative – or, in the intra-scientific form of the variability thesis, paradigm-relative – may be explicable in a similar way; as lying, that is, in a complex mesh of further disagreements in background beliefs, rather than in any deep divergence of standards of evidence.

There is a relevant ambiguity in 'what counts as evidence'. In one sense, there is much divergence in 'what counts as evidence'; in what one counts as *relevant* evidence, which depends on one's other beliefs. In another sense, perhaps, after all, there is not much divergence in 'what counts as evidence'; in appraising the security of a belief, pre-scientific as well as scientific peoples, and converts to the new paradigm as well as defenders of the old, may be assessing its fit to their experience and to their other beliefs. (This is not to deny that other, non-evidential, factors may be important in determining what belief or what paradigm is accepted.) If we think of criteria of justification at the appropriate level of generality, of framework principles rather than material content, of the constraints of experiential anchoring and explanatory integration rather than of specific judgements of relevance, there may, after all, be commonality rather than divergence.[5]

Some may feel that this is just too bland adequately to represent the difference between 'scientific' and 'pre-scientific' cultures. But this dissatisfaction may be deflected by the suggestion that what distinguishes scientific cultures might be better thought of, not as a matter of different standards of evidence, in the sense at issue, but as a matter of greater willingness to submit beliefs to criticism, a greater awareness of alternatives, and hence more openness to questions of justification. Perhaps in closed, pre-scientific cultures people aren't much concerned with how secure this or that belief is; this doesn't mean that the question of justification doesn't make sense *of* them, only that it may not be very salient *to* them.[6] (Implicit in this is the thought that 'scientific versus pre-scientific' is not so sharp a distinction as is sometimes assumed.)

Perspectivalism is the thesis that judgements of justification are inherently perspectival, in that what evidence one takes to be relevant to the degree of justification of a belief unavoidably depends on other beliefs one has; so that, since people differ in their background beliefs, they will differ in their judgement of how justified this or that belief is, the more radically, the more radically their background beliefs differ.

In place of the pluralism of criteria of justification that lies behind both contextualism and tribalism, I am suggesting an underlying commonality of criteria of evidence masked, but not erased, by the perspectival character of specific assessments of justification. And when I offer the foundherentist theory as an explication of what is implicit in 'our appraisals of evidence', I am hoping to have captured the underlying commonalities.

It is not absolutely essential to the success of this chapter that the foundherentist theory should represent, as I perhaps immodestly hope, something common to different cultures and communities; but, if it does, this would be supportive of my thesis that what reassurance we can have of the truth-indicativeness of the foundherentist criteria rests in part on facts about human beings, about *all* normal humans, that is.

A quite unexpected source of confirmation for my aspiration turns up in an argument offered by Annis, an argument which is supposed to show that contextualism need not lead to the repudiation of objectivism, to conventionalism. 'From the fact that justification is relative to the norms and social practices of a group', according to Annis, 'it does not follow that they cannot be criticized nor that justification is somehow subjective'. The argument is, first, that the relevant practices and norms are epistemic, so that their goals are 'truth and the avoidance of error'; then, that they can be criticized if they fail to achieve those goals. Annis refers to the Kpelle, who, he reports, rely on the authority of elders more than we do; but this, he continues, 'could be criticized if they found it led to too many false perceptual beliefs'.[7] The argument certainly doesn't show what Annis claims it does. If Annis were saying only that some norms accepted by a group may be criticized on the basis of other norms accepted by the group, the authority of the elders on the basis of conformity to perception, for example, *or* conformity to perception on the basis of the authority of the elders, this would be compatible with his contextualism, but would not reconcile it with objectivism. If, on the other hand, Annis is saying that there are community-independent criteria, specifically, conformity to what is perceived, by which to judge whether the epistemic norms and practices of some community are succeeding with respect to 'truth and the avoidance of error', this would indeed constitute a commitment to objectivism, but would undermine contextualism. Looking back, I note that the failure of this argument confirms a claim made in chapter 9, that contextualism leads to conventionalism. But, more important, looking forward, I am struck by the fact that even a contextualist like Annis appeals to *perception* as the basis for criticizing 'epistemic practices and norms'. For this supports the idea I have been developing here, that concern for experiential anchoring (and, I should say, also, for explanatory integration) is not a local quirk of 'our' criteria of evidence, in any parochial sense of 'our'.

In fact I am much in sympathy with something like the idea Peirce expresses by saying that perceptual judgements are, though not infallible, involuntary.[8] I would prefer to put it, avoiding the terminology of 'perceptual judgement', like this: though we soon learn that we cannot always trust our senses, trusting them prima facie is natural to us. (This deliberately recalls an observation of Alexander Bain's that I, like Peirce, find notable: that human cognition is a matter of 'innate credulity tempered by checks'.)[9]

To make the relevance of these thoughts to the ratification of foundherentism clearer, I must ask the reader first to bear with me through some rather complex manoeuvring.

II

Descartes's 'proof' that what he clearly and distinctly perceives is true is, I said, a classic ratificatory effort; but it should already be clear that what I am aiming for is much less ambitious. I don't aim to show that all or most of our presumed knowledge is indeed knowledge, nor to offer proof of the truth-indicativeness of the foundherentist criteria. The goal was stated in terms of 'giving what reassurance I can' that the foundherentist criteria are truth-indicative, because I think there are limits, not only to what I can do, but to what can be done, in this direction. (This indicates the particular unCartesian spin I would like to give the quotation from James which opens the chapter.)

All these disclaimers also indicate that I regard the problem of ratification as hard. Scarcely, you might think, a controversial claim – but, interestingly enough, one a reliabilist would have to deny. If a reliabilist explication is correct, the problem of ratification is trivial. For reliabilism explicates 'A is justified in believing that p' along the lines of 'A arrived at the belief that p by a reliable process [a process that produces true results more than 50 per cent of the time]'; it follows immediately that a belief which is justified is probably [more probably than not] true. At first blush, it may sound like a significant advantage of reliabilism that it deals at a stroke with a formerly intractable problem. At second blush, one realizes that this is not after all so impressive an achievement. For one thing, the problems about how to individuate belief-forming processes which have always dogged reliabilists are now starting to nip at their heels again.[10] For another, it is becoming only too apparent that the trivialization of the problem of ratification is one side of a coin the other side of which is the failure of reliabilism to give any substantive account of justification, only the purely schematic truth-conduciveness formula.

What I have just said, it might be thought, could backfire. In chapter 7, I argued against the attributive character of reliabilism, the way it connects justification to whatever is in fact truth-conducive, rather than to *what we take to be* truth-conducive (or, rather, what we take to be truth-*indicative*, but this is not the point presently at issue). Now, a reliabilist of a revisionist stripe – a reliabilist who does not claim, as Goldman does, that reliabilism represents the criteria of justification we actually have, but who wants to *replace* our criteria of justification by reliabilist standards – might argue that the replacement he proposes has the great advantage of telescoping the question of ratification and the question of explication together; surely, he can be expected to urge, a significant economy. I think the advantage is illusory; for, unlike the evidentialist criteria of justification we actually have, the reliabilist criterion is just not the kind of thing we *could* use to appraise a person's justification; all we *can* do is work on the basis of *what we take to be* truth-indicative, i.e., use the criteria of evidence that the revisionist reliabilist wants to replace.

There is a more general point here, besides the specific point about reliabilism. In general, the problem of establishing that satisfaction of these or those criteria of justification is appropriately related to the truth of justified beliefs is substantial, and formidable, unless one has opted for a characterization of the criteria of justification, or of truth, or of the desired relation between them, which is designed precisely to guarantee the result. Attempts to ratify coherentist criteria of justification by relying on a coherence theory of truth provoke something of the same kind of dissatisfaction as the trivialization of the project of ratification that results from a reliabilist explication. It is dissatisfaction of much the same kind, again, as many readers felt when Strawson proposed to dissolve the problem of induction by observing that conforming to inductive patterns is 'part of what we mean by "rational"'.[11]

Actually, I am not convinced that it *is* 'part of what we mean by "rational"' that conforming to inductive patterns is rational; and anyway neither 'induction' nor 'rational' is prominent in my epistemological vocabulary. But there is a class of trivial epistemological truths which deserves mention in this context. As Lewis's habit of using 'likely' or 'probable' interchangeably with 'credible' or 'justified' indicates, 'likely' and related expressions have specifically epistemic uses. 'How likely E makes it that p' can mean 'how supportive E is with respect to p'; and 'how likely it is that p' can mean something like 'how justified someone would be in believing that p on the best evidence presently available'. (It seems possible, by the way, that some of the superficial plausibility of reliabilism may derive from a confusion of the epistemic 'likely' with a frequentist conception.) So, assuming these epistemic uses, such formulae as 'supportive evidence with respect to p is evidence which makes it likely that p', and 'the more justified someone would be in believing that p on the best evidence available, the likelier it is that p', are trivially true. The natural response to the Strawsonian claim is: maybe so, but why should we care about being rational, in that sense? And the verbal truths mentioned in this paragraph are equally powerless to give the reassurance we are seeking. They raise the question: why, given that we care about the truth of our beliefs, should we care about the likelihood, in this epistemic sense, of what we believe?

From my perspective, the problem of ratification is substantial: the foundherentist criteria of justification are not so characterized as to guarantee their truth-indicativeness, and I shall not rely, either, on an account of truth which guarantees it. And I am looking for a ratification which is specific to foundherentism, i.e., which latches onto its details as no appeal to tautologies to the effect that justified beliefs are likely to be true could do.

Let me illustrate what I mean by 'latching onto the details' by asking what would be required to ratify criteria which were, not foundherentist, but foundationalist. I consider specifically an infallibilist foundationalism according to which A is justified in believing that p iff either this belief is infallibly guaranteed to be true by his present experience, or it is derived, directly or indirectly, from some belief(s) which is (are) so guaranteed. To show that a belief's being justified by these criteria is an indication that it is true would call for an argument along the lines, first, that experience guarantees the truth of the beliefs supposed to be basic; second, that beliefs inductively supported by true beliefs are probably true, and that beliefs deductively implied by true beliefs are true. The former would be needed to give reassurance with respect to input, the latter to give reassurance with respect to transmission.

The model is instructive, because what will be required for the ratification of the foundherentist criteria will differ just as foundherentism differs from infallibilist foundationalism. An initial, simplified way to look at it would be to see the foundherentist criteria as holding, in effect, that A is the more justified in believing that p the better this belief is anchored in experience and supported by other beliefs by being integrated into an explanatory story the components of which are also anchored in experience and supported by other beliefs . . . etc. To show that the extent to which a belief is justified according to these criteria is an indication of its truth would call for something which latches on to experiential anchoring and supportiveness/explanatory integration – the foundherentist's analogues of the input and transmission aspects distinguished in the previous paragraph – and shows how they are indicative of truth.

This makes it apparent why I don't anticipate that the project of ratification can be undertaken wholly a priori; for, although the part of the argument that relates to supportiveness and explanatory integration may be expected to have at least a quasi-logical character, the part that relates to experiential anchoring can be expected to be empirical in nature.

The last observation is intended to be neutral with respect to the question, whether there is any a priori knowledge; with respect to which I had better say candidly that I have at present no answer to offer. That would require a theory of the a priori, and – here I borrow a delightfully wry phrase from Fodor – I seem to have mislaid mine. (Perhaps it is worth saying, though, that a priori knowledge would presumably require true beliefs the justification of which needs no support from experience, i.e., that what is called for is, specifically, a theory of a priori *justification*.) The intention is not, however, to be neutral with respect to the question, whether there is a priori knowledge of empirical matters; I am assuming there is not. Actually, nothing even this strong is quite required; for the kind of statement which has recently been suggested as having the mixed status of contingent a priori, such as 'the standard metre bar is one metre long', is not remotely the sort of thing to which ratificatory arguments are likely to need to appeal. But I am in any case persuaded that the supposed mixed status of such statements is probably an illusion.[12]

The alert reader will notice that this means that I cannot motivate my commitment to the thesis of the continuity of philosophy and *science* by pointing to arguments for repudiating the a priori. The picture that attracts me is, rather, one which acknowledges that both philosophy and *science* include both synthetic and analytic elements. It is common enough to hear it said that some basic principles in physics, say, have turned into tautologies by becoming definitory of key theoretical concepts. I confess that I am persuaded, in fact, by less recherché examples, such as this trivial medical truth: diastolic blood pressure is lower than systolic.[13] Anyhow, I see philosophy as depending, as *science* does, on experience; unlike it rather in the degree of indirection of the dependence, and in the kind of experience on which it depends – in requiring special attention to features of experience so ubiquitous as to go almost unnoticed, rather than on special efforts and apparatus to allow us to experience what is not available to everyday, unaided observation. (This conception is significantly closer to Peirce's than to Quine's.)[14]

So, here goes. What reassurance can be given of the truth-indicativeness of the foundherentist criteria? There are two rather different ways one might go about this: by trying to relate COMPLETE justification to decisive indication of the truth of the belief in question, or by trying to relate lesser degrees of justification to grades of truth-indicativeness. It seems appropriate to describe the former strategy as 'from above', the latter as 'from below'.[15] Since I can do neither entirely satisfactorily, prudence demands that I attempt both.

Conventionalists deny that the question of ratification makes sense. Sceptics allow that it makes sense, but think it is soluble only negatively, i.e., that it is *not* possible to connect satisfaction of our criteria of justification with truth-indicativeness. In effect, the 'from below' part of what follows will constitute my (rather oblique) response to pre-Cartesian, i.e., less than fully global, styles of scepticism, and the 'from above' part my (slightly less oblique) response to Cartesian, global scepticism.

According to the foundherentist criteria, the ultimate evidence with respect to empirical beliefs is experiential evidence, sensory and introspective. So the truth-indicativeness of the foundherentist criteria requires it to be the case that our senses give us information about things and events around us and that introspection gives us information about our own mental goings-on. It doesn't require that the senses or introspection be *infallible* sources of information, but it does require that they *be* sources of information.

This is why I was concerned, towards the end of chapter 5, not only to articulate the picture of human beings as organisms equipped with sensory organs which detect information afforded by things around them (which is, I take it, the commonsense picture, and the picture our conception of evidence presupposes), but also to point out how this picture is embedded in plausible psychological theorizing which is itself congruent with plausible biological theorizing (with an evolutionary approach).

As usual, I am focusing my arguments on perception, and allowing introspection to tag along.

Additionally, the argument offered here will require the further proposition that experiential evidence, sensory and introspective, is the *only* ultimate evidence we have with respect to empirical beliefs; that we don't have powers of clairvoyance, telepathy, or extra-sensory perception. These, no less obviously than the theses that one's senses are sources of information about the world, and introspection a source of information about one's own mental goings-on, are empirical theses; they are theses to which *scientific* investigations of (supposedly) 'paranormal phenomena' have a strong contributory relevance.

It may be asked whether my arguments should be interpreted as also requiring that we do not have religious experiences, in the sense, that is, not of being profoundly impressed by the wonder and complexity of the universe, but of being in some kind of direct interaction with a deity. The question reveals an interesting unclarity in what is meant by 'empirical' in 'empirical beliefs'; if one takes it as 'to do with the natural world', the question of religious experience can perhaps be put aside as not relevant, whereas if one takes it as 'not purely logical, to do with how things contingently are', the question cannot be avoided. Since the present task is already formidable, I shall take the easier path, and construe 'empirical' narrowly enough to keep the issue of religious experience at bay.[16]

The crossword analogy isn't much help with the project of ratification, since there is no analogue of the possibility of checking my solution against the one published in the next day's paper. But it does help to think of COMPLETE justification on the analogy of having completed all the entries intersecting with the entry in question, and with it, and all those intersecting entries, optimally fitting their clues, and the entries intersecting with them . . . etc. For someone to be COMPLETELY justified in believing that p, his C-evidence with respect to p must be conclusive and comprehensive, and his C-reasons themselves COMPLETELY justified. In other words, that belief would have to be optimally supported by experience and all other relevant propositions, themselves optimally supported by experience and all other relevant propositions . . . etc. No one actually has such a thing, of course, but we can conceive of a hypothetical ideal theory, a theory which is maximally experientially anchored and explanatorily integrated; and C-beliefs in which someone is COMPLETELY justified would belong to this hypothetical ideal theory. (The appropriateness of the description 'ideal' depends on the assumption that experience is, and is all, the ultimate empirical evidence available to us.)

This suggests one possible 'from above' strategy: to rely on something like Peirce's definition of truth as the ultimate opinion, the hypothetical ideal theory capable of surviving all experiential evidence and full logical scrutiny.[17] This strategy has merit; but another, slightly more oblique and somewhat less reassuring, which does not depend on our accepting this definition of truth, also deserves consideration.

The alternative strategy (which is still, I think, Peircean in spirit) runs like this. Either there is a unique ideal theory, or there isn't. And if there is, either it is appropriate to identify that theory with the truth, or it isn't. If there is a unique ideal theory, and that theory is the truth, then COMPLETE justification is decisive indication of the truth of a belief. If there isn't a unique ideal theory, or if there is, but it could be false, then even COMPLETE justification would not guarantee that a belief is true. But it is, nevertheless, the best to which we could aspire; if COMPLETE justification isn't enough, nothing is. Unless COMPLETE justification is truth-indicative, in other words, inquiry would be futile. I would not say that 'all men by nature desire to know', in the sense Aristotle intended; but a disposition to investigate, to inquire, to try to figure things out, *is* part of our makeup, though not, for many people, an overriding part. And if we are to inquire at all, we can only proceed in the hope that our best *is* good enough.

If we compare these two strategies, it becomes apparent that we are faced with a choice between a stronger style of ratificatory argument which is made possible by compromising realism in the account of truth, and a weaker style of ratificatory argument compatible with a realist view of truth.

The vocabulary is different, but the problem-situation is the same as with our response to Cartesian scepticism, to the Evil Demon hypothesis. The Demon is supposed to be capable of making it seem to us exactly as if p, when in fact not-p; and it is essential to Descartes' argumentative strategy that the deception hypothesized be *absolutely undetectable by us*. One possible response, the response made explicitly by O. K. Bouwsma and implicitly by Peirce,[18] is to maintain that the Demon hypothesis is covertly unintelligible; that it really makes no sense to suppose that things could seem to us, however deeply we probed, in all possible respects as if p, and yet p be false – we only think it makes sense because we imagine less comprehensive deceptions, deceptions we could detect. Another possible response is to allow that the hypothesis makes sense, but to point out that, since the deception it hypothesizes would be absolutely undetectable, it is, for us, epistemically absolutely idle. It is a merely logically possible danger against which, *ex hypothesi*, we can take no precautions.

One might wonder whether one couldn't somehow split the difference between these two approaches. After all, one might argue, the thought that motivates the pragmatist character of Peirce's account of truth, that it makes no sense to suppose either (i) that a proposition which belongs to the hypothetical ideal theory should not be true, or (ii) that there should be truths not part of the hypothetical ideal theory, has two components, the first error- and the second ignorance-oriented. And if, as one might, one felt the former more compelling than the latter, one might wonder whether it would be possible to work with the idea that the hypothetical ideal theory could not be false, but could fail to be the whole truth. This line of thought is appealing; but it is not clear to me whether it can, in the end, be made to work, because, as the comprehensiveness condition makes clear, the error- and ignorance-oriented aspects of our fallibility, though distinguishable, are pervasively interdependent. What one doesn't know, simply, lessens the security of what one does. The more robust argument available seems to be the second, more realist but less reassuring, approach 'from above'.

But we are seldom, if ever, COMPLETELY justified in any of our beliefs, so the approach 'from below', focusing on lesser degrees of justification, also needs to be explored. I am not trying to prove that if one is justified to degree n in some belief, then in n per cent of cases one's belief will be true. Rather, I want to try to answer the question: why, if what we care about is whether our beliefs are true, should we prefer to have beliefs which are more, rather than less, justified? This does not presuppose that all we care about is security; we care about interest, importance, substantial content too. It only presupposes that our concern with justification is linked to the desire for security rather than the desire for substance.

The underlying idea is the same as I used in the argument from above: that all we have to go on, in figuring out how things are, is our experience and the explanatory stories we devise to account for it. But now the structural details of the characterization of supportiveness will be prominent, for while COMPLETE justification requires conclusive and comprehensive evidence, lesser degrees do not, so the focus shifts to degrees of comprehensiveness and supportiveness. How justified A is in believing that p, according to my account, depends on how supportive his C-evidence with respect to p is, how comprehensive it is, and how independently secure his C-reasons are. The third clause, independent security, need not be considered here; since it concerns the degree to which A is justified in believing his C-reasons with respect to p, it depends on the supportiveness and comprehensiveness of his C-evidence with respect to those reasons – and on the independent security of his reasons with respect to his reasons, but this reference to independent security will eventually drop out as we reach experiential C-evidence. The thought, then, is this. Let E* be all the relevant evidence with respect to p. Then how comprehensive E is, is a measure of how close it is to E*. And the Petrocelli Principle, which guides the characterization of supportiveness, tells us that how supportive E is with respect to p depends on how little room E leaves for competitors of p. So the more justified A is in believing that p, *the closer his evidence is to all the relevant evidence,* and (provided my explication has, as intended, conformed to what is expressed metaphorically in the Petrocelli Principle) *the less room his evidence leaves for rivals to p.* And if so, then degree of justification, by the foundherentist criteria explicated in chapter 4, looks to be as good an indication of truth as one could have.

Readers who recall that what replaces 'inductive argument' in my explication is 'supportive evidence' will not need to be told that the argument just given is what replaces 'the justification of induction' in my ratification. (Actually, the more familiar project would better be called the '*meta-*justification of induction', which incidentally makes it clear that when a Popperian says 'induction is unjustifiable' he must be suspected of eliding 'it can't be shown that induction is truth-conducive' into 'induction can be shown not to be truth-conducive'.)

My reconceptualization has, I hope, shifted the focus onto a more tractable problem. For one thing, it has made it clear that the part of the ratificatory argument which focuses on supportiveness has a quasi-deductive character. I say 'quasi-' only because I have had to do some hand-waving on account of the vagueness of the characterization of supportiveness so far developed; if I were able to give a precise explication of the notions of supportiveness and explanatory integration, it ought to be possible to make this part of the ratificatory argument more rigorous. Some may suspect that this is a dangerous admission, urging that we have known since Hume that a deductive [meta]-justification of induction won't work. I concede, of course, that there is no way to show an inductive argument deductively valid, nor, more to the present point, to show supportive-but-not-conclusive evidence conclusive; but it doesn't follow that arguments of a deductive character can't show that the supportiveness of E with respect to p is, on the assumption of the truth of E, an indication of the truth of p. (In chapter 4, I argued that the notion of supportiveness does not look to be logical, in the sense of 'syntactically characterizable'. This is quite compatible with the present point, which is that *meta*-arguments about the truth-indicativeness of supportive evidence do look to be of a logical, deductive character.) But, it may be objected, if my argument *is*, or would be if it could be made rigorous enough, of a deductive character, doesn't that mean that it is trivial, uninformative? I don't think so; deductive arguments certainly can, *pace* Wittgenstein, be informative – informative, that is, about the hidden but discoverable complexities of our concepts. That is, indeed, exactly why it is hard to make the argument more rigorous than I have so far done, because it would require a deeper analysis of supportiveness and explanatory integration than I can presently manage.

Like the argument from above, the argument from below relies (*inter alia*) on two propositions about human cognitive capacities: (1) that experience (sensory and introspective) is a source of empirical information and (2) that it is the only ultimate source of such information available to us. Thus far I have accorded these propositions more or less equal treatment. But I don't really think they are exactly equal either in their independent security or in their bearing on the arguments. Without the first, there would be no way to devise *any* kind of ratificatory argument for the foundherentist criteria, for those criteria are essentially experientialist in character. Without the second, though the arguments I have offered could not stand unmodified, it would still be possible to devise arguments that satisfaction of the foundherentist criteria is, if not necessarily the *best* indication of truth, at least *an* indication (if any indication is available to us). Luckily, the first proposition is not only more essential, but also more secure, than the second. It is not hard to imagine how we might (though I think, as things stand, we don't) come to have reason to think that there is, after all, telepathy, or that dreams foretell the future. Nor is it hard to imagine how we might come to have reason to think that the senses are less reliable than we now suppose; but it requires enormous imaginative effort, to put it mildly, to construct a scenario on which we might be forced to the conclusion that our senses aren't a means of detecting information about things around us *at all*. Quine's imaginative effort in this direction is instructive:

> Experience might still take a turn that would justify [the sceptic's] doubts about external objects. Our success in predicting observations might fall off sharply, and concomitantly with this we might begin to be somewhat successful in basing predictions upon dreams and reveries.[19]

What interest me about this, in the present context, is that Quine's description of the possibility of our finding predictions based on dreams and reveries beginning to be more successful has to be understood as referring to predictions *about what will be observed*; so that his attempt to imagine how we might have other ultimate evidence besides the sensory works much better than his attempt to imagine how sensory evidence might be displaced altogether.

This is where the thoughts offered in section I, that concern for experiential anchoring is not a local or parochial quirk but common to different times and cultures, and that it is human nature to rely, prima facie, on the information conveyed by one's senses, interlock with the ratificatory arguments.

No: I haven't forgotten that there are notorious difficulties with Descartes's ratificatory project which, it might be anticipated, would arise for *any* attempted ratification of criteria of justification. Probably these notorious difficulties have had some readers thinking for some time, 'fools rush in . . .'. Before I explain how I escape the most notorious difficulty, I want to say something about a less notorious, but still troublesome, problem that arises in Descartes's enterprise.

Descartes's 'proof', if it worked, would overshoot the mark; it leaves him with the embarrassing question: how, given that one's faculties were created by an omnipotent and non-deceiving God, does it come about that one *ever* makes mistakes? And his answer, that human reason is limited but the will unlimited, and that error arises when the will prompts one to go beyond the limits of one's reasoning capacities, leaves him with the further embarrassing question: why did God not create us with unlimited powers of reasoning, or with reason and will in better harmony? And his answer: that God's purposes are beyond human comprehension, is completely unsatisfying.[20] I don't face anything analogous to this problem, because I don't claim that anyone is more than very rarely, if ever, COMPLETELY justified in believing anything, nor that *complete* justification is any guarantee of truth.

But some may suspect that, if Descartes's argument overshoots the mark, mine undershoots it. I made a point of distinguishing the question on which this chapter is focused: are our criteria of justification truth-indicative? from the question: are our beliefs mostly true? The observation that people have many beliefs in which they are not, or not much, justified, with which the second question was put aside, hints, though it doesn't say explicitly, that people also have beliefs in which they *are* justified. And it is a legitimate question, certainly, what reasons there are for even this degree of optimism. On this issue, it may be feasible to appeal to evolutionary considerations. As I observed in chapter 9, compared with other animals, human beings are not especially fast or strong; their forte is, rather, their greater cognitive capacity, their ability to represent the world to themselves and hence to predict and manipulate it. Unlike Descartes's appeals to a divine creator, this line of thought has no tendency to suggest that our cognitive capacities can be expected to be perfect; only that we can be expected to have a minimal competence at least with respect to matters most closely linked to the conditions of survival. I am inclined to think that evolutionary considerations might offer some modest reassurance, for example, that our innate dispositions to classify certain things as of a kind by and large approximately pick out real kinds, which would support the idea that we have some minimal explanatory competence, on which, by revising and correcting our beliefs in the face of further experience, we can build; on which, indeed, we have built SCIENCE.

The reference to evolution in the last paragraph, by the way, constitutes a second reason why mine counts, though only in the least demanding sense, as an evolutionary epistemology; the first being that the congruence of a Gibsonian, ecological approach to perception conformable with a focus on the adaptedness of organisms to their environments, was noted (chapter 5, section V) as contributing to its plausibility and hence, even more indirectly, to the plausibility of the conception of perception built into foundherentism.

Returning, now, to the main thread of the argument, let me repeat that my sights are set *much* lower than Descartes's; I have aspired only to give reasons for thinking that, if any truth-indication is available to us, satisfaction of the foundherentist criteria of justification is as good an indication of truth as we could have. Even this very significant lowering of aspirations, however, will not in itself constitute any reply to the more notorious difficulty with Descartes's enterprise: the vicious circle into which it is generally supposed Descartes got himself. Aren't my ratificatory arguments, however hedged, however modest in what they aspire to do, bound to be viciously circular?

I don't think so.

First: I have not offered an argument with the conclusion that the foundherentist criteria are truth-indicative, one of the premises of which is that the foundherentist criteria are truth-indicative.

Second: nor have I (like those who hope for an inductive meta-justification of induction) used a certain method of inference or belief-formation to arrive at the conclusion that that very method is a good, truth-conducive method.

I have offered reasons for thinking that, if any truth-indication is possible for us, satisfaction of the foundherentist criteria is the best truth-indication we can have. If the suspicion lingers that there is something unhealthily self-dependent here, it may be the legacy of foundationalism, which imposes an epistemological ordering I do not respect, or of *foundationalism*, which imposes a meta-epistemological ordering I do not respect. But I have argued that neither foundationalism nor *foundationalism*, and hence, neither kind of epistemological priority, is well-supported.

This is probably not enough to allay all suspicions. 'Yes, but how do you *know* that the senses are a source of information about things in one's environment, that introspection is a source of information about one's own mental goings-on?', I may be asked, echoing the familiar challenge to Descartes, 'How do you *know* that God exists and is not a deceiver?' The question will be put, no doubt, in a tone which suggests that the only response available to me is, 'because my evidence satisfies the foundherentist criteria', echoing the anticipated answer from Descartes, 'because I clearly and distinctly perceive it to be true'. I shall put aside the question whether Descartes has any recourse against this challenge,[21] and concentrate on my own defence. For simplicity, let 'R' abbreviate all the direct reasons I have offered in my ratificatory argument. The anticipated question, 'Yes, but how do you know that R?' is rhetorical, a challenge rather than a simple request for information, and it may be taken in either of two ways: (1) as a challenge to give my reasons for believing that R, or: (2) as a challenge to show that my reasons for believing that R are good enough for my belief to constitute knowledge. I cannot meet the second challenge without articulating my standards of evidence and showing that my evidence with respect to R satisfies them, and, at least arguably though not quite so obviously, without offering reassurance that my standards of evidence are truth-indicative; and if so, I cannot meet it, in the present context, without circularity. But I can meet the first challenge simply by giving my reasons for believing that R. And this is enough. My reasons are good reasons if they are independently secure and they genuinely support R; and I am justified in believing those reasons, and hence in believing that R, if my evidence for believing them is good evidence. And if I am justified in believing that R, then (assuming that R is true, and whatever else is needed to avoid Gettier paradoxes) I know that R. And if I do and if R (and the indirect reasons on which it depends) are good reasons for believing that the foundherentist criteria are truth-indicative, I know that, too. Even if I can't know that I am justified in my weakly ratificatory conclusion, I can be justified in it nonetheless; and even if I can't know that I know it, I can know it nonetheless.[22]

By my lights, of course, justification is not categorical, but comes in degrees; so, to avoid any possible misunderstanding, perhaps I need to repeat that I don't claim that the considerations I have offered in ratification of the foundherentist criteria are even close to being conclusive, comprehensive, or COMPLETELY independently secure. If I *am* justified in believing that, if any truth-indication is possible for us, the foundherentist criteria are the best truth-indication we can have, it is only to a relatively modest degree. But isn't that a good deal better than nothing?

Epistemology, as I conceive it, and its meta-theory, are integral parts of a whole web of theories about the world and ourselves, not underpinning but intermeshing with other parts. Standards of evidence are not hopelessly culture-bound, though judgements of justification are always perspectival. And we can have, not proof that our criteria of justification are truth-guaranteeing, but reasons for thinking that, if any truth-indication is available to us, they are truth-indicative; reasons no less fallible than those parts of our theories about the world and ourselves with which they interlock, but no more so, either.

The old *foundationalism* aspired to a certitude impossible for fallible human inquirers; but the new conventionalism and the new tribalism surrender to a 'factitious despair'.[23] Though we must settle for less reassurance than Descartes hoped to achieve, we need not give up the quest or hope of truth itself.

When Descartes's epistemological story ended, 'happily ever after', we knew it was too good to be true. Perhaps it is appropriate to end my story – combining, as it does, a pervasive fallibilism with a modest optimism about our epistemic condition – 'hopefully ever after'.

Notes

INTRODUCTION

1 The starting point of this nest of issues is Gettier, 'Is Justified True Belief Knowledge?', though the essential point was anticipated by Russell in 'Knowledge, Error and Probable Opinion'; Shope, *The Analysis of Knowing*, exhaustively surveys the state of play as of 1983. My attitude to these issues has something in common with a thought expressed by Ayer, before the publication of Gettier's paper, in *The Problem of Knowledge*, p. 34:

> The main problem is to state and assess the grounds on which ... claims to knowledge are made ... It is a relatively unimportant question what titles you then bestow upon them

and something in common with the conclusion, though less with the arguments, found in Kirkham, 'Does the Gettier Problem Rest on a Mistake?'.
2 See e.g. papers by Flax and Hartsock in Harding and Hintikka, *Discovering Reality*; Harding, *Whose Science? Whose Knowledge?*, pp. 41, 278, 280; Jaggar, 'Love and Knowledge: Emotion in a Feminist Epistemology', p. 146; Haraway, 'Situated Knowledges'. In 'Epistemological Reflections of an Old Feminist' I argue that 'feminist epistemology' is misconceived. Cf. also my review of Harding and Hintikka, *Discovering Reality*, and 'Science "From a Feminist Perspective"'.
3 Dewey, *Reconstruction in Philosophy*.
4 Peirce, *Collected Papers*, 7.51.

CHAPTER 1 FOUNDATIONALISM VERSUS COHERENTISM

1 Sellars, 'Empiricism and the Philosophy of Mind', p. 170.
2 See e.g., Cornman, 'Foundational versus Nonfoundational Theories of Empirical Justification'; Goldman, A. H., *Empirical Knowledge*, chapter 7;

Lehrer, *Knowledge*, chapters 4–8; Pollock, 'A Plethora of Epistemological Theories' and *Contemporary Theories of Knowledge*, chapters 2 and 3.

3 Cf. Alston, 'Two Types of Foundationalism', and 'Level-Confusions in Epistemology'.

4 Cf. Alston, 'Varieties of Privileged Access' and 'Self-Warrant: a Neglected Form of Privileged Access'.

5 My thesis that foundationalism and coherentism do not exhaust the options is not new (though the intermediate theory I propose is). See e.g., Annis, 'A Contextualist Theory of Epistemic Justification'; Kornblith, 'Beyond Foundationalism and the Coherence Theory'; Sosa, 'The Raft and the Pyramid'.

6 Cf. Sosa, 'The Raft and the Pyramid'.

7 Cf. Foley, 'Justified Inconsistent Beliefs'.

CHAPTER 2 FOUNDATIONALISM UNDERMINED

1 Goodman, 'Sense and Certainty', pp. 162–3.

2 All page references in the text of this chapter are to this book of Lewis's.

3 Goodman, 'Sense and Certainty'; Reichenbach, 'Are Phenomenal Reports Absolutely Certain?'; Firth, 'Coherence, Certainty and Epistemic Priority', 'The Anatomy of Certainty' and 'Lewis on the Given'; Quinton, 'The Foundations of Knowledge' and *The Nature of Things*, pp. 155ff.; Pastin, 'C. I. Lewis's Radical Foundationalism' and 'Modest Foundationalism and Self-Warrant'; BonJour, *The Structure of Empirical Knowledge*, chapter 4.

4 These thoughts are anticipated in Firth, 'Coherence, Certainty and Epistemic Priority', p. 551.

5 Goodman, 'Sense and Certainty', pp. 161–2.

6 Sellars, 'Empiricism and the Philosophy of Mind', p. 165.

7 Opthalmologists distinguish 'objective' vision tests, where the patient's eyes are examined directly, and 'subjective' tests, where the patient is asked to report on how things look to him. Objective tests are used to check the results of subjective tests, and vice versa. Subjective tests are standardly repeated, to allow for the possibility that the patient's report is mistaken. See Asher, *Experiments in Seeing*, chapter 10.

Both Reichenbach and Goodman make the point that phenomenal beliefs must be consistent with other beliefs. See Goodman, 'Sense and Certainty', p. 163, Reichenbach, 'Are Phenomenal Reports Absolutely Certain?', p. 155.

8 Lewis, 'The Given Element in Empirical Knowledge', p. 173.

9 Cf. Reichenbach, 'Are Phenomenal Reports Absolutely Certain?', p. 156.

10 Lewis, 'The Given Element in Empirical Knowledge', pp. 172–3.

11 Ibid., p. 173.

12 Ibid., p. 168.

13 Ibid., p. 173.

14 They are developed in more detail in Haack, 'C. I. Lewis', pp. 230ff.

CHAPTER 3 COHERENTISM DISCOMPOSED

1 Lewis, 'The Given Element in Empirical Knowledge', pp. 168–9.
2 All page references in the text of section I of this chapter are to this book.
3 All page references in the text of section II of this chapter are to this paper.
4 Alston raises doubts about the internalism/externalism dichotomy in 'Internalism and Externalism in Epistemology' and 'An Internalist Externalism'; and, though I am not sure he has quite got to the bottom of it, I am convinced that he is right to question whether there is any simple dichotomy here.
5 BonJour, 'Externalist Theories of Empirical Knowledge', p. 55.
6 Davidson, 'Afterthoughts', p. 134.
7 I shall not discuss Quine's views on the distinction between observation sentences and theoretical sentences here, though I think it a bit less straightforward than Davidson takes it to be; cf. Quine and Ullian, *The Web of Belief*, p. 17:

> A trace of fallibility, indeed, there is [with observation sentences]. Normally, observation is the tug that tows the ship of theory; but in extreme cases the theory pulls so hard that observation yields.

8 Quine, *Word and Object*, p. 59. In a footnote he attributes the expression, 'principle of charity' to Wilson, 'Substances Without Substrata'.
9 Quine, *Word and Object*, p. 69.
10 Davidson, 'The Method of Truth in Metaphysics', p. 201.
11 Ibid., p. 201.
12 For the next part of the argument I am indebted to Burdick, 'On Davidson and Interpretation', sections 5 and 6, which I follow closely.
13 Davidson, 'Radical Interpretation', p. 135.
14 Davidson, 'Belief and the Basis of Meaning', p. 152.
15 Davidson, 'On the Very Idea of a Conceptual Scheme', p. 19.
16 However, Turnbull reports that one of the obstacles he encountered in his study of the Ik was that his informants made it a kind of game constantly to lie to him; 'but anthropologists', he continues, 'have their ways of worming the truth out of reluctant informants' (*The Mountain People*, p. 35).
17 Cf. Burdick, 'On Davidson and Interpretation', section 5, for an incisive, and more comprehensive, discussion of the problems with Davidson's empirical constraints. (McGinn, in 'Charity, Interpretation and Belief ', and Vermazen, in 'The Intelligibility of Massive Error', also criticize Davidson's principle of charity, though, in my view, less successfully.)
18 Quine, 'The Nature of Natural Knowledge', p. 68.
19 Not that Quine's position on these matters is unambiguous; cf. chapter 6 below.
20 My thanks to Norman Armstrong for drawing this to my attention.

CHAPTER 4 FOUNDHERENTISM ARTICULATED

1 Quine, 'Epistemology Naturalized', p. 75.

2 Quine and Ullian, *The Web of Belief*, p. 79.

3 After I coined the term 'evidentialist' to describe my approach, I learned that it was already current in the literature. Feldman and Conee's sense, in 'Evidentialism', in which the expression refers to theories which explicate justification in terms of the subject's evidence, which must be something of which the subject is aware, and contrasts with 'reliabilism', is very close to my conception. My account is also evidentialist in the sense used by Calvinist proponents of 'Reformed epistemology' – for I shall require (section III below) that A is justified in believing that p only if he has good evidence with respect to p; whereas some Reformed epistemologists hold that belief in God is justified in the absence of evidence. See Plantinga, 'Reason and Belief in God'.

   The distinction of evidentialist versus extrinsic theories is the nearest analogue, in my terminology, of the rejected dichotomy of internalism versus externalism.

4 My first, clumsy attempt to articulate this distinction was made in 'Epistemology *With* a Knowing Subject'. Dewey's description of belief as 'Mr Facing-both-ways' ('Beliefs and Existences', p. 169) is apropos.

5 Two caveats are needed here. The first is that S-beliefs which belong to the causal nexus of A's S-belief that p, not in virtue of their sustaining or inhibiting some S-belief which sustains or inhibits the S-belief that p, but in virtue of their causal relations to some non-belief state in the causal nexus of A's S-belief that p, should be excluded from A's S-evidence. The second is that it may be necessary to exclude evidential states which are causally related to A's S-belief that p, but in the wrong way. ('Deviant causal chains' are a logical possibility dear to philosophers' hearts, but casually enough disregarded in our pre-analytical conceptual scheme. Cf. the discussion of testimonial evidence at the end of this section.)

6 According to Mintz, 'Gentlepeople: Sharpen Your Pencils', p. 15, the crossword puzzle 'was born in 1913 as "word cross"' (my thanks to Ralph Sleeper for drawing this article to my attention).

   The analogy of clues/experiential evidence suggested here should not be allowed to encourage too simple-minded a picture in which each empirical belief has its own, distinctive, simple bit of direct experiential evidence – a danger I believe I have avoided in what follows. (My thanks to John Clendinnen for help here.)

7 This is why, rather than saying, as I did in 'Rebuilding the Ship While Sailing on the Water', that the conception of justification is partly causal and partly logical, I now prefer to say that it is partly causal and partly evaluative. Cf. chapter 5, section III, on the (false) dichotomy of inductivism versus deductivism.

8 My thanks to Christopher Peacocke for pressing the question of the relation of my account to the idea of inference to the best explanation.

9 My thanks to Andrew Swann for prompting me to get this clear.

10 This loose talk of 'a lot' and 'just a bit' of evidence will rightly raise suspicions that a problem of relativity to language may impede further explication here.

11 Cf. Hardwig, 'Epistemic Dependence'.

12 'A wise man, therefore, proportions his belief to the evidence', *Enquiry Concerning Human Understanding*, section X, 87, p. 110. Note that my analogue of this maxim, unlike Hume's version, has no tendency to suggest that belief, or degree of belief, is voluntary.

CHAPTER 5 THE SENSES: REFUTATIONS AND CONJECTURES

1 Peirce, *Collected Papers*, 8.144 and 5.185.

2 Popper, 'Epistemology Without a Knowing Subject', pp. 108ff.

3 All page references in the text of section II of this chapter are to this book.

4 Quinton, 'The Foundations of Knowledge', section XI.

5 Ayer, 'Truth, Verification and Verisimilitude'.

6 Popper, 'The Verification of Basic Statements' and 'Subjective Experience and Linguistic Formulation'; the quotation is from p. 1114 of the latter.

7 Popper, 'Epistemology Without a Knowing Subject', pp. 119ff., and 'On the Theory of the Objective Mind', section 4.

8 All page references in the text of the rest of this chapter are to this book.

9 Watkins prefers to say (pp. 249 and 254) 'quasi-inductive', since he realizes that the inferences involved need not be of the forms usually called 'inductive'; on this point Watkins acknowledges Ayer, *The Problem of Knowledge*, p. 80.

10 See especially Peirce's 'Perception and Telepathy', *Collected Papers* 7.597ff.

11 The quotation, which is on p. 257, is from Gregory, *Eye and Brain*, p. 222.

12 See Gibson, *The Senses Considered as Perceptual Systems; The Ecological Approach to Visual Perception*; and 'New Reasons for Realism'. Cf. also Kelley, *The Evidence of the Senses*.

Churchland, 'Explanation: a PDP Approach', p. 228, observes, as I have done, that – though some writers have supposed that somehow there must be there is no conflict between Peirce's conception of perceptual judgement as a kind of abduction, and Gibson's ecological approach. (Churchland does not observe, however, that, as the passages that open this chapter make clear, Peirce himself holds, as Gibson does, that perception is of things around us.)

I note that the realist aspect of my account of the evidence of the senses aligns me not only with Peirce and Gibson, but also with Davidson.

13 Gibson, *The Senses Considered as Perceptual Systems*, p. 1.

CHAPTER 6 NATURALISM DISAMBIGUATED

1 Russell, *Our Knowledge of the External World*, p. 71.

2 I shall return to it, very briefly, in chapter 7, section II.

3 Quine, 'Five Milestones of Empiricism', p. 72.
4 Putnam, 'Why Reason Can't be Naturalized', p. 19.
5 Quine, *Word and Object*, pp. 22–3.
6 Putnam, 'Meaning Holism', p. 425.
7 Quine, 'Reply to Putnam', pp. 430–1; in the offset passage Quine is quoting from his 'Facts of the Matter'.
8 Quine, 'The Nature of Natural Knowledge', pp. 67–8.
9 Quine, *The Roots of Reference*, pp. 2–3.
10 Quine, 'Things and Their Place in Theories', p. 22.
11 Quine, 'Epistemology Naturalized', p. 82.
12 Quine, 'Things and Their Place in Theories', p. 21.
13 Quine, *The Roots of Reference*, p. 3.
14 Quine and Ullian, *The Web of Belief*, first edition, p. 7.
15 1978. My thanks to Dirk Koppelberg for drawing this to my attention.
16 Quine, 'Epistemology Naturalized', pp. 82–3.
17 Quine's naturalism is construed as descriptivist by Siegel, in 'Justification, Discovery and the Naturalization of Epistemology', by Goldman, in the introduction to *Epistemology and Cognition*, and by Kim, in 'What is "Naturalized Epistemology"?'.
18 Quine, 'Epistemology Naturalized', p. 75.
19 Putnam, 'Why Reason Can't be Naturalized', p. 19.
20 Quine, 'Epistemology Naturalized', pp. 87–8.
21 Quine, 'Reply to White', pp. 664–5. For those readers who find 'scouting' puzzling, here is the *OED*'s definition:
      scout, v.t. reject (proposal, notion) with scorn or ridicule. [cf. ON *skúta* a taunt, Sw *skujta* to shoot; prob. cogn. w. SHOOT].
22 Quine, *Word and Object*, p. 22; *Ontological Relativity*, pp. 75, 82–3; 'The Nature of Natural Knowledge', p. 68.
23 Quine, *Word and Object*, pp. 9ff.; Quine and Ullian, *The Web of Belief*, p. 79.
24 See e.g., Sosa, 'The Raft and the Pyramid', p. 14 (Quine as critic of foundationalism), Goldman, *Epistemology and Cognition*, p. 107, and Nelson, *Who Knows: From Quine to a Feminist Empiricism*, pp. 25–8 (Quine as coherentist); Cornman, 'Foundational versus Nonfoundational Theories of Empirical Justification', p. 250 (Quine as foundationalist).
25 Quine, 'Epistemology Naturalized', p. 84.
26 Quine, *The Roots of Reference*, p. 2.
27 Ibid., p. 3.
28 Quine, 'Natural Kinds', p. 126.
29 Quine, *The Roots of Reference*, pp. 19–20.
30 Quine, 'Natural Kinds', p. 116.
31 Ibid., p. 116.
32 Peirce, *Collected Papers*, 1.15ff., 6.619ff., 8.7ff. See also Haack, ' "Extreme Scholastic Realism;" its Relevance to Philosophy of Science Today' (when I wrote this paper, however, I was myself somewhat disposed to assimilate the concepts of natural kind and similarity – a disposition of which I was cured by David Savan).

33 Goodman, 'The New Riddle of Induction', p. 74.
34 Quine, 'Epistemology Naturalized', pp. 87–8.
35 For amplification, see Haack, 'Science "From a Feminist Perspective"', section I.

CHAPTER 7 THE EVIDENCE AGAINST RELIABILISM

1 Price, *Belief*, p. 92.
2 Ramsey, *The Foundations of Mathematics*, p. 199.
3 Lycan, on the dust jacket of *Epistemology and Cognition*.
4 Donnellan, 'Reference and Definite Descriptions'.
5 This point is discussed in detail in chapter 10, section II.
6 Goldman, 'What is Justified Belief?', p. 10; *Epistemology and Cognition*, pp. 103ff.
7 Goldman, 'What is Justified Belief?', pp. 13–14.
8 Ibid., pp. 16–18.
9 Ibid., p. 18.
10 Ibid., p. 20.
11 Ibid., p. 20.
12 Ibid., p. 10; cf. *Epistemology and Cognition*, p. 104. I note also that on p. 9 of 'What is Justified Belief?' Goldman concedes the relevance to justification of states which causally sustain (as well as of the processes which causally originate) beliefs; this insight also slips out of reach of his theory as the paper proceeds.
13 Goldman, *Epistemology and Cognition*, chapters 4 and 5.
14 Ibid., p. 106.
15 Ibid., p. 92.
16 Goldman refers to BonJour, 'Externalist Theories of Empirical Justification'; see also BonJour, *The Structure of Empirical Knowledge*, chapter 3.
17 Goldman, *Epistemology and Cognition*, pp. 53ff.
18 Ibid., p. 63.
19 Ibid., pp. 111ff.; my paraphrase.
20 Ibid., p. 113.
21 Ibid., p. 115.
22 Goldman, 'What is Justified Belief?', p. 16.
23 Goldman refers to Cohen, 'Justification and Truth'; see also Foley, 'What's Wrong With Reliabilism?'.
24 Goldman, *Epistemology and Cognition*, p. 107.
25 Ibid., p. 108.
26 Ibid., p. 109.
27 Goldman, 'What is Justified Belief?', p. 1; *Epistemology and Cognition*, p. 109.
28 See Goldman, 'Epistemics: the Regulative Theory of Cognition'.
29 Goldman, *Epistemology and Cognition*, pp. 194ff.
30 Ibid., pp. 182, 184, 278ff., 305ff.
31 Ibid., pp. 194ff.

32 Ibid., pp. 299ff.
33 Ibid., pp. 1, 4–5. I shall not discuss this distinction of Goldman's directly; but my arguments for a different, though related, distinction between the project of giving criteria of justification and the project of giving rules for the conduct of inquiry (chapter 10 section I), are germane.
34 At any rate, this is the impression I get, though not quite so clearly as I would like, from the introduction to *Epistemology and Cognition*.
35 Goldman, 'Epistemics: the Regulative Theory of Cognition', p. 523.

CHAPTER 8 REVOLUTIONARY SCIENTISM SUBVERTED

1 Fodor, *Representations*, p. 121.
2 Stich, *From Folk Psychology to Cognitive Science: the Case Against Belief*, p. 2.
3 Ibid., pp. 5–10.
4 Churchland, P. Smith, 'Epistemology in the Age of Neuroscience', pp. 544–5, 546, 547.
5 Stich, *From Folk Psychology to Cognitive Science*, pp. 229–30.
6 Churchland, P. M., *Scientific Realism and the Plasticity of Mind*, sections 12–16; 'Eliminative Materialism and the Propositional Attitudes', section II.
7 Churchland, P. M., 'The Continuity of Philosophy and the Sciences'.
8 Stich, *From Folk Psychology to Cognitive Science*, pp. 230–7; Nisbett and Wilson, 'Telling More Than We Can Know: Verbal Reports on Mental Processes'; Wilson, 'Strangers to Ourselves: the Origins and Accuracy of Beliefs About One's Own Mental States'. The reader will notice some points of contact between my critique and Horgan and Woodward's in 'Folk Psychology is Here to Stay'.
9 Nisbett and Wilson, 'Telling More Than We Can Know', p. 231; Wilson, 'Strangers to Ourselves', p. 16. My italics.
10 Churchland, P. M., *Matter and Consciousness*, p. 79.
11 Stich, *From Folk Psychology to Cognitive Science*, p. 238.
12 Minsky, 'K-Lines: a Theory of Memory'; the quotation is from p. 100. On p. 88 Minsky warns: 'The idea proposed here – of a primitive 'disposition representing' structure – would probably serve only for a rather infantile dispositional memory; the present theory does not go very far toward supporting the more familiar kinds of cognitive contructs we know as adults . . .
I doubt that human memory has the same, uniform, invariant structure throughout development'.
13 Minsky, 'Frame-System Theory'; 'A Framework for Representing Knowledge'. For the characterization of frames, the allusion to Kuhn, and the contrast with logistic models, see the latter, pp. 96–7 and 123–28.
14 Winograd, 'Frame Representations and the Declarative-Procedural Controversy'; 'What Does It Mean to Understand Language?'. The discussion of Maturana is on pp. 284ff. of the latter; unfortunately, Winograd's reference

for the quotation from Maturana seems to be mistaken, and I have been unable to locate the source.

15 Winograd, 'What Does It Mean to Understand Language?', p. 249.
16 Cf. Wooldridge, *The Machinery of the Brain*, cited in Dennett, *Brainstorms*, pp. 65–6, on the behaviour, or 'behaviour', of the *sphex* wasp.
17 Churchland, P. M., *Scientific Realism and the Plasticity of Mind*, p. 134.
18 Winograd, 'What Does It Mean to Understand Language?', p. 250.
19 Hobbes, T., *Human Nature*, in Woodridge, *Hobbes Selections*, p. 23. (What I say about the role of language here is intended to be neutral with respect to the question, whether any non-human animals are capable of language use.)
20 Churchland, P. M., 'The Ontological Status of Observables', pp. 150–1.
21 Churchland, P. M., 'Folk Psychology and the Explanation of Behavior', pp. 125–7; the extended quotation is from p. 127.
22 Churchland, P. M., 'On the Nature of Theories', pp. 163ff.
23 Polanyi, *Personal Knowledge* and, especially, *The Tacit Dimension*.
24 Kosslyn and Koenig, *Wet Mind*, pp. 401ff.
25 Fodor, 'Fodor's Guide to Mental Representation'.
26 Stich, *From Folk Psychology to Cognitive Science*, p. 164.
27 Ibid., p. 164.
28 Ibid., p. 166.
29 Ibid., p. 166.
30 Price, *Belief*, pp. 267ff.
31 Cf. Fodor, *Representations*, p. 5.
32 Bain, *The Emotions and the Will*, pp. 505–535; Peirce, *Collected Papers*, 5.12. Cf. Haack, 'Descartes, Peirce and the Cognitive Community', section I.
33 I am, of course, making things easy for myself by choosing an example of a belief of highly practical character; mathematical or metaphysical beliefs would not fit the picture so neatly. But I think the ascription of highly theoretical beliefs is secondary, that we can ascribe such beliefs only against a background of ascriptions of beliefs more like my example.
34 Goschke and Koppelberg, 'Connectionist Representation, Semantic Compositionality, and the Instability of Concept Structure', p. 268.
35 Churchland, P. M., 'Eliminative Materialism and the Propositional Attitudes', pp. 12–17.
36 Cf. Horgan, 'From Cognitive Science to Folk Psychology: Computation, Mental Representation and Belief' for a distinction of 'tractable' versus 'non-tractable' reduction.
37 Orwell, *Nineteen Eighty-Four*, Appendix.
38 Daley, *A Faint Cold Fear*, p. 6.
39 Fodor, *Representations*, p. 6.
40 See Burge, 'Individualism and the Mental'.
41 Stich, *From Folk Psychology to Cognitive Science*, pp. 54ff.
42 Burdick, 'A Logical Form for the Propositional Attitudes'. This need not leave me with the problem that now C-beliefs are not representable, as the account of the appraisal of C-evidence given in chapter 4 requires,

sententially, since one can use Burdick's technique for re-presenting what is held-true in sentential form.

43 Stich, *From Folk Psychology to Cognitive Science*, p. 192.

44 Churchland, P. M., *Matter and Consciousness*, p. 1.

45 Churchland, P. M., 'Eliminative Materialism and the Propositional Attitudes', pp. 13–14.

46 Ibid., p. 21.

47 Churchland, P. M., *Matter and Consciousness*, p. 48, and 'Eliminative Materialism and the Propositional Attitudes', pp. 21–2; he refers to Churchland, P. Smith, 'Is Determinism Self-Refuting?' as the source of his reply to the objection.

48 True, on p. 18 of 'Eliminative Materialism and the Propositional Attitudes', Churchland tells us that a declarative sentence to which a speaker would give assent is 'a one-dimensional projection of a four- or five-dimensional solid that is an element in his true kinematical state'. To the (limited) extent that I understand this, I *think* it says that assent to a sentence (and, I presume, assertion of a sentence) *does* express an inner state, only not fully or perfectly.

49 Heil, 'Intentionality Speaks for Itself', p. 346.

CHAPTER 9   VULGAR PRAGMATISM: AN UNEDIFYING PROSPECT

1 My thanks to David Stove for reporting this dialogue.

2 All page references in the text of section I of this chapter are to this book of Rorty's. Rorty is by no means the first, of course, to argue that epistemology is misconceived; cf., for example, Nelson, 'The Impossibility of a "Theory of Knowledge"'.

3 See Rorty, 'Unfamiliar Noises', and cf. Haack, 'Surprising Noises: Rorty and Hesse on Metaphor' and 'Dry Truth and Real Knowledge: Epistemologies of Metaphor and Metaphors of Epistemology'.

4 See Sellars, 'Empiricism and the Philosophy of Mind'.

5 See Quine, 'Two Dogmas of Empiricism'.

6 At any rate, everything in Davidson's work before 1987 is strongly opposed to any such idea. Perhaps, in 'Afterthoughts', Davidson sounds a little wobbly, describing himself, on p. 134, as a 'pragmatist' about truth. By his Dewey Lectures of 1990, 'The Structure and Content of Truth', however, though he has repudiated the idea that Tarski's is a correspondence theory, it is once again clear that he is by no stretch of the imagination sympathetic to 'pragmatism' in Rorty's vulgar sense. (On Tarski and correspondence, by the way, cf. Haack, 'Is It True What They Say About Tarski?' and ' "Realism" '.)

7 Rorty, *Contingency, Irony and Solidarity*, p. 73.

8 An accusation made explicitly in *Essays on Heidegger and Others*, p. 86.

9 All page references in the text of section II of this chapter are to this book of Stich's.

10 Rorty, *Objectivity, Relativism and Truth*, p. 21.

11 Stich gets this conceit from Schiffer, 'Truth and the Theory of Content'.

12 Hallen and Sodipo, *Knowledge, Belief and Witchcraft*.

13 Russell, 'Knowledge, Error and Probable Opinion'.

14 As does Goldman in 'Stephen P. Stich: *The Fragmentation of Reason*', pp. 190–1.

15 Stich, 'The Fragmentation of Reason: a Precis of Two Chapters', p. 179.

16 Peirce, *Collected Papers*, 8.143.

17 Ibid., 1.34, 1.235, 2.135.

18 James, *Pragmatism*, pp. 107ff.; *The Meaning of Truth*, pp. 3, 143. Cf. Haack, 'Can James's Theory of Truth Be Made More Satisfactory?'.

19 James, *The Will to Believe*, p. 11: '*our passional nature . . . must decide an option between propositions, whenever it is a genuine option that cannot by its nature be decided on intellectual grounds.*' See also James's letter to Kallen in Perry, *The Thought and Character of William James*, p. 249.

20 James, *Pragmatism*, p. 112.

21 Cf. Haack, 'Pragmatism', for a more detailed analysis of the epistemologies of pragmatism, and 'Philosophy/philosophy, an Untenable Dualism' for a detailed critique of Rorty's interpretation of Peirce.

In the text I have confined my discussion to James, whom both Rorty and Stich, I believe, seriously misinterpret. Scholars may observe that, although Stich's one quotation from James (*The Fragmentation of Reason*, p. 160, quoting James's *Pragmatism*, p. 42) is carefully, and tendentiously, edited in an attempt to make James appear to say what Stich says he does, even the bowdlerized version makes clear James's commitment to the instrumental value of truth.

A more difficult question, pressed upon me by Sidney Ratner, is how closely Rorty's anti-epistemological stance resembles Dewey's critique, in *The Quest for Certainty*, of the 'spectator theory of knowledge'. For now, I shall say only that Dewey seems to me quite ambiguous, but that one (though not the only) way to read him is as urging a more naturalistic epistemology – and that on this interpretation, of course, he is quite unlike Rorty.

CHAPTER 10 FOUNDHERENTISM RATIFIED

1 James, *The Will to Believe*, p. 17.

2 So my way of making the distinction between individual and social aspects of epistemology is rather different from Goldman's.

3 Cf. my review of Code, *Epistemic Responsibility*.

4 *Character as Indicated by Handwriting*, by Rosa Baughm, 'author of "The Handbook [sic] of Palmistry", "Chirogomancy", and papers on Physiogony'.

5 My articulation here grew out of correspondence with Hilary Putnam, who is more disposed to pluralism in this regard than I am.

6 In thinking about these issues I have found Horton, 'African Traditional

Thought and Western Science' and Wiredu, 'How Not to Compare African Thought With Western Thought', illuminating.

7 Annis, 'A Contextualist Theory of Epistemic Justification', p. 216.

8 Peirce, *Collected Papers*, 5.115ff.

9 Bain, *The Emotions and the Will*, pp. 511ff.

10 Problems well articulated by Feldman in 'Reliability and Justification'.

11 Strawson, *Introduction to Logical Theory*, pp. 233ff.

12 Kripke, *Naming and Necessity*; cf. Casullo, A., 'Kripke on the A Priori and the Necessary' and Frapolli, M-J, 'Identity, Necessity and *A Prioricity*: The Fallacy of Equivocation'.

13 Rosenfield, *The Complete Medical Exam*, p. 140.

14 Peirce, *Collected Papers*, 6.2.

15 I borrow the terminology from Quine's 'On the Reasons for the Indeterminacy of Translation'.

16 This manoeuvre, no doubt, will be regarded as profoundly unsatisfactory by Calvinist proponents of 'Reformed epistemology', whose attitude, I dare say, will be as expressed in this quotation from Marsden, 'The Collapse of American Evangelical Academia', p. 257:

> [S]in creates a widespread abnormality. Trust in God which ought to be a spontaneous act providing us with intuitive first principles of knowledge is lacking in most people. Christians should not be embarrassed to say frankly that this is the issue. If one trusts in God, one will view some evidence differently than a person who basically denies God.

17 Peirce, *Collected Papers*, 5.565.

18 Bouwsma, 'Descartes' Evil Genius'; Haack, 'Descartes, Peirce and the Cognitive Community'.

19 Quine, 'Things and Their Place in Theories', p. 22.

20 Descartes, *Meditation* IV.

21 But see Van Cleve, 'Foundationalism, Epistemic Principles, and the Cartesian Circle', for illuminating discussion of this issue.

22 Cf. Peirce's distinction between 'perfect' and 'sure' knowledge, *Collected Papers*, 4.62–3.

23 '. . . the philosophy which is now in vogue embraces and cherishes certain tenets, the purpose of which . . . is to persuade men that nothing difficult . . . can be expected from art or human labour . . . which . . . tend[s] . . . to a deliberate and factitious despair, which . . . cuts the sinews and spur of industry . . . And all for the sake of having their art thought perfect, and for the miserable vainglory of making it believed that whatever has not yet been discovered and comprehended can never be discovered or comprehended hereafter'. Bacon, *The New Organon*, Book One, Aphorism LXXXVIII.

Bibliography of Works Cited

Alston, W. P., 'Varieties of Privileged Access', *American Philosophical Quarterly*, 8.3, 1971, 223–41.

Alston, W. P., Self-Warrant: a Neglected Form of Privileged Access', *American Philosophical Quarterly*, 13.4, 1976, 257–72.

Alston, W. P., 'Two Types of Foundationalism', *Journal of Philosophy*, LXXIII.7, 1976, 165–85.

Alston, W. P., 'Level-Confusions in Epistemology', *Midwest Studies*, v, 1980, 135–50.

Alston, W. P., 'Internalism and Externalism in Epistemology', *Philosophical Topics*, XIV.1, 1986, 179–221.

Alston, W. P., 'An Internalist Externalism', *Synthese*, 74, 1988, 265–83.

Annis, D., 'A Contextualist Theory of Epistemic Justification', *American Philosophical Quarterly*, 15.3, 1978, 213–19.

Armstrong, D. M., *Belief, Truth and Knowledge*, Cambridge University Press, Cambridge, 1973.

Asher, H., *Experiments in Seeing*, Basic Books, New York, 1961.

Ayer, A. J., *The Problem of Knowledge*, Penguin Books, Harmondsworth, Middlesex, 1956.

Ayer, A. J., 'Truth, Verification and Verisimilitude' in Schilpp, ed., *The Philosophy of Karl Popper*, 684–91.

Bacon, F., *The New Organon* (1620), ed. Anderson, F. H., Bobbs Merrill, Indianapolis, IN, and New York, 1960.

Bain, A., *The Emotions and the Will*, Longmans, Green, London, third edition, 1875.

Baughm, R., *Character as Indicated by Handwriting*, L. Upcott Gill, London, n.d.

BonJour, L., 'Externalist Theories of Empirical Knowledge', *Midwest Studies in Philosophy*, v, 1980, 53–73.

BonJour, L., *The Structure of Empirical Knowledge*, Harvard University Press, Cambridge, MA and London, 1985.

Bouwsma, O. K., 'Descartes' Evil Genius', *Philosophical Review*, LVIII, 1949, and in Sesonske and Fleming, eds, *Meta-Meditations*, 26–36.

Burdick, H., 'A Logical Form for the Propositional Attitudes', *Synthese*, 52, 1982, 185–230.

Burdick, H., 'On Davidson and Interpretation', *Synthese*, 80, 1989, 321–45.

Burge, T., 'Individualism and the Mental', *Midwest Studies*, IV, 1979, 73–122.

Casullo, A., 'Kripke on the A Priori and the Necessary', *Analysis*, 37, 1977, 152–9, and in Moser, P. K., ed., *A Priori Knowledge*, Oxford University Press, Oxford, 1987, 161–9.

Churchland, P. M., *Scientific Realism and the Plasticity of Mind*, Cambridge University Press, Cambridge, 1979.

Churchland, P. M., 'Eliminative Materialism and the Propositional Attitudes', *Journal of Philosophy*, LXXXVIII.2, 1981, 67–89; page references to the reprint in *A Neurocomputational Perspective*, 1–22.

Churchland, P. M., 'The Ontological Status of Observables', *Pacific Philosophical Quarterly*, 63.3, 1982, 226–35; page references to the reprint in *A Neurocomputational Perspective*, 139–51.

Churchland, P. M., *Matter and Consciousness: A Contemporary Introduction to the Philosophy of Mind*, Bradford Books, MIT Press, Cambridge, MA, 1984.

Churchland, P. M., 'The Continuity of Philosophy and the Sciences', *Mind and Language*, 1.1, 1986, 5–14.

Churchland, P. M., 'Folk Psychology and the Explanation of Behaviour', *Proceedings of the Aristotelian Society*, Supplement, 62, 1988, 209–22; page references to the reprint in *A Neurocomputational Perspective*, 111–27.

Churchland, P. M., 'On the Nature of Theories', in Savage, C. W., ed., *Scientific Theories, Minnesota Studies in the Philosophy of Science*, 11, University of Minnesota Press, Minneapolis, MN, 1989, 59–101; page references to the reprint in *A Neurocomputational Perspective*, 153–96.

Churchland, P. M., 'Explanation: a PDP Approach' (not previously published) in *A Neurocomputational Perspective*, 197–230.

Churchland, P. M., *A Neurocomputational Perspective: The Nature of Mind and the Structure of Science*, Bradford Books, MIT Press, Cambridge, MA and London, 1989.

Churchland, P. Smith, 'Is Determinism Self-Refuting?', *Mind*, 90, 1981, 99–101.

Churchland, P. Smith, 'Epistemology in the Age of Neuroscience', *Journal of Philosophy*, LXXXIV.10, 1987, 544–53.

Cohen, S., 'Justification and Truth', *Philosophical Studies*, 46, 1984, 279–95.

Cornman, J., 'Foundational versus Nonfoundational Theories of Empirical Justification', in Pappas and Swain, eds, *Essays on Knowledge and Justification*, 229–52.

Daley, R., *A Faint Cold Fear*, Warner Books, New York, 1990.

Davidson, D., 'On the Very Idea of a Conceptual Scheme', *Proceedings of the American Philosophical Association*, XLVII, 1972–3, 5–20.

Davidson, D., 'Radical Interpretation', *Dialectica*, 27, 1973, 313–28, and in *Inquiries into Truth and Interpretation*, 125–40; page references to *Inquiries*.

Davidson, D., 'Belief and the Basis of Meaning', *Synthese*, 27, 1974, 309–23; and in *Inquiries into Truth and Interpretation*, 145–51; page references to *Inquiries*.

Davidson, D., 'The Method of Truth in Metaphysics', *Midwest Studies in Philosophy*, II, 1977, and in *Inquiries into Truth and Interpretation*, 199–214; page references to *Inquiries*.

Davidson, D., 'Reply to Foster', in *Truth and Meaning*, eds Evans, G. and McDowell, J., Clarendon Press, Oxford, 1976, 33–41, and in *Inquiries into Truth and Interpretation*, 171–80; page references to *Truth and Meaning*.

Davidson, D., *Inquiries into Truth and Interpretation*, Clarendon Press, Oxford, 1984.

Davidson, D., 'A Coherence Theory of Truth and Knowledge', in *Kant oder Hegel?*, ed. Henrich, Dieter, Klett-Cotta, Stuttgart, 1983, 423–38, reprinted in *Reading Rorty*, ed. Malachowski, A. R., 120–34; page references to *Reading Rorty*.

Davidson, D., 'Afterthoughts [on 'A Coherence Theory of Truth and Knowledge'], 1987', in Malachowski, ed., *Reading Rorty*, 134–7.

Davidson, D., 'The Structure and Content of Truth' (the Dewey Leatures), *Journal of Philosophy*, LXXXVII.6, 1990, 279–328.

Dennett, D., *Brainstorms*, Harvester, Hassocks, Sussex, 1979.

Descartes, R., *Meditations on First Philosophy*, (1641), trans. Haldane, E. and Ross, G. R. T., Cambridge University Press, Cambridge, 1911.

Dewey, J., 'Beliefs and Existences' (1905), in *The Influence of Darwin on Philosophy*, Henry Holt and Company, New York, 1910, 169–97.

Dewey, J., *Reconstruction in Philosophy*, Henry Holt and Co., 1920, and Beacon Press, Boston, MA, 1957.

Dewey, J., *The Quest for Certainty* (1929), Capricorn Books, G. P. Putnam's Sons, New York, 1960.

Donnellan, K., 'Reference and Definite Descriptions', *Philosophical Review*, 75.3, 1966, 281–304.

Feldman, R., 'Reliability and Justification', *The Monist*, 68.2, 1985, 159–74.

Feldman, R. and Conee, E., 'Evidentialism', *Philosophical Studies*, 48, 1985, 15–34.

Firth, R., 'Coherence, Certainty and Epistemic Priority', *Journal of Philosophy*, LXI.19, 1964, 545–57.

Firth, R., 'The Anatomy of Certainty', *Philosophical Review*, LXXVI.1, 1967, 3–27.

Firth, R., 'Lewis on the Given', in *The Philosophy of C. I. Lewis*, ed. Schilpp, P. A., 329–50.

Fodor, J. A., *Representations: Philosophical Essays on the Foundations of Cognitive Science*, Bradford Books, MIT Press, Cambridge, MA, and London, 1981.

Fodor, J. A., 'Fodor's Guide to Mental Representation: the Intelligent Auntie's Vade Mecum', *Mind*, 94, 1985, 76–100.

Foley, R., 'Justified Inconsistent Beliefs', *American Philosophical Quarterly*, 16.4, 1979, 247–57.

Foley, R., 'What's Wrong With Reliabilism?', *The Monist*, 68.2, 1985, 188–202.

Frapolli, M-J., 'Identity, Necessity and *A Prioricity*: The Fallacy of Equivocation', *History and Philosophy of Logic*, 13, 1992, 91–109.

Gibson, J. J., *The Senses Considered as Perceptual Systems*, Houghton Mifflin, Boston, MA, 1966.

Gibson, J. J., 'New Reasons for Realism', *Synthese*, 17, 1967, 162–72.

Gibson, J. J., *The Ecological Approach to Visual Perception*, Houghton Mifflin, Boston, MA, 1979; reprinted by Lawrence Erlbaum Associates, Hillsdale, NJ, and London, 1986.

Goldman, A. H., *Empirical Knowledge*, University of California Press, Berkeley, Los Angeles, CA, and London, 1988.

Goldman, A. I., 'Epistemics: the Regulative Theory of Cognition', *Journal of Philosophy*, 75, 1978, 509–23.

Goldman, A. I., 'What is Justified Belief?', in Pappas, ed., *Justification and Knowledge*, 1–23.

Goldman, A. I., *Epistemology and Cognition*, Harvard University Press, Cambridge, MA, and London, 1986.

Goldman, A. I., 'Strong and Weak Justification', in Tomberlin, ed., *Philosophical Perspectives, 2: Epistemology*, 51–70.

Goldman, A. I., 'Stephen P. Stich: *The Fragmentation of Reason*', *Philosophy and Phenomenological Research*, LI.1, 1991, 189–93.

Goschke, T. and Koppelberg, D., 'Connectionist Representation, Semantic Compositionality, and the Instability of Concept Structure', *Psychological Research*, 52, 1990, 253–70.

Goodman, N., 'Sense and Certainty', *Philosophical Review*, 61, 1952, 160–7.

Goodman, N., 'The New Riddle of Induction' (1953), in *Fact, Fiction and Forecast*, 59–83.

Goodman, N., *Fact, Fiction and Forecast*, Bobbs-Merrill, Indianapolis, New York, Kansas City, second edition, 1965.

Gregory, R. L., *Eye and Brain: the Psychology of Seeing*, Wiedenfield and Nicholson, London, 1966 and 1972; page references to second, 1972, edition.

Haack, S., 'The Relevance of Psychology to Epistemology', *Metaphilosophy*, 6, 1975, 161–76.

Haack, S., 'Is It True What They Say About Tarski?', *Philosophy*, 51.197, 1976, 323–36.

Haack, S., 'Epistemology *With* a Knowing Subject', *Review of Metaphysics*, XXXIII.2, 1979, 309–36.

Haack, S., 'Descartes, Peirce and the Cognitive Community', *The Monist*, 65.2, 1982, 156–82; reprinted in Freeman, E., ed., *The Relevance of Charles Peirce*, Open Court, La Salle, IL, 1983, 238–63.

Haack, S., 'Theories of Knowledge: an Analytic Framework', *Proceedings of the Aristotelian Society*, LXXXIII, 1982–3, 143–57.

Haack, S., 'Can James's Theory of Truth be Made More Satisfactory?', *Transactions of the Charles S. Peirce, Society*, XX, 3, 1984, 269–78.

Haack, S., 'C. I. Lewis', in *American Philosophy*, ed. Singer, Marcus G., Royal

Institute of Philosophy Lecture Series, 19, Cambridge University Press, Cambridge, 1985, 215–39.

Haack, S., Review of Harding and Hintikka, eds, *Discovering Reality*, *Philosophy*, 60.232, 1985, 265–70.

Haack, S., '"Realism"', *Synthese*, 73.2, 1987, 275–299.

Haack, S., 'Surprising Noises: Rorty and Hesse on Metaphor', *Proceedings of the Aristotelian Society*, LXXXVIII, 1987–8, 179–87.

Haack, S., 'Recent Obituaries of Epistemology', *American Philosophical Quarterly*, 27.3, 1990, 199–220.

Haack, S., 'Rebuilding the Ship While Sailing on the Water', in *Perspectives on Quine*, eds Barrett, R. and Gibson, R., Blackwell, Oxford, 1990, 111–27.

Haack, S., Critical Notice of Code, *Epistemic Responsibility, Canadian Journal of Philosophy*, 21.1, 1991, 91–108.

Haack, S., 'What is "the Problem of the Empirical Basis", and Does Johnny Wideawake Solve It?', *British Journal for the Philosophy of Science*, 42, 1991, 369–89.

Haack, S., '"Extreme Scholastic Realism": its Relevance to Philosophy of Science Today', *Transactions of the Charles S.Peirce Society*, XXVIII.1, 1992, 19–50.

Haack, S., 'Science "From a Feminist Perspective"', *Philosophy*, 67, 1992, 5–18.

Haack, S., 'Double-Aspect Foundherentism: a New Theory of Empirical Justification', *Philosophy and Phenomenological Research*, LII.1, 1993, 113–28.

Haack, S., 'The Two Faces of Quine's Naturalism', *Synthese*, 94, 1993, 335–56.

Haack, S., 'Pragmatism', in *Handbook of Epistemology*, eds Sosa, E. and Dancy, J., Blackwell, Oxford, 1992, 351–7.

Haack, S., 'Philosophy/philosophy, an Untenable Dualism', *Transactions of the Charles S.Peirce Society*, XXIX.3, 1993.

Haack, S., 'Dry Truth and Real Knowledge: Epistemologies of Metaphor and Metaphors of Epistemology', forthcoming in *Approaches to Metaphor*, ed. Hintikka, J., *Synthese* library, Kluwer, Dordrecht, the Netherlands.

Haack, S., 'Epistemological Reflections of an Old Feminist', *Reason Papers*, 18, Fall 1993.

Hahn, L. and Schilpp, P. A., eds, *The Philosophy of W. V. Quine*, Open Court, La Salle, IL, 1986.

Hallen, B. and Sodipo, J., *Knowledge, Belief and Witchcraft*, Ethnographica, London, 1986.

Haraway, D., 'Situated Knowledges: *The Science Question in Feminism* and the Privilege of Partial Perspective', *Feminist Studies*, 14.3, 1988, 575–600.

Harding, S., and Hintikka, M., eds, *Discovering Reality: Feminist Perspectives on Epistemology, Metaphysics, Methodology and the Philosophy of Science*, Reidel, Dordrecht, the Netherlands, 1983.

Harding, S., *Whose Science? Whose Knowledge?*, Cornell University Press, Ithaca, NY, 1991.

Hardwig, J., 'Epistemic Dependence', *Journal of Philosophy*, LXXXII, 1985, 335–49.

Heil, J., 'Intentionality Speaks for Itself', in Silvers, ed., *Rerepresentations*, 345–68.

Hobbes, T., *Human Nature* (1650); page references to Woodridge, J. E., ed., *Hobbes Selections*, Charles Scribner's Sons, New York, Chicago, Boston, 1936.

Horgan, T., 'From Cognitive Science to Folk Psychology: Computation, Mental Representation and Belief', *Philosophy and Phenomenological Research*, LII.2, 1992, 449–84.

Horgan, T. and Woodward, J., 'Folk Psychology is Here to Stay', *Philosophical Review*, 94, 1985, 197–226.

Horton, R., 'African Traditional Thought and Western Science', *Africa*, 37, numbers 1 and 2, 1967, 50–71 and 155–87; reprinted in Wilson, B. R., ed., *Rationality*, Blackwell, Oxford, 1970, 131–72.

Hume, David, *Enquiry Concerning Human Understanding* (1748), ed. Selby-Bigge, L. A., from the posthumous edition of 1777, revised by Nidditch, P. H., Clarendon Press, Oxford, 1975.

Jaggar, A., 'Love and Knowledge: Emotion in a Feminist Epistemology', in Garry, A. and Pearsall, M., eds, *Women, Knowledge and Reality*, Unwin Hyman, Boston, MA, 1989, 129–55.

James, W., *The Will to Believe*, (1897), Dover, New York, 1956.

James, W., *Pragmatism* (1907), eds Burkhardt, F. and Bowers, F., Harvard University Press, Cambridge, MA, and London, 1975.

James, W., *The Meaning of Truth* (1909), eds Burkhardt, F. and Bowers, F., Harvard University Press, Cambridge, MA, and London, 1975.

Kelley, D., *The Evidence of the Senses*, Louisiana State University Press, Baton Rouge, LA, and London, 1986.

Kim, J., 'What is "Naturalized Epistemology"?', in Tomberlin, ed., *Philosophical Perspectives, 2: Epistemology*, 381–406.

Kirkham, R., 'Does the Gettier Problem Rest on a Mistake?', *Mind*, XCIII, 1985, 501–13.

Kornblith, H., 'Beyond Foundationalism and the Coherence Theory', *Journal of Philosophy*, LXXII.10, 1980, 597–612; reprinted in *Naturalizing Epistemology*, 115–28.

Kornblith, H., ed., *Naturalizing Epistemology*, MIT Press, Cambridge, MA, 1985.

Kosslyn, S.M. and Koenig, O., *Wet Mind: The New Cognitive Neuroscience*, Free Press, New York, 1992.

Kripke, S., *Naming and Necessity*, Blackwell, Oxford, 1980.

Kuhn, T. S., *The Structure of Scientific Revolutions*, University of Chicago Press, Chicago, IL, 1962; enlarged edition, 1970.

Lehrer, K., *Knowledge*, Clarendon Press, Oxford, 1974.

Lewis, C. I., *An Analysis of Knowledge and Valuation*, Open Court, La Salle, IL, 1946.

Lewis, C. I., 'The Given Element in Empirical Knowledge', *Philosophical Review*, 61, 1952, 168–75.

Malachowski, A. R., ed., *Reading Rorty*, Blackwell, Oxford, 1990.

Marsden, G., 'The Collapse of American Evangelical Academia', in Plantinga and Wolterstorff, eds, *Faith and Rationality*, 219–63.

McGinn, C., 'Charity, Interpretation and Belief', *Journal of Philosophy*, 74, 1977, 521–35.

Minsky, M., 'K-Lines: a Theory of Memory', in Norman, D., ed., *Perspectives on Cognitive Science*, 87–103.

Minsky, M., 'Frame-System Theory', in Wason, P. and Johnson-Laird, P., eds, *Thinking*, Cambridge University Press, Cambridge, 1977, 355–76.

Minsky, M., 'A Framework for Representing Knowledge', in Haugeland, J., ed., *Mind Design*, Bradford Books, MIT Press, Cambridge, MA, 1981, 94–128.

Mintz, S. B., 'Gentlepeople: Sharpen Your Pencils', *Columbia*, Winter 1992, 14–19.

Nelson, L., 'The Impossibility of a "Theory of Knowledge"', first published in German in 1908, reprinted in English in *Socratic Method and Critical Philosophy*, trans. Thomas K. Brown III, New York, NY, 1969, 185–205.

Nelson, L. Hankinson, *Who Knows: From Quine to a Feminist Empiricism*, Temple University Press, Philadelphia, PA, 1990.

Nisbett, R. and Wilson, T. D., 'Telling More Than We Can Know: Verbal Reports on Mental Processes', *The Psychological Review*, 84.3, 1977, 321–59.

Norman, D., ed., *Perspectives on Cognitive Science*, Ablex, Norwood, NJ, 1981.

Orwell, G., *Nineteen Eighty-Four* (1949), Penguin, Harmondsworth, Middlesex, 1954.

Pappas, G., and Swain, M., eds, *Essays on Knowledge and Justification*, Cornell University Press, Ithaca, NY, and London, 1978.

Pappas, G., ed., *Justification and Knowledge*, Reidel, Dordrecht, Holland, Boston, MA, and London, 1979.

Pastin, M., 'C. I. Lewis's Radical Foundationalism', *Noûs*, 9, 1975, 407–20.

Pastin, M., 'Modest Foundationalism and Self-Warrant', *American Philosophical Quarterly* monograph series, 4, 141–9, and in Pappas and Swain, *Essays on Knowledge and Justification*, 279–88.

Pearson, K., *The Grammar of Science*, Adams and Charles Black, London, second edition, 1900.

Peirce, C. S., *Collected Papers*, eds Hartshorne, C., Weiss, P. and Burks, A., Harvard University Press, Cambridge, MA, and London, 1931–58. References by volume and paragraph number.

Perry, Ralph Barton, *The Thought and Character of William James*, Harvard University Press, Cambridge, MA, 1948.

Plantinga, A. and Wolterstorff, N., eds, *Faith and Rationality*, University of Notre Dame Press, Notre Dame, IN, and London, 1983.

Plantinga, A., 'Reason and Belief in God', in *Faith and Rationality*, eds Plantinga and Wolterstorff, 16–93.

Polanyi, M., *Personal Knowledge*, Routledge and Kegan Paul, London, 1958.

Polanyi, M., *The Tacit Dimension*, Doubleday, Garden City, NY, 1966.

Pollock, J., 'A Plethora of Epistemological Theories', in Pappas, ed., *Knowledge and Justification*, 93–114.

Pollock, J., *Contemporary Theories of Knowledge*, Rowman and Littlefield, Savage, MD, 1986, Hutchinson, London, 1987.

Popper, K. R., *The Logic of Scientific Discovery*, Hutchinson, London, 1959.

Popper, K. R., *Objective Knowledge: An Evolutionary Approach*, Clarendon Press, Oxford, 1972.

Popper, K. R., 'Epistemology Without a Knowing Subject', in *Objective Knowledge*, 106–52.

Popper, K. R., 'On the Theory of the Objective Mind', in *Objective Knowledge*, 153–90.

Popper, K. R., 'The Verification of Basic Statements' and 'Subjective Experience and Linguistic Formulation', in Schilpp, ed., *The Philosophy of Karl Popper*, 1110–11 and 1111–14.

Price, H. H., *Belief*, Allen and Unwin, London, 1969.

Putnam, H., 'Why Reason Can't be Naturalized', *Synthese*, 52, 1982, 3–23.

Putnam, H., 'Meaning Holism', in Hahn and Schilpp, eds, *The Philosophy of W. V. Quine*, 405–26.

Quine, W. V., 'Two Dogmas of Empiricism' (1951), in *From a Logical Point of View*, 20–46.

Quine, W. V., *From a Logical Point of View*, Harvard University Press, Cambridge, MA, 1953; Harper Torchbooks, Harper and Row, New York and Evanston, 1963; page references to the latter.

Quine, W. V., *Word and Object*, MIT Press, Cambridge, MA and London, 1960.

Quine, W. V., *Ontological Relativity and Other Essays*, Columbia University Press, New York and London, 1969.

Quine, W. V., 'Epistemology Naturalized', in *Ontological Relativity and Other Essays*, 69–90.

Quine, W. V., 'Natural Kinds', in *Ontological Relativity and Other Essays*, 114–38.

Quine, W. V., 'On the Reasons for the Indeterminacy of Translation', *Journal of Philosophy*, LXVII.6, 1970, 178–83.

Quine, W. V., *The Roots of Reference*, Open Court, La Salle, IL, 1973.

Quine, W. V., 'The Nature of Natural Knowledge', in Guttenplan, S., ed., *Mind and Language*, Clarendon Press, Oxford, 1975, 67–82.

Quine, W. V., 'Facts of the Matter', in Shahan, R., and Merrill, K., eds, *American Philosophy from Edwards to Quine*, University of Oklahoma Press, Norman, OK, 1977, 176–96.

Quine, W. V., *Theories and Things*, Belknap Press of Harvard University Press, Cambridge, MA, and London, 1981.

Quine, W. V., 'Things and Their Place in Theories', in *Theories and Things*, 1–23.

Quine, W. V., 'Five Milestones of Empiricism', in *Theories and Things*, 67–72.

Quine, W. V., 'Reply to Putnam', in Hahn and Schilpp, eds, *The Philosophy of W. V. Quine*, 427–32.

Quine, W. V., 'Reply to White', in Hahn and Schilpp, eds, *The Philosophy of W. V. Quine*, 663–5.

Quine, W. V. and Ullian, J., *The Web of Belief*, Random House, New York, 1970; second edition, 1978.

Quinton, A. M., 'The Foundations of Knowledge', in *British Analytical Philosophy*, eds Williams, B. and Montefiore, A., Routledge and Kegan Paul, London, 1966, 55–86.

Quinton, A. M., *The Nature of Things*, Routledge and Kegan Paul, London, 1973.

Ramsey, F. P., *The Foundations of Mathematics*, ed. Braithwaite, R. B., Routledge and Kegan Paul, London, 1931.

Reichenbach, H., 'Are Phenomenal Reports Absolutely Certain?', *Philosophical Review*, 61, 1952, 147–59.

Reid, T., *Essays on the Intellectual Powers* (1785), in Beanblossom, R. E. and Lehrer, K., eds, *Thomas Reid: Inquiry and Essays*, Hackett, Indianapolis, IN, 1983.

Rorty, R., *Philosophy and the Mirror of Nature*, Princeton University Press, Princeton, NJ, 1979.

Rorty, R., 'Unfamiliar Noises: Hesse and Davidson on Metaphor', *Proceedings of the Aristotelian Society*, Supplement, 61, 1987, 283–96, and in *Objectivity, Relativism and Truth*, 162–74.

Rorty, R., *Contingency, Irony and Solidarity*, Cambridge University Press, Cambridge, 1989.

Rorty, R., *Objectivity, Relativism and Truth: Philosophical Papers, 1*, Cambridge University Press, Cambridge, 1991.

Rorty, R., *Essays on Heidegger and Others: Philosophical Papers, 2*, Cambridge University Press, Cambridge, 1991.

Rosenfield, I., *The Complete Medical Exam*, Newsweek Books, New York, 1978.

Russell, B., 'Knowledge, Error and Probable Opinion', in *The Problems of Philosophy*, Oxford University Press, Oxford, 1912.

Russell, B., *Our Knowledge of the External World as a Field for Scientific Method in Philosophy*, Allen and Unwin, London, 1914.

Schiffer, S., 'Truth and the Theory of Content', in Parret and Bouverese, eds, *Meaning and Understanding*, Walter de Gruyter, Berlin, 1981.

Schilpp, P. A., ed., *The Philosophy of C. I. Lewis*, Open Court, La Salle, IL, 1968.

Schilpp, P. A., ed., *The Philosophy of Karl Popper*, Open Court, La Salle, IL, 1974.

Sellars, W., 'Empiricism and the Philosophy of Mind', in *Science, Perception and Reality*, Routledge and Kegan Paul, London, 1963, 127–96.

Sesonske, A. and Fleming, N., eds, *Meta-Meditations: Studies in Descartes*, Wadsworth, Belmont, CA, 1965.

Shope, R. K., *The Analysis of Knowing*, Princeton University Press, Princeton, NJ, 1983.

Siegel, H., 'Justification, Discovery, and the Naturalization of Epistemology', *Philosophy of Science*, 47, 1980, 279–320.

Silvers, S., ed., *Rerepresentations: Readings in the Philosophy of Mental Representation*, Kluwer Academic Publishers, Dordrecht, the Netherlands, Boston, MA, and London, 1989.

Sosa, E., 'The Raft and the Pyramid', *Midwest Studies in Philosophy*, v, 1980, 3–25.

Stich, S. P., *From Folk Psychology to Cognitive Science*, Bradford Books, MIT Press, Cambridge, MA, and London, 1983.

Stich, S. P., *The Fragmentation of Reason*, Bradford Books, MIT Press, Cambridge, MA, and London, 1990.

Stich, S. P., 'The Fragmentation of Reason: a Precis of Two Chapters', *Philosophy and Phenomenological Research*, LI.1, 1991, 178–83.

Strawson, P. F., *Introduction to Logical Theory*, Methuen, London, 1952.

Tomberlin, J., ed., *Philosophical Perspectives, 2: Epistemology*, Ridgeview, Atascadero, CA, 1988.

Turnbull, C., *The Mountain People*, Picador, London, 1974.

Van Cleve, J., 'Foundationalism, Epistemic Principles, and the Cartesian Circle', *Philosophical Review*, LXXXVIII.1, 1979, 55–91.

Vermazen, B., 'The Intelligibility of Massive Error', *Philosophical Quarterly*, 33.138, 1983, 69–74.

Watkins, J. W. N., *Science and Scepticism*, Hutchinson, London, 1984.

Wilson, N. L., 'Substances Without Substrata', *Review of Metaphysics*, 12, 1959, 521–39.

Wilson, T. D., 'Strangers to Ourselves: the Origins and Accuracy of Beliefs About One's Own Mental States', in Harvey, J. H. and Weary, G., eds, *Attribution: Basic Issues and Applications*, Academic Press, Orlando, FL, 1985, 1–35.

Winograd, T., 'Frame Representations and the Declarative-Procedural Controversy', in Bobrow, D. G. and Collins, A., eds, *Representation and Understanding*, San Francisco, New York and London, 1975, 188–210.

Winograd, T., 'What Does It Mean to Understand Language?', in Norman, ed., *Perspectives on Cognitive Science*, 231–63.

Wooldridge, D. E., *The Machinery of the Brain*, MacGraw Hill, New York, 1963.

Wiredu, K., 'How Not to Compare African Thought With Western Thought', in *African Thought*, ed. Wright, R. A., University Press of America, New York, 1984, 149–62.

Wittgenstein, L., *On Certainty*, ed. Anscombe, G. E. M. and von Wright, G. H., with English translation by Paul, G. A. and Anscombe, G. E. M., Blackwell, Oxford and Harper and Row, New York, 1969.

Index

* by a page number indicates where the definition of a term is to be found in the text.

A name in square brackets after an entry indicates the author responsible for the terminology concerned, or whose use of the terminology is discussed.

References to 'the Cartesian approach', 'the Kuhnian position', etc., are indexed under Descartes, Kuhn, and so on.